ROUTLEDGE LIBRARY EDITIONS:
TRADE UNIONS

I0124934

Volume 19

TRADE UNIONS
AND THE LAW

TRADE UNIONS
AND THE LAW

R. W. RIDEOUT

Routledge
Taylor & Francis Group

LONDON AND NEW YORK

First published in 1973 by George Allen & Unwin Ltd.

This edition first published in 2023
by Routledge
4 Park Square, Milton Park, Abingdon, Oxon OX14 4RN

and by Routledge
605 Third Avenue, New York, NY 10158

Routledge is an imprint of the Taylor & Francis Group, an informa business

British Library Cataloguing in Publication Data
A catalogue record for this book is available from the British Library

ISBN: 978-1-032-37553-3 (Set)
ISBN: 978-1-032-38510-5 (Volume 19) (hbk)
ISBN: 978-1-032-38518-1 (Volume 19) (pbk)
ISBN: 978-1-003-34540-4 (Volume 19) (ebk)

DOI: 10.4324/9781003345404

Publisher's Note
The publisher has gone to great lengths to ensure the quality of this reprint but points out that some imperfections in the original copies may be apparent.

Disclaimer
The publisher has made every effort to trace copyright holders and would welcome correspondence from those they have been unable to trace.

Trade Unions and the Law

by R. W. Rideout

London   George Allen & Unwin Ltd
Ruskin House   Museum Street

ISBN 0 04 331054 0 hardback
      0 04 331055 9 paperback

Printed in Great Britain
in 10 point Times Roman type
by The Aldine Press, Letchworth

Preface

I am painfully aware that the trade unionist has never had much time for the law and now, no doubt, has less than normal. In consequence, partly of a high degree of ignorance of that law, unions have in the past fallen foul of it to their considerable expense, monetarily, and in terms of their public image. As a result, they have reviled it the more, as one might revile a machine one did not know how to operate because it produced disastrous results.

This book has, therefore, been prepared as an attempt to present the law in as readable and non-technical form as possible, at the same time attempting to lose none of the accuracy such a presentation should have. Footnotes and case references, which, for the lawyer, denote the value of a book, have been eliminated. In their place, I have tried to insert, necessarily briefly, background information and comment. The law is, as it were, a top dressing. What one thinks of it as such is as variable as most people's approach to manure. If, as trade unionists often think, their field is covered with a verdant pasture, it may seem out of place. One thing is clear, however. The effect it has depends entirely on its peculiar context. Libraries of books have been written, many of them for publication by my publishers, on this context. I can only hope to draw attention to what seem to me some of the more relevant aspects of it.

Once upon a time, life for the lawyer in this area was relatively peaceful, and, so long as one was not attempting to make a living by practice in it, pleasant. Now development upon development surprises, alarms and, sometimes, but rarely, pleases the writer who desperately attempts to keep up to date. Necessarily much will have happened between this book going to print and publication. I have tried to state the position as at 14th February 1973.

My thanks are due to my publishers, who have been very patient

PREFACE

and very efficient, and to sundry typists who struggled to produce a typescript which a publisher might possibly accept. This time most of this task has fallen upon Miss Sylvia New, whose interest in it has been a considerable encouragement.

R. W. RIDEOUT

University College, London

Contents

Preface   7

1 Legal Institutions and Methods
  Sources of Law   13
  Courts with Jurisdiction in Industrial Matters   16
    The Supreme Court   16
    The National Industrial Relations Court   17
    Industrial Tribunals   23
  Common Law

PART I   MEMBERSHIP AND INTERNAL AFFAIRS
OF TRADE UNIONS

2 Trade Union Organization
  Definitions   25
  Registration   28
  Rules   32
  Legal Status   38

3 Trade Union Membership
  Membership as a Condition of Employment   41
    'Encouragement'   42
    The Nature of the 'Agency Shop'   43
    Approved Closed Shop   44
    Procedure   45
  Admission to Membership of an Organization   48
  Discipline—Substantive Offences   51
  Disciplinary Procedure   54
  Appeal Procedures   59
  Complaints by Members   61

4 Internal Government
  Funds, Property and Accounts   67
  Other Administrative Requirements   70
  Offences and Penalties   70
  Liabilities of Funds   71

CONTENTS

The Political Fund   72
Elections   75
Dissolution and Amalgamation   77
Government   81

PART II   INDUSTRIAL ACTION

5 Definitions

Strikes   82
'Irregular Industrial Action Short of a Strike'   84
The Lock-out   86
Industrial Disputes   87

6 Unfair Industrial Practices

'Supporting' Practices   91
Other Unfair Industrial Practices   96
   Inducement to Breach of Contract   96
   Sympathetic Action   99
   Secondary Action   100
Complaints Procedures   102
   Before Industrial Tribunals   102
   Before the NIRC   103
Remedies   106
Effectiveness of the 'Unfair Practice' Sanction   110

7 The Common Law Residue

Inducement to Breach of Contract   116
Other 'Economic' Torts   119
Statutory Protection   123
Picketing—Civil Liability   127
Criminal Liability   131

8 Emergency Procedures   133

PART III   INDUSTRIAL RELATIONS

9 Collective Bargaining

Sole Bargaining Agents   143
Contractual Effect of Collective Agreements   159
Remedial Procedure   166
Information   169

10 Official Instruments of Collective Bargaining

The Wages Council	172
The Industrial Arbitration Board	174
The Commission on Industrial Relations	180
The National Industrial Relations Court	183
Conciliation and Arbitration	187
Conciliation	187
Arbitration	189
Enquiry	190

PART IV INDIVIDUAL EMPLOYMENT

11 Dismissal

The Basis of the Workers' Protection	192
Common Law Remedies Depending on Contract	193
Sickness	195
Suspension	196
Notice	197
Statutory Remedies Depending on the Concept of Unfair Dismissal	199
Procedure	203
Alternative Procedure	205
Remedies	206
The Code of Practice and Dismissal Procedures	209

12 Redundancy

Scope of the Scheme	213
Dismissal	214
Redundancy	217
Lay-off and Short Time	222
Alternative Offers	223
Continuity	226
1. Change of Employer	226
2. Temporary Breaks in the Employment Contract	227
Calculation of Payment	231
Overtime	231
Shift and Rota Workers	233
No fixed Hours	233
Alternative Schemes	234

CONTENTS

13 Compensation for Industrial Injury
    The Nature of Liability   235
    Vicarious Liability   240
    Negligence   244
    Breach of Statutory Duty   248
    Fault Liability   251

Comparative Index of Major Statutory Provisions   253

Labour Law Books   267

Index   269

Chapter 1

Legal Institutions and Methods

SOURCES OF LAW

The Law in Great Britain comes from three principal sources: legislation passed by Parliament or delegated legislation made by statutory authority; judicial decisions of the higher courts; and custom.

It will be obvious that each of these plays a different part in legal development. Legislation is the most speedy and the most radical way of introducing new law or changing existing law. As everyone knows, in this country, at least until the present time, every piece of legislation can be freely repealed or amended by a subsequent Act of Parliament. It is not quite so widely realized that there is a much larger body of delegated legislation. Roughly speaking this is the sub-rules and regulations which deal in more detail with what the authorizing Act sets out in outline. This does not mean that delegated legislation consists only of minor provisions. Some of it can be very general in its application. Nor must it be supposed that the sole purpose of delegated legislation is to expand the provisions of Acts of Parliament. It is often used to amend the provisions of the statute itself. The great advantages of leaving matters to be worked out in detail by delegated legislation, rather than by passing an Act through Parliament, lie in the fact that much of the detail is of a technical nature best understood by experts. It can be, though it does not follow that it always is, brought into force much more quickly than the parliamentary process would allow. Partly because of this and partly because of its nature, it can be changed more readily. In the British system the practice of a public discussion stage in the first draft of a Bill in Parliament does not exist. White papers or consultative documents give some opportunity for a discussion of principles, but rarely of details. Delegated legislation is, however, frequently subject to such discussion in draft, either in practice or by reason of a statutory direction.

So it is that by legislation and sub-legislation much of the law, both in general and in detail, is made. In a sense, however, it can be said to be theoretical at this stage. That is to say, it is not usually specifically referred to particular fact situations. It has, therefore, an appearance of inflexibility. So we may find a statutory provision stating: 'Every dangerous part of any machinery . . . shall be securely fenced.' The provision looks simple enough. Suppose, however, that we apply it to a situation in which a man's hand is injured by the fan blade in the engine of a run-about truck in a factory. Suppose, further, that other parts of the engine made it extremely unlikely that he would have been able to approach the fan with his hand; but, nevertheless, he managed it. We may say at once that the truck is a 'machine', but if it is, can it really have been the intention of the legislature that there should have been a fence right round it to stop its dangerous tendency to move from causing injury? The absurdity of such a suggestion may lead us to suppose that it is not a 'machine' for the purposes of the Act, and we may explain this by drawing a distinction between a vehicle and a machine. Because we are not too sure of the soundness of this reasoning, especially as the injury has arisen from its mechanical and not its vehicular character, we may go further in our argument to say, 'Well anyway, the rest of the engine was a "fence".' A fence does not have to be in the form of a wire grill. Anything that stops us getting somewhere may be called a fence. But the man argues that even if this is so, the fence was not 'secure' because he got past it. We must then decide whether 'security' imposes an absolute standard so that the mere fact that someone is injured proves that the protection was not secure, or whether, alternatively, the legislation intended 'secure' to mean 'secure against any foreseeable event'. Eventually, having decided all these points, we are in a position to declare the state of the law arising from the statutory provision as it applies to the particular problem; yet it will be seen that the statute has at most only provided this detailed answer by drawing conclusions from general provisions. These conclusions may often be governed by policy and the social and economic undesirability of deciding otherwise.

This is exactly how the courts deal with statutory provisions and so we may say that the courts have made law. They also make law by another process. Much of the law of England and Scotland did not start with a statute at all. Someone came to the courts, for instance, and said, 'I have a field. Every morning my neighbour brings his cows past it on their way to milking, opens the gate and allows the cows to enter and eat the grass in my field for an hour or so while my neighbour has his breakfast.' The court would take the view that land ownership must mean that one had an exclusive right to use the land, or it would be something less than ownership. A rule concerning trespass to land thus came into existence.

Whether we take such a case, or the type of case we previously examined of statutory interpretation, we shall move to another situation. The neighbour this time, just for spite, stands on the roadway and sprays my grass with sodium chlorate which not only destroys the grass but also causes my pregnant cow, which ate some of the grass, to abort. Alternatively, a factory machine happens to have wheels which are driven by a small motor so that occasionally it can be moved from place to place. A new though related fact has been introduced into a situation covered by the law. The courts are asked to develop the law one stage further. In doing so they will interpret and apply what they themselves said in former cases where the facts are somewhat similar. In doing so it would obviously be unacceptable that they should freely be able to say that the previous case was wrong because they would, looking back, have come to a different conclusion. The point is that people regulate their conduct according to the law and they want to be able to rely upon the statements of lawyers, looking at statutes and past decisions, as to what that law is. There is bound to develop, therefore, a respect for previous decisions which in this country, at least, has reached a high peak where one judge will tend to accept a previous decision even though he is not too sure that he would have come to the same conclusion. He will usually consider himself *bound* to accept the decision of a court superior to his own, i.e. a court of appeal.

Custom is that process whereby what began as common practice has been so consistently followed that it can now be said to be a rule. People continue to do the same thing, no longer primarily because it is convenient but because, for as long as they can remember, it has been done that way. Custom plays less and less part as a source of law, if only because, as time passes, customs tend to become the subject of case or statute law, or to be superseded by them. Some trade customs continue to be significant in the law of employment because they become the basis of implied contractual terms governing the conditions of employment of individual workers. So, for instance, wage rates have, in the past, been governed by the custom of the trade; although few will now be found remaining outside the sphere of collective agreements. Again, it may be customary to deduct so much from piece rates for bad work and the courts, if persuaded that this is so, will hold that to be a term of the agreed contract of employment. In time it may be formulated in a collective agreement.

COURTS WITH JURISDICTION IN INDUSTRIAL MATTERS

THE SUPREME COURT

Until 1971 all litigation in labour matters in the United Kingdom went through the ordinary common law courts, or the national insurance and industrial tribunals, introduced in 1946 and 1963 respectively.

Cases concerning contracts of employment disputes might even begin as low as the magistrates courts, but more often the lowest point in the structure was the County Court. The decisions of these courts are not systematically or extensively reported and the lowest court which actually made law on labour matters was the High Court. None of the vast new structure under the Industrial Relations Act depends on these courts, and indeed most of their old jurisdiction over contracts of employment will be transferred to new institutions established by that Act.

The two courts at the top of the common law structure, however, that is to say, the Court of Appeal and the House of Lords (sitting as the highest court of appeal in the country), retain their importance and also assume the same position as final courts of appeal on matters arising under the new legislation. Only a small number of cases that begin in the new National Industrial Relations Court will reach the House of Lords, and a minute fraction of those beginning in industrial tribunals will reach the Court of Appeal, let alone the House of Lords. These will, however, tend to be those involving the most difficult, or the most significant, points of law and it is important to realize that the decisions of these appeal courts will have to be followed as law by all the lower courts and tribunals because the English legal system operates what is known as the system of 'binding judicial precedent'.

Both these courts consist of judges, three in the Court of Appeal and, normally, five in the House of Lords, trained in the ordinary law, not particularly expert in labour matters and available to hear any case on any legal point.

THE NATIONAL INDUSTRIAL RELATIONS COURT

This court, which is equal in status to the divisions of the High Court, was established by the Industrial Relations Act 1971. It is in many ways radically different from any existing court and partakes of many of the characteristics of a tribunal. When sitting, each branch of it will consist of a legally trained judge and two members with knowledge or experience of industrial relations matters. (The court may have up to four lay members or, if the parties consent, only one.) One of the legally qualified judges is appointed President of the court as a whole. There is a branch operating for Scotland under a judge appointed from the Court of Session. The judges are appointed for life (i.e. they remain, normally, until retirement, which must take place at the age of 75) whilst the other members are appointed for a given term of not less than three years and may be reappointed. They may retire, or may be removed by the Lord Chancellor and the Secretary of State for Employment on the ground of incapacity or misbehaviour. It is interesting to note that this is the only higher court in the country some of whose members may be removed so easily.

The court may sit anywhere in the country. It is probable that most of its sittings will be in London but it is anticipated that, if it would be unduly expensive or troublesome for this to take place, the hearing may be at the place where the matter arose.

Most significantly, the court is required to exercise its jurisdiction so as to allow the parties to avail themselves of opportunities for conciliation, and particularly the services of a conciliation officer. On the face of it this looks wider than a somewhat similar requirement attaching to industrial tribunals since it envisages that, even after proceedings have begun, they may be adjourned for conciliation. It is narrower in the sense that conciliation can only occur if the parties desire it; whereas the conciliation officer operating under an industrial tribunal may intervene on his own initiative if he thinks it would be valuable. Of course any issue in the High Court or any other court may be settled by agreement. The difference in the NIRC is that that court must actively seek to facilitate such agreement.

The court is required to avoid formality so far as it appears to it appropriate to do so. It is not bound by the rules of admissible evidence which are followed in other courts. So, for instance, it can listen to hearsay, that is to say a second-hand report of what someone else said (though it need not give it much weight). The court has powers to compel people to attend and give evidence and produce documents. It also has power to administer oaths. It may review its own decisions and vary its orders. This may produce a confused picture since the NIRC may be asked to consider whether it was right, and after its second decision the matter may still go on appeal to the Court of Appeal. As if to emphasize the absence of formality, a litigant before the court is permitted to appear in person or to be represented by any person, whether a lawyer or not. This is the first time since the development of a recognizable legal profession that the right of audience in a superior court has been given to a representative other than a member of the legal profession. Whereas the trade union official should not underrate his ability to compete with lawyers in legal argument, particularly in matters concerning industrial relations upon which he may be more expert, he should not overrate it. Very many fine legal points arise under the Industrial Relations Act and surrounding law. Occasionally points not normally connected with labour law will intrude. The court may help the lay representative procedurally, but it cannot teach him the substantive law so that he may plead his case properly. Furthermore, despite the statutory requirement to avoid excessive formality a good deal of formal procedure is already apparent.

For at least the last one hundred years all courts with power to make an order to carry out or cease any act have had power to make what is known as an interim order. The object of such an order is speedily to prevent a continuation of the alleged improper conduct pending the final determination of the case after full argument. In this period much damage might be done and even if the court were prepared to conduct a final hearing at once the parties would normally want time to prepare their case. Common law courts take this interim order one stage further so as to permit it to be made *ex parte*, that is to say without hearing the parties or their witnesses but merely by examining the sworn affidavits of both sides as to what the facts are. By this means it is often possible to obtain an interim order *ex parte* in no more than twenty-four hours. It follows that all the claimant is required to do in such a procedure is to show that there is a prima facie case for saying that the activities of which he complains are illegal. He does not have to prove the matter finally. Nor does he have to face cross-examination on his allegations. Normally this is a useful jurisdiction, but in industrial matters it had a grave defect in that even a temporary cessation of industrial action in furtherance of an industrial dispute would normally mean that there was no practicable possibility of recommencing the industrial action if it was held finally to be permissible. Most interim orders granted in this field in the last ten years have not been followed by any final hearing.

The National Industrial Relations Court may make an interim order but may not do so unless 'all reasonable steps have been taken with a view to securing that notice of the application and an opportunity for making representations relating to that application have been given' to the person against whom the order is made. This does not necessarily mean that such representations need be permitted to be made orally. The rules of the court require an oral hearing when dealing with matter primarily involving a charge of misconduct as in allegations of unfair industrial practice.

Unlike any other higher court in the country, the National Industrial Relations Court cannot normally make orders for costs against one party. An order that one party should pay the costs and expenses of the other can only be made where, in the opinion of the court, the proceedings were unnecessary, improper or vexatious or there has been unreasonable delay or other unreasonable conduct in bringing or conducting the proceedings. This is the same power as that possessed by the industrial tribunals. (Although, rather strangely, the Act gives power to authorize the industrial tribunals to give costs on a much wider basis, it is not proposed to use that power.) The justification for this limitation is that a party should not be deterred from bringing his claim by the fear that if he loses, he will be ordered to pay the costs of the other side. In the case of industrial tribunals, where the party can keep his own costs to a low minimum, this idea is reasonable. It may be, however, that since the National Industrial Relations Court will inevitably be more expensive, the fact that a claimant must pay his own costs, even for a good claim which he wins, will act as a deterrent to him. Since appeal lies now from industrial tribunals to the NIRC (and no longer to the Divisional Court of the Queen's Bench Division which could award costs), the claimant may even be deterred for this reason from commencing a case before the industrial tribunals. It should be mentioned that legal aid can be obtained for actions before the NIRC, but the financial limits for this are now low in relation to average earnings.

Finally, the National Industrial Relations Court is peculiar in having a relatively short time limit of six months for the presentation of complaints about the commission of unfair industrial practices.

The work of the court may be divided into two main parts, namely, (i) that concerning the commission of all unfair industrial practices under the Industrial Relations Act 1971, with the exception of those concerning purely individual matters of infringement of trade union freedoms, unfair dismissal and breach of the guiding principles relating to the conduct of trade unions; (ii) a diverse range of matters concerning industrial relations generally which will be dealt with in Chapters 8 and 9.

The court has also become the appeal court on points of law from decisions of the industrial tribunals, which formally went to a Divisional Court of the Queen's Bench Division. The NIRC also hears all appeals from decisions of the registrar concerning political fund rules of organizations of workers and, as to applications for registration, from organizations of workers, or employers, or organizations desiring registration on the special register.

The Industrial Court, when dealing with complaints of the commission of unfair industrial practices, has power to make an order determining the rights of the parties, and an order instructing the person against whom the complaint is made to refrain from continuing the practice and to refrain from taking any other action of a like nature in relation to the complainant. This order, however, does not require him to take any steps in relation to the unauthorized conduct of others. The court may also award compensation. The amount of this is to be determined by what the court considers just and equitable in all the circumstances, having regard to the loss sustained by the complainant in consequence of the matters of which he complains, in so far as the loss was attributable to action taken by or on behalf of the party against whom the complaint is made. The complainant must, however, as in ordinary actions for breach of contract, take reasonable steps to mitigate (i.e. reduce) his loss. If he does so the amount mitigated will, of course, not be included in the loss. If he fails to do so the court will assess what could have been saved by such steps and deduct that from the amount of the loss sustained. The court may also deduct from the amount of compensation such amount as it considers just and equitable in relation to the extent to which the matters complained of were caused or contributed to by any action of the complainant. This is a most significant provision. It remains to be seen, for instance, whether it will permit a trade union to reply to the claim of an employer on the ground that the dispute from which the actions in question arose was caused by bad management. In the case of complaints against registered trade unions, the maximum amount of compensation awarded to each complainant must not exceed £5,000 for a union of 5,000 members or less, £25,000 for a union of not more than 25,000 members, and £100,000 for a union of more than 100,000 members.

INDUSTRIAL TRIBUNALS
Industrial tribunals were first established under the Industrial Training Act 1964. Their jurisdiction was originally confined to matters arising under that Act, which largely concerned the assessment of the training levy by the relevant training board. Had they been established with this type of employer/authority dispute solely in mind the vast extension of their work without radical reorganization of their structure would have seemed to produce impossible strain. At that time it is possible that the thinking that led to the Redundancy Payments Act 1965 was in being. There is no doubt that from their inception the tribunals were visualized as the embryo of a system of labour courts into which they have now developed.

The tribunals sit in centres throughout the country and it is planned that there should generally be one within twenty miles of any place of work. At present, three sit centrally in London, but it was estimated that there would need to be fifteen to deal with the new work under the Industrial Relations Act.

The matters on which the tribunals now have jurisdiction are as follows:

Employers' appeals against levies made under the Industrial Training Act 1964.

*Questions arising under the Redundancy Payments Act 1965, as to the employees' right to payment of compensation, and the amount thereof, or the employers' right to a rebate from the central fund.

*Questions arising under the Equal Pay Act 1970.

*Disputes concerning redundancy payments or compensation under certain former statutes applying, for instance, to civil servants and local government employees.

The determination of whether specified work is 'dock work' under the Docks and Harbours Act 1966, designed to regulate the employment of dock workers and to license employers of dock labour.

(Formerly, questions as to whether a business falls within the Selective Employment Payments Act 1966 so as to be required to pay tax on a *per capita* basis on employees. This legislation has now been phased out.)

*Claims that an employee has been unfairly dismissed within the provisions of the Industrial Relations Act 1971.

*Claims of an unfair industrial practice involving in discrimination against, or dismissal of, a worker because of the exercise of his trade union rights under section 5 of the Industrial Relations Act 1971.

*Claims against industrial organizations of breach of rules or guiding principles either after reference of the registrar (if the organization is registered), or directly (whether the organization is registered or not).

Provision is also made in the Industrial Relations Act 1971 for the Lord Chancellor, by order, to permit claims for damages for breach of contract of employment (other than damages in respect of personal injuries or death) to be brought before an industrial tribunal. Such claims may be permitted to be brought concurrently with any other proceedings before the tribunal. This jurisdiction, if conferred, will be concurrent with any common law jurisdiction

* On matters marked thus, appeal will lie on a question of law to the National Industrial Relations Court.

over contracts of employment subject to any rules of court allowing such actions to be stayed pending the determination of an industrial tribunal.

In the case of any complaint concerning unfair dismissal or discrimination because of the exercise of trade union rights which is presented to an industrial tribunal, it is the duty of a conciliation officer acting under the relevant tribunal to endeavour to promote a settlement of the complaint, either if he is requested to do so by the parties or, in the absence of such a request, if he considers he could act with a reasonable prospect of success. Unfortunately, the statutory provision is so worded that the conciliation officer can only act after a complaint has been presented; or on a joint request of the parties without such formal complaint but after the employee has ceased to be employed by that employer. This means that, in the case of dismissal, the dismissal must actually take effect before formal conciliation can commence. The NIRC has indicated that conciliation should be permitted during prolonged notice periods. The task of the conciliation officer in particular is to seek to secure reinstatement in employment on terms appearing to him to be equitable. Failing that, and only if the parties so desire, to seek to promote agreement between them as to the amount of compensation.

COMMON LAW

The jurisdiction of the common law courts (what might be called the old industrial law) remains, superficially, unchanged. It is still possible for a member, or expelled member, to bring a common law action for breach of trade union rules or for an employee to sue for breach of his contract of employment, and thus for 'wrongful' as distinct from 'unfair' dismissal. Actions in tort arising from industrial activity can be brought, in practice only where the activity is not in contemplation or furtherance of an industrial dispute. In practice little attempt is likely to be made to use these methods. In the last two cases provision is made for the formulation of rules of court to provide power to stay a common law action wherever the matter could be the subject of complaint to an industrial tribunal or to the NIRC. The High Court has already refused to grant an injunction arising from picketing where the matter was concurrently before the NIRC. In the first case the procedure for complaint to an industrial tribunal is likely to prove far easier, cheaper and more attractive than the common law procedure.

One possible source of continued common law jurisdiction to deal with certain types of industrial action remains. The unfair industrial practices specified in the Industrial Relations Act 1971 are only available in situations where the activity in question is in contemplation or furtherance of an industrial dispute as defined in the Act. In particular, this definition does not include disputes between one group of workmen and another, or disputes of a political nature. In such cases the only available action would be the common law action for tort which, because there was no industrial dispute, would enjoy no statutory protection from the law of tort.

It is unlikely, however, that any substantial number of these situations will arise, far less that there will be any rivalry between the remedies offered by the two jurisdictions.

Part I

Membership and Internal Affairs
of Trade Unions

Chapter 2
Trade Union Organization

DEFINITIONS

Before we go further into the subject of internal trade union government, it is desirable to clarify the terms we shall be using, particularly as some of them bear statutory meanings different from those in popular use.

The general term for organizations in this field, which is employed in the Industrial Relations Act 1971, is 'industrial organization'. This category is subdivided into 'organizations of workers' and 'organizations of employers'. An organization of workers is any organization, temporary or permanent, which consists wholly or mainly of workers and whose principal objects include the negotiation of relations between workers of the description for which it caters, and employers and organizations of employers. A federation of such organizations is also within the definition.

It will be noted that so far as this definition extends there is no requirement of independence from employer control, nor of registration. The term 'trade union' on the other hand is now properly confined to organizations of workers which have registered with the Registrar of Trade Unions under the 1971 Act. In order to register, and thus become a trade union within the statutory definition, the organization must be independent (meaning that it shall not be under the domination or control of an employer or group or organization of employers) and have power, without the concurrence of a parent organization, to alter its own rules and to control application of its own property and funds.

A federation may also register as a trade union but only if all its constituent or affiliated member organizations are registered, either as trade unions or upon the special register.

This is confusing and may well need later statutory amendment. Undoubtedly the term 'trade union' will continue to be used generally. Difficulties will arise in the case of largely autonomous sections of trade unions which cannot register separately because of some residual control of their funds.

The term 'worker' is defined at some length in the 1971 Act: 'worker' (subject to the following provisions . . .) means an individual regarded in whichever (if any) of the following capacities is applicable to him, that is to say, as a person who works or normally works or seeks to work:

(*a*) under a contract of employment, or

(*b*) under any other contract (whether express or implied, and, if express, whether oral or in writing) whereby he undertakes to perform personally any work or services for another party to the contract who is not a professional client of his, or

(*c*) in employment under or for the purposes of a government department (otherwise than as a member of the naval, military or air forces of the Crown of any women's service administered by the Defence Council) in so far as any such employment does not fall within either of the preceding paragraphs.

Class (*a*) refers to the type of person normally called an employee. The former term 'contract of service' has been abandoned, no doubt as having emotive undertones. It is important to note, however, that while it is sensible to let 'contract of employment' take its place, this phrase has in the past been used in some statutes as a neutral term to cover anyone engaged to do work whether under a contract of service (i.e. as an employee) or on a self-employed basis. Class (*b*) comprises those normally termed self-employed, but excludes from that category those who, in popular terms, would not so describe themselves because they are regarded as professional men dealing with clients. This last is a very imprecise type of phrase. The banker would regard himself as a professional man but the clearing banks deal with 'customers'. It is obviously sensible to include those in ordinary banking within the Act, whilst the professional merchant banker would no doubt be excluded. So it is important to emphasize the existence both of a profession and of clients. The professions are, however, an ill-defined class. Are they to include estate agents, for example? If so, what happens when the estate agent deals with professional clients one day and private house purchasers the next? It remains to be seen whether this definition will permit courts to take finer points such as, for instance, to accept an argument that a self-employed man who undertakes that the work shall be done, probably but not necessarily by him personally, is within class (b). Class (c) merely includes civil servants within the meaning of the term 'worker'. They would probably have come within class (a) in any event, but there is some doubt about this on technical legal grounds.

We shall see that at later stages in the Industrial Relations Act 1971, and indeed in other parts of the law, a distinction has to be made between employees and the self-employed. Surprisingly, the legal test of the existence of a contract of employment (service) and a contract of self-employment (services) is indistinct. It appears that the most modern approach is as follows. The court arrives at a prima facie conclusion by the application of certain fundamental guide-lines. The most significant of these are, firstly, whether the alleged employer is in a position to control the manner in which the work is done and, secondly, whether the work must be performed personally or can be performed by some person to whom it is delegated. This prima facie conclusion is then checked by examining the elements of the relationships which were inconsistent with it. These elements are numerous, since they notionally include anything that one might not expect to find in a contract of employment. All of them are merely evidence of the existence of one type of contract or another, and the existence of some inconsistencies need not mean that any one type of contract is rejected. So the court will look again at the element of control, it will consider who provides the tools and machinery by which the work is done, how the wages are paid, whether the work must be done at a particular time and even what the parties themselves say about the nature of the relationship they intended. In this examination it may allow itself to be influenced by what one might expect to find in the trade. So one would expect the production-line worker to be employed, but the prevalence of self-employment in the construction industry would produce a greater readiness to find self-employment there. A very important factor to consider is whether the worker stands to gain or lose by good or bad management of the work. This factor was originally expressed by asking who bears the chance of profit and the risk of loss, but obviously a piece-rate worker could be classified as self-employed on this broadly expressed basis. The courts emphasize that they are looking for a factor which points to the small businessman and away from the dependent employee. Finally, it must be emphasized that the factors taken into account and the weight given to them will vary according to the purpose for which the definitition is required. If, for instance, the court is asked to decide whether a man is employed, so as to cast upon the alleged employer the burden of civil liability for the man's faults during employment, the element of control will play a large part. If one is deciding in which class a person is to be placed for the purpose of national insurance benefits and contributions, the element of economic independence, demonstrated by the profit and loss factor, will be of more significance.

REGISTRATION

Three registers exist to cover industrial organizations within the meaning of the Industrial Relations Act.

(a) the register of trade unions;
(b) the register of employers' associations;
(c) the special register.

The provisional register was a wholly transitional arrangement to contain all organizations which had been registered under the earlier system introduced in 1871 (with the exception of such organizations which themselves requested their removal), and any organization which applied for inclusion within six months of the beginning of October 1971 when this part of the Act took effect. Within six months of entry upon the provisional register the Registrar had to determine whether the organization fell within the definition of an organization of workers, or of employers, and had the requisite degree of independence to be registered. At present he appears to construe 'independence' as anything not involving economic dependence on contributions by employers to the funds of the organization. Employer influence does not seem necessarily to be a disqualification. If so satisfied, he was to cancel provisional registration and issue a certificate of full registration. Provisional registration conferred a few of the protective advantages available to fully registered organizations, but did not permit those organizations only provisionally registered to use the statutory machinery for establishing bargaining agencies, agency shops, and so on. An organization might remain on the provisional register for a maximum of a further six months if the Registrar was not satisfied of its eligibility for full registration. If, during this further period, he was satisfied that such elibigility could be achieved by a change of rule and that the organization was taking all necessary steps to alter its rules, he could permit it to remain on the provisional register for such further period as he considered appropriate to achieve this end. Otherwise, before the end of the extra six-month period, he was to cancel the provisional registration. Once all such organizations had been removed from the provisional register it ceased to exist.

Thereafter the ordinary process of direct application to be placed on the permanent register takes over. An applicant must apply in the prescribed form accompanying the application with:

(a) a copy of its rules and list of its officers (once registered, a note of any change in either matter must be sent to the Registrar within one month and, in the case of a change of rules, must be accompanied by a fee of £10);

(b) the names and addresses of its branches (if any);

(c) a return of its finances similar to the annual return required of a registered trade union (unless the organization has not been in existence for a year).

The full registration is then made when the Registrar is satisfied that the organization satisfies the same requirements as it was necessary to satisfy for transfer from the provisional register, and upon the payment of a £25 fee.

The precise purpose of the *special register* is obscure. It seems to have been designed for those bodies which satisfied the definitions of a trade union (i.e. it is not open to organizations of employers) but did not wish to register as such. Organizations applying to be placed on this register must be incorporated by charter or letters patent of the Crown. It is also provided that a company registered under the Companies Act 1948, which also satisfies the definition, is eligible for special registration, but it is difficult to imagine many organizations in this category since an organization which had among its principal objects the regulation of industrial relations would have been ineligible for registration under the Companies Act. Some organizations, despite this prohibition, are known to have secured double registration before 1971. These chartered, and otherwise incorporated, bodies are normally professional institutes, colleges and other associations which would have considered designation as a trade union to impair their professional status. An organization desiring special registration must send with the application a copy of its rules, a list of its officers and the names and addresses of its branches. At no time does it have to submit annual statements of its accounts.

An organization on the special register is an organization of workers within the meaning of the Industrial Relations Act. It is not a 'trade union' within the statutory definition, but it is able to make use of any of the statutory machinery provided for use by a 'trade union'.*

Every registered trade union must keep proper accounts of its transactions, assets and liabilities and must establish and maintain a satisfactory system of control of its accounts, cash holdings, receipts and remittances. The account must be such as to give a true and fair view of its state of affairs and to explain its transactions. The organization must also maintain a register of its members. A trade union must submit to the Registrar an annual statement of its affairs, before 1 June in any year, relating to the last preceding year unless the Registrar directs some other period or date. Unless the organization is very small (Schedule 5(9)) the accounting section must be audited by an appointed auditor who must be a member of a body of auditors recognized for the purpose of the Companies Act 1948 section 161(i)(a). The accounting section must include revenue accounts indicating the income and expenditure for the period, a balance sheet and such other accounts

* There must remain some doubt on this point. Section 86(2) seems to say that all the provisions of the Act apply to a specially registered union as if it were a trade union. But section 86(3) says that the definition section in relation to trade unions does not apply. This might seem to prevent the organization using any provision of the Act expressly reserved for trade unions. Such a construction is suggested by the provision in section 86(4) of only certain specified sections in which use of the term 'trade union' shall indicate organizations in the special register. Exclusion from use of the remainder of the Act would, however, appear to be nonsense.

as required by the Registrar which shall give a true and fair view of the matters to which they relate. The annual return must additionally include the auditor's report and any other matters the Registrar may require. This may well be considered in practice the most burdensome part of registration. Before 1971 few trade unions kept accounts which would have stood up to professional auditing.

Unless exempt by the Registrar on the ground that the smallness of its membership would make the task unduly onerous, a registered trade union must publish in every calendar year a report relating to its activities. It may do this either by supplying a free copy to every member or by including it in a journal relating to its affairs and activities and available (not necessarily free) to all its members. The report must include the annual return in full and any other prescribed information. If the union is exempt from this requirement it must, in every such exempt year, supply free to each member a copy of its annual return.

A trade union must supply to any person at a reasonable charge a copy of its rule book and, at a 'prescribed charge', a copy of its latest annual report.

A registered trade union which is maintaining a members' superannuation scheme must arrange for its examination by a qualified actuary who must report to the union (a copy of the report must be sent to the Registrar within three years of the commencement of the Act) within two years of the commencement of operation of the relevant part of the Act. If a suitable actuarial examination of such a scheme has been made within two years before the commencement of the Act this two-year period may be extended to five years. (This commencement date is presumably the coming into operation of the registration provision, so the time limit is October 1973.)

The report of the actuary must state whether, in his opinion, the premium or contribution rates are adequate and the accounting or funding arrangements are suitable, and whether the fund (where separately maintained) is adequate. A separate fund *must* be maintained for all new schemes, and for *all* schemes after a period of five years from the commencement of the Act. After the commencement of this part of the Act, no registered trade union may begin to maintain a superannuation scheme unless the proposals have been examined beforehand by a qualified actuary and a copy of his report has been sent to the Registrar. The Registrar may revocably exempt a scheme from these requirements if he considers satisfaction unnecessary because of the small number of members covered, or for some other special reason. Periodical re-examination of schemes is required at intervals not greater than five years and the report must be sent to the Registrar within one year from the date of examination. Again, these are regulations which, in the current state of union pension funds, will not usually be easy to satisfy.

RULES

Quite apart from the general applicable statutory requirements in section 65, a registered trade union must have rules covering the following matters:

1. The name of the organization.
2. The address of its principal office (any change in this must be notified within one month).
3. The objects for which it was established.
4. The fact that it has branches (if this is so), and the extent and manner of control on those branches.
5. The election of the governing body at reasonable intervals.

This raises an interesting problem. The requirement is clearly meant to apply to the national executive committe. Most union rules, however, refer to the annual (or other) conference as the 'governing body'. This may well consist of elected representatives; but it is more likely to consist of representatives by reason of their holding of some other office, or simply of all the members. It seems likely that the Registrar will adhere to the plain intent of the legislature and read the requirement as imposing an obligation to elect the national executive at reasonable intervals.

6. The manner of removal from office of members of the governing body.

There is no requirement here that the union should have any particular officers as there used to be, but;

7. The rules must make provision for the election or appointment of officers and the manner of their removal. The same requirement applies to officials who are not officers, such as shop stewards or their equivalents. Previously many rule books of unions with shop stewards have not contained any provision for election or appointment.

8. The powers and duties of:

(*a*) the governing body;

(*b*) the officers;

(*c*) the officials; and

9. The manner in which business meetings are to be convened and conducted.

10. The rules must specify any body by which, and any official (which term includes an officer) by whom, instructions may be given to members of the organization on its behalf for any kind of industrial action, and the circumstances in which any such instructions may be given. This is a vital requirement, but one almost impossible to satisfy. An unregistered union will, of course, be liable for the acts of its officials which it authorizes, but the official will also remain liable. In the case of a registered union, however, liability under the Industrial Relations Act 1971 for the commission of unfair industrial practices falls on the union but *not* on the official when his acts are within his authority. The official of a registered union, if acting within his authority on behalf of the union, will avoid liability altogether, for both himself and his union, for the major unfair industrial practice of knowingly inducing a breach of contract in contemplation or furtherance of an industrial dispute (section 96). It will, therefore, be necessary to ascertain as clearly as possible the scope of authority of an individual official, but in practice any attempt to frame a comprehensive rule of this nature with any degree of precision capable of legal application will be beyond most draftsmen.

11. The manner in which elections are to be held or ballots taken for any purposes of the organization. This includes:

(*a*) eligibility to vote;

(*b*) preparatory procedure;

(*c*) procedure for counting and sorting; and

(*d*) procedure for declaration or notification of the result.

12. In the case of a registered federation the circumstances (if any) in which the organization has power to enter into agreement on behalf of its constituents or affiliated organizations.

13. The manner in which any rules can be made, altered or revoked.

14. The manner in which the organization can be dissolved.

15. The distribution of the property of the union in the event of such dissolution.

16. The descriptions of persons who are eligible for membership.

17. The procedure for dealing with applications for membership.

18. The provision of an appeal against a decision upon such an application.

These last three matters are of considerable importance because of the guiding principle, applicable to all industrial organizations, which makes it an unfair industrial practice, by exclusion from membership, arbitrarily or unreasonably to discriminate against a worker of one of the descriptions of which the organization is intended wholly or mainly to consist and who is appropriately qualified for employment as a worker of that description. This is an imprecise standard but whatever decisions are taken by courts upon its meaning much will depend on the union's own definition of the classes of members of which it consists.

19. The contributions payable in respect of membership, including an admission or re-admission fee, and the amount thereof.

20. The procedure and penalties in the case of default.

According to the guiding principles such procedure need not include a hearing, but must involve reasonable notice of any proposal which involves termination of membership, on financial grounds and the reason for the proposal.

21. Specification of descriptions of conduct for which disciplinary action may be taken.

22. The nature of the disciplinary action in respect of each description.

Such action must not, in any particular case, be unfair or unreasonable. Disciplinary action may not be taken against a member by reason of his refusing or failing to take part in any action which would constitute an unfair industrial practice, or of his refusal to take part in any strike, or irregular industrial action short of a strike called, organized or financed other than in contemplation or furtherance of any industrial dispute or in such circumstances that the strike would constitute an unfair industrial practice on the part of the organization or the person concerned. It may well be that this disability to discipline the strike-breaker where the strike constitutes an unfair practice will prove in practice one of the major sanctions against industrial action.

23. The procedure for taking disciplinary action, including appeals procedure. Apparently there must be such an appeals procedure.

This procedure must include written notice of the charges in reasonable time to allow preparation of a defence, a full and fair hearing and a written statement of the findings. The first two requirements already existed in the common law.

24. Specification of any other circumstances in which membership can be terminated, and the procedure.

25. Specification of a procedure for inquiry into any complaint by a member that action contrary to the rules has been taken by the organization or an official of it.

26. Provision must be made as to the purposes for which and the manner in which any property or funds of the organization are authorized to be applied or invested.

This is again a vital provision. In the case of an award of compensation against a registered trade union, payment may be enforced against all the unions' property except property which is, or has been, in any fund precluded by the union rules from being used for financing strikes, lock-outs or other industrial action. We shall examine the scope of this provision in due course, but the essential starting point of such examination will always be the nature of the rules enabling use of the funds.

Finally, a registered trade union must make provision as to amounts of benefits (if any) and the circumstances in which they are payable to members. Rules must be made for all accounts to be properly recorded, prepared and audited in accordance with the provisions already noted. The rules must provide for the right of members to inspect the accounts and the register of members.

The Registrar may waive any of these requirements where it appears to him that its enforcement would be inappropriate by reason of particular circumstances relating to that trade union. Otherwise the fact that the rules of a registered trade union do not fulfil such a requirement will not invalidate that rule. The effect of this is that the rule can be relied on between the member and his union, subject to the possibility that observance of it will constitute a breach of the guiding principles applicable to all workers' organizations and so be an unfair industrial practice. The Registrar may, however, require alteration of the rule to comply, subject to the ultimate sanction of de-registration.

As soon as practicable after issuing a certificate of registration, or after registration of any change of rules, the Registrar must examine the rules submitted to him to see whether they comply with the guiding principles and with the particular requirements we have just noted. It must be noted, therefore, that suitable rules are not a precondition of registration. If he finds a defect he must serve a notice indicating that an alteration is necessary and specifying a reasonable period, fixed by him, for this to be done. This period may if the Registrar thinks fit be extended once for a further reasonable period, if during the first period the union submits fresh rules which still do not comply with the statutory requirement. The Act does not restrict this extension to a situation in which a genuine attempt has been made to comply with the Registrar's requirements. In practice, no doubt, the Registrar would not grant a further extension in circumstances where no reasonable attempt to comply could be shown.

It should be noted that the directive of the Registrar is required merely to show that alterations are necessary and not what those alterations should be. In practice it is probable that the Registrar will follow past policy and give advice, at least where he is asked to do so. If no satisfactory amendments are made, or no rules are submitted at all, the Registrar may, but apparently need not, apply to the National Industrial Relations Court for cancellation of the registration. In early drafts of the Act provision was made for the Registrar to carry out the cancellation himself, but this was altered when it was appreciated that cancellation of registration by an administrative (as distinct from a judicial) decision is contrary to an ILO convention. The NIRC, if such application is made, can direct cancellation but may alternatively allow a further period for alteration and resubmission of rules as it thinks appropriate.

Alternatively, if at any of the stages of submission of the rules the Registrar does not approve, the union itself may apply to the NIRC for an order directing approval, or allowing an extension of time to comply. The effect of this is that successive applications can be made to the NIRC for extensions of time to permit requisite amendments to be made. Wherever a required change of rules could not be made in the specified time because of a provision in the union's rules, that restrictive provision may be ignored for this purpose.

Apart from requesting cancellation of registration for failing to

APPLICATION TO REGISTER

Prescribed form accompanied by copy of rules, list of officers, list of branches, and financial return

ORGANIZATION

REGISTRATION

On one of the following registers:
(a) register of trade unions
(b) register of employers' associations
(c) special register

Registrar must be satisfied that organization satisfies the appropriate definition and is independent

Fee of £25

REGISTRAR

EXAMINATION OF RULES

To ascertain whether they comply with:
(a) the guiding principles
(b) the statutory requirements as to content content of rules

Notice of defect   *REGISTRAR*

APPROVAL OF RULES AT:

First time limit for amendment

←— REGISTRAR —→

APPROVAL OF RULES AT:

Second time limit for amendment

ORGANIZATION

ORGANIZATION   *REGISTRAR*

Application to NIRC to CANCEL registration

(a) for failure to amend rules
(b) for breach of any other statutory requirement as to registration
(c) for obtaining registration by fraud or mistake
(d) for becoming ineligible by reason of change of rules or of circumstance

APPROVAL OF RULES AT:

Further extension of time to amend rules or otherwise comply

←— COURT —→
- - ORGANIZATION - -

satisfy the requirements as to contents of the rules, the Registrar may apply to the NIRC for cancellation on any of the following grounds:

(a) that registration was obtained by fraud or mistake;
(b) that by reason of a change of its rules or of circumstance the organization has ceased to be eligible for registration;
(c) that the organization has refused or failed to comply with any other statutory requirement as to registration and has persisted in the default after the expiry of a period of at least two months fixed by notice of the Registrar specifying the default.

If the application is made on this last ground, the NIRC may alternatively, if it considers it appropriate, extend the time for remedying the default.

The Registrar himself must cancel registration of a union:

(a) if he is requested by the organization to do so; or
(b) if the Registrar is satisfied that the organization has ceased to exist;

and in either of these cases he must publish a notice of cancellation in the London and Edinburgh Gazettes.

LEGAL STATUS

English law recognizes both natural and artificial persons. Artificial legal entity is acquired by way of what is known as incorporation. This can be conferred by statute or by the exercise of the royal prerogative by way of charter or letters patent. There are a few customary corporations which have enjoyed this status for so long that the law assumes it must have been conferred upon them, and there are also certain offices which carry corporate status in the sense that the office is recognized as embodied in the particular individual holding it (corporations sole).

Apart from this, in theory nothing else exists which is capable of possessing rights and owing duties. An organization which is not a corporation is strictly merely a collection of the individual persons who comprise it for the time being. It follows that though a limited company (which is a statutory corporation) can, for instance, own property, the village cricket club (which is usually an unincorporated association) cannot. If an unincorporated association desires to own property that property would be regarded in law as belonging to some individual or group of individuals (such as the committee). In many cases this ownership on behalf of a group of individuals might be formally established by a device known as a trust under which the legal owner is required to administer the property only on behalf of the objects of a trust. He is then called a trustee.

In the same way something which does not exist cannot, again in theory, sue or be sued in a legal action, although, as regards its property, its trustees might be sued on its behalf.

Originally a trade union was regarded wholly as an unincorporated association, and for this reason the Trade Union Act 1871 required its property to be owned and managed by trustees. At the beginning of the century as a forerunner of a change of lega thought that eventually spread to other unincorporated associa tions, it was said that a sharp line should not always be drawn between incorporated and unincorporated associations. Where an unincorporated association was popularly recognized as having an existence of its own, such as is the case of a trade union, the House of Lords took the view, on two occasions separated by an interval of fifty years, that it should be possible to bring an action against it in its own name and, if no statutory protection stood in the way, that its funds should be available to satisfy a judgment.

The Industrial Relations Act 1971 has produced a series of certain rules:

(a) A registered trade union becomes a full incorporated body upon registration. It has an independent and continuous existence of its own, is known by the name specified in the certificate and has a 'common seal' which it uses, as it were, by way of signature to indicate the existence of its authority and actions.

(b) Upon incorporation all property held on trust for the organization becomes, without more, the property of the organization. That is to say that all trusts of a registered union's property cease to exist. The funds merely become the general property of the organization arranged in funds for special purposes. There does not seem to be anything to prevent the organization re-establishing trusts for itself, for general or particular purposes, if it thinks there is any value in so doing.

(c) As a legal person the registered trade union can be sued in its own name and its funds (subject to the limitations already noticed on funds not available for financing industrial action) become liable to satisfy any judgment against it. This is so whether the funds remain in its own name or are placed in the names of trustees.

(d) An unregistered organization is in the strict sense, not a legal person. It cannot own its property, but must continue to benefit from it by way of trusts. On the other hand, so that it should not acquire an advantage over a registered union, it is expressly provided that any civil action can be brought by or against it in its own name and judgment satisfied against its funds, whether held on trust for it or otherwise, as if it were incorporated. It is, therefore, in an intermediate position between an unincorporated association and a full legal entity.

Although it is easy to state these rules, it is likely that they will be the cause of the application to trade unions of a number of the intricate rules or concepts characteristic of company law. There is no point, in a book of this nature, in speculating as to these consequences before they arise. It may be suggested, however, that there are no advantages to be gained as such from retaining the intermediate stage of the unregistered trade union and that some disadvantages will be felt. Most commonly these will stem from property holding by trustees and the administrative work involved in a change of trustee.

Chapter 3

Trade Union Membership

MEMBERSHIP AS A CONDITION OF EMPLOYMENT

The closed shop agreement (in any of its forms) or, more commonly, the understanding between employers and unions that the former would maintain 100 per cent trade union membership had, by 1971, become a not uncommon feature of the organized section of British industry. Since the 1920s the courts had taken the clear position that such an agreement was not in unreasonable restraint of either the right of the individual freely to offer himself for employment or the right of the employer freely to employ whom he chose. In the 1960s the courts, led by the Master of the Rolls, Lord Denning, cast some doubt on the continued validity of this view. The right to maintain closed shop agreements (normally without seeking contractual validity for them) and to impose them upon the individual worker was never directly challenged in the courts, largely because to do so one would first have to establish a right to work and no such basic right had ever been clearly recognized in English law before 1971.

The Industrial Relations Act, however, provided as a basic rule that every worker (including the self-employed worker) had, as against his employer, a right to join any registered trade union he chose or a right to remain outside any organization of workers or any particular organization of workers; such, for instance, as one designated by the employer. For the employer to enforce a closed shop agreement of any kind in the case of a worker not willing to join the designated union will infringe this basic right and amount to an unfair industrial practice of which the worker can complain to an industrial tribunal. The Act, however, permits some exceptions which may first be summarized before more detailed discussion:

(*a*) An employer, without resorting to suggestions of reward or penalty, may encourage a worker to join a registered trade union which he recognizes as having negotiating rights with him.

(*b*) An employer may, by voluntary agreement or use of the statutory procedure, enter into an agency shop agreement with a registered trade union or a group of registered trade unions. If this happens the individual may normally either join the agency union, or one of them, or remain outside but pay the equivalent of union dues to such union, or one of them.

(*c*) Upon a joint application by an employer and a registered trade union (or group of registered trade unions) a specially permitted post-entry closed shop agreement may be approved if it can be shown that nothing less would prevent the breakdown of organization and collective bargaining in the group of workers covered by the application. This arrangement is known in the Act as an 'approved closed shop'.

It will be seen that there is no provision to permit the continuance of a *pre-entry* closed shop; that is to say, an agreement precluding the engagement of workers who are not members of some, or some particular, organization of workers; or, even more strictly, who have not been recommended for employment by an organization of workers. Any such agreement is said to be void, and may be so declared by the NIRC upon the application of any worker who can satisfy the court that he was refused employment because of such an agreement. This is a vital difference. A pre-entry closed shop allows the union to control entry to the trade. A post-entry closed shop leaves such control in the hands of the employer but ensures strong collective representation of employees.

'ENCOURAGEMENT'

It will be observed that the Act only permits 'encouragement' to join a *recognized registered* trade union. There can, however, be no objection to an employer giving advice on how a right should be exercised without infringing the freedom to exercise that right. It is not difficult to conceive of circumstances where something that could be described as encouragement would amount to an infringement of the ultimate freedom of choice if it had not been specifically permitted; but on the other hand there are many situations where advice could safely be given. No doubt, however, there are matters very close to the borderline of discrimination which (providing they amount neither to reward or penalty) are more clearly permissible when described as 'encouragement' than when described merely as non-interference with the freedom of choice. It must be clearly understood that it is not permissible to use a device such as equalizing the pay of non-members and union members after deduction of their union dues. Even if this deduction was made in both cases by the employer at source it would amount to discrimination against the non-unionist who received no benefit in return for the deduction from his pay. If done without agreement with the worker it would, in many cases, be a breach of the Truck Acts and, therefore, void. Manual workers who had not agreed to such a deduction could claim its repayment.

THE NATURE OF THE 'AGENCY SHOP'
The term 'agency shop' is a somewhat artificial one coined by the statute to describe an agreement whereby the worker is given a choice of three alternatives:

(a) he can become a member of one of the registered unions with whom the agreement exists;
(b) he may decline such membership but pay the equivalent of union dues to one such union. In that case he can be a member of some other organization of workers if he chooses, or he may remain outside any organization;
(c) he may allege a conscientious objection to union membership which, if established by acceptance by the agency unions or the finding, upon application, of an industrial tribunal, entitles him to remain a non-unionist so long as he pays the equivalent of union dues to a charity agreed upon between himself and the unions or, in the case of dispute, resolved by an industrial tribunal.

The onus of choice is on the worker and he must inform his employer of his choice, but it is not for him to ensure that the appropriate payments are made. A conscientious objector, or a person who wishes merely to make the equivalent of union contributions, satisfies the statutory requirements for exemption from membership while a request from him to the employer to make the appropriate deductions is in force.

APPROVED CLOSED SHOP

Where a successful application for a specially permitted post-entry closed shop has been made, the worker must join one of the trade unions with which the agreement is made unless he is specially exempt by reason of a conscientious objection to trade union membership. In the latter case, again, he must request the employer to make salary deductions equivalent to union dues and pay them to charity. The onus is on other workers to apply for membership of an appropriate trade union within three months of the agreement coming into force. Newly employed workers must apply within one month of the commencement of employment. A post-entry closed shop agreement is not specifically declared to be void unless specially permitted, but any attempt to put into practice an unauthorized agreement by dismissing or penalizing a worker who refused to join one of the unions party to it would amount to an unfair industrial practice on the part of the employer. Any person taking or threatening to take industrial action knowingly to induce an employer to commit such an unfair practice would himself be guilty of an unfair practice. On the other hand, where a permitted closed shop, or an agency-shop, agreement exists it is not an unfair industrial practice for an employer to dismiss, penalize or otherwise discriminate against a worker on the ground that he is not a member and has refused or failed (which must mean failed to request the employer) to make the appropriate alternative contributions. In the case of a closed shop agreement the same freedom applies to action against a worker whose membership application has been rejected or who has been expelled and had an appeal against expulsion rejected, or who has allowed the time in which such an appeal could be made to expire. In the case of an agency shop such a person could avoid dismissal or other penalization by requesting payment to a union of sums equivalent to union dues. The union could not refuse such a right.

It is important to emphasize again that the trade union rights apply equally to applicants for jobs. An applicant cannot, therefore, be rejected on the ground of exercise of such rights without the employer committing an unfair practice. It is permissible to reject the application of, or otherwise penalize or discriminate against, an applicant who refuses to satisfy one of the alternatives open to him or, in the case of an approved closed shop agreement, who has been excluded from the union and exhausted his right of appeal. Presumably an excluded applicant who was in the process of appealing ought, strictly speaking, to be taken on subject to the outcome of the appeal.

PROCEDURE

Voluntary negotiation of an agency shop agreement is permitted so long as all the unions concerned are registered and none has been rejected by a statutory ballot less than two years before. If the employer is unwilling to enter into an agreement voluntarily, one or more registered trade unions, or a joint negotiating panel, may make an application to the NIRC specifying the descriptions of worker to be covered and the unions which would form the agency. An employer may also apply but, like the unions, is not entitled to do so unless there is a desire to enter into such an agreement on the part of the unions. Normally, therefore, an employer would use the statutory procedure when he was subjected to conflicting claims.

The NIRC must be satisfied that the application is not made by a union within two years of the report of the rejection of an application by any union, or the statutory revocation of an existing agency in respect of the same, or partly the same, group of workers. The court must also be satisfied that the specified organization is already recognized by the employer as having negotiating rights in respect of the workers covered by the application. So recognition, either voluntarily or by statutory means, must always precede an agency shop. Once satisfied, it must refer the application to the CIR. The CIR must postpone consideration of the application until after the designation of a sole bargaining agent if it appears that such a question is in dispute and that an agency shop agreement is likely to be ineffective until the dispute is settled. Otherwise, it must take steps to hold a ballot among the defined classes of worker, or a wider or narrower group if it considers this desirable. If a majority of those eligible to vote, or two-thirds of actually voting, favour the establishment of the proposed agency shop, the employer must take all such action as is requisite on his part for the purpose of entering into and carrying out an agency shop agreement. No order of the NIRC is required to complete the process.

It is an unfair industrial practice to seek, by industrial action or the threat of it, knowingly to induce the employer not to enter into the agreement or not to carry it out. It would similarly be an unfair practice on the employer's part not to do so. But a somewhat abnormal procedure exists for dealing with this matter.

If the requisite majority of those voting do not favour the agreement, neither a statutory nor a voluntary agency shop agreement may be entered into between the employer and any of the unions concerned, in respect of any of the workers specified, for two years from the date of the CIR report to that effect. No other union may use the statutory machinery in that time, but a voluntary agency shop agreement with another union would be valid.

At any time during the subsistence of a voluntary agreement, or at any time not earlier than two years after the report of a ballot leading to an agreement, any person may apply to the NIRC for termination of the agreement. The application must be supported in writing by not less than one-fifth of the workers to whom the agreement applies. The CIR must then arrange a ballot on the question of termination. If neither a majority of those eligible to vote, or two-thirds of those voting, support the continuation of the agreement, it must be terminated. For two years from the result of a termination ballot no statutory application for an agency shop can be made by any union in respect of any of the workers covered and no voluntary agreement may be entered into with any of the rejected unions. If the ballot confirms the contination of the agreement no further application to terminate it can be made for two years from the date of the report to that effect.

It is an unfair industrial practice for an employer, by lock-out or threat thereof, to attempt to induce anyone to refrain from applying for an agency shop or for a termination order. In turn, it is an unfair practice for anyone, by industrial action or threat thereof, to attempt to induce an employer to enter into an agency shop agreement after a statutory applicaton covering the same group of workers has been made (save after the successful ballot), or not to apply for such an agreement.

A joint application may be made to the NIRC for approval of a proposed post-entry closed shop agreement. Such an application must be accompanied by a copy of the proposed agreement, and may not be made within two years of making a similar application or within two years of the date of the report of a ballot for an agency shop covering the same workers. If the NIRC is satisfied that the application is not disqualified, the matter must then be referred to the CIR which must consider whether such a closed shop, as distinct from the lesser form of agency shop, is necessary for the purposes:

(a) of enabling the workers covered, to be organized, or to continue to be organized, in independent trade unions organized as representative, responsible and effective bodies for regulating relations between employers and workers;

(b) of maintaining reasonable terms and conditions of employment and reasonable prospects of continued employment for those workers;

(c) of promoting or maintaining stable arrangements for collective bargaining relating to those workers; and

(d) of preventing collective agreements relating to those workers, which have been or may thereafter be, made by the applicants from being frustrated.

In short the closed shop must be required to prevent the breakdown of labour organization. If the CIR reports that the conditions have been satisfied and recommends the establishment of the agreement, the NIRC may make an order allowing between one and three months for an application for a ballot to be made. If no such application is made an order to establish the agreement must be made. Thus in this case the ballot is being used in reverse by those who do not favour a closed shop. An application for a ballot, supported in writing by one-fifth of the relevant workers, may be made. If a majority of those eligible to vote, or two-thirds of those voting, support the agreement a similar order must be made. Otherwise, no application for an approved closed shop may be made for two years from the date of the report of failure of the ballot in respect of any description of workers covered by the defeated application.

Once an agreement has been made it may not be compulsorily revoked for two years from the date of the report of the approving ballot (or, presumably, the order of the Court if there is no such ballot, although the Act does not say this). After that time the same revocation procedure applies as for agency shop agreements.

Where an approved closed shop agreement exists it is not an unfair industrial practice to dismiss, penalize, otherwise discriminate against, or refuse to engage a worker who is, or would be, one who refused to join a relevant union or, as a conscientious objector, refused to pay the equivalent of union dues to an agreed charity.

ADMISSION TO MEMBERSHIP OF AN ORGANIZATION

Before the passing of the Industrial Relations Act 1971, the common law had afforded very little assistance to a rejected applicant for trade union membership. It is fair to say that British trade unions were not noted for their tendency to reject applicants but there is a little evidence to suggest that some branches were more discriminatory than the general policy of their union would suggest. The law takes the view that the rights of a member of an association like a trade union arise from a contract between the organization (or each of its other members) and the individual member. The terms of this contract will generally be derived from the rules of the organization, whether written or customary. The significance of this approach lies in the fact that an applicant for membership has no contract. He is not even regarded as in the position of having, by applying, accepted an offer by the organization to enter into a contract. The applicant is making the offer; the organization is considering whether or not to accept it. It followed from this that even if the organization had rules as to admission procedure, or specified that certain types of applicant were entitled to admission, it was under no contractually enforceable obligation to the applicant to follow those rules. It had been said in one case that an applicant was entitled to have his application considered in good faith. That case actually concerned periodic application for renewal of membership (and that, of the stock exchange) and it is difficult to see upon what basis a fresh applicant could have established even this relatively valueless right.

Various writers had suggested that some other ground of action might emerge. If it could be said that a man had a right freely to seek such employment, then it could be argued that any interference with that right of free search was a civil wrong (i.e. a tort). This was often described as the establishment of a right to work, but it was, of course, nothing of the sort. It was never suggested that there was any right to a particular job, nor even to employment generally, if no employer ready and willing to employ could be found. The common law was in some difficulty in designating the freedom to seek work as a right of property since it had persistently refused to recognize that a worker had any property right in a job even when he had found one. None the less, in two decisions the Court of Appeal eventually suggested that interference with the freedom to seek work was actionable as such; at least when that interference amounted to the absolute denial, as by operation of a closed shop agreement, of the opportunity of work to non-members of a particular association. The view accepted by the court was that the law had always recognized that a contract which *unreasonably* restrained freedom to trade or offer one's labour on the market was void. This recognition depended on acceptance of the proposition that the public interest required the free flow of labour and trade. If, therefore, the law considered that a contractual restriction could not be enforced it ought to consider that a non-contractual restriction, which was unreasonable, was likewise contrary to public policy. The way to secure public policy in such a case would be to compel removal of the restriction by admission to the privileged organization. It must be noted that such a remedy would only have applied where the restriction was unreasonable. It would not have applied to the ordinary operation of closed shop agreements which could be justified (although the courts would be the arbiters of what was justified). It would also have been necessary, before the doctrine could have been applied to restrictions imposed by trade unions (within the definition then in force), to overcome the statutory provision then in force to the effect that agreements and trusts of trade unions should not be considered void merely because they were in unreasonable restraint of trade. This, however, would not have been difficult since the court would not have been declaring void an agreement, but rather the refusal to enter into an agreement.

It is not too much, therefore, to suggest that the common law was on the verge of establishing a right to admission where it could be shown to have been unreasonably refused; the courts to decide what was reasonable. It was saved the trouble by the provision of a statutory power of a similar nature in the Industrial Relations Act. That Act provides that:

'Any person who applies for membership of the organization, or of a branch or section of the organization and who –

(*a*) is a worker of the description, or (as the case may be) of one of the descriptions, of which, in accordance with the rules of the organization the organization or that branch or section, as the case may be, is intended wholly or mainly to consist, or of which it wholly or mainly consists, and

(*b*) is appropriately qualified for employment as a worker of that description,

shall not, by way of any arbitrary or unreasonable discrimination, be excluded from membership of the organization, or of the branch or section of it.

As we have seen, in the case of a registered organization an appeal procedure must be provided in respect of application for admission to membership. But the basic right to admission extends to all organizations of workers, whether or not they are registered trade unions, and whether or not they operate any form of closed, or agency, shop, or other restriction on the freedom of non-members to accept employment. In that respect it is wider than the rule which the common law was developing. It requires the determination of three principal questions:

(*a*) Is the applicant a worker of a description for which the organization caters?

(*b*) Is the applicant appropriately qualified for employment as a worker of that description?

(*c*) Does the rejection of his application amount to an arbitrary or unreasonable discrimination?

If the applicant supposes that an affirmative answer might be given to all these he would be justified in making an application, apparently either to an industrial tribunal or to the NIRC as he sees fit (or to the registrar if the organization is registered), alleging that the organization has committed an unfair industrial practice.

It will be impossible, for some time, to give reliable guidance on what the courts would consider to be a reasonable rejection. Rejection of applicants on the ground that they lacked the requisite skills would be considered justified for failure by the applicant to show an 'appropriate qualification'. It must not, however, be supposed that the organization is free to specify its own appropriate qualifications. If a union consists, *inter alia*, of cabinet makers a requirement that an applicant should have served an apprenticeship might well be considered permissible on the ground that this was merely a way of making sure that he was appropriately qualified. Such a requirement in the case of a refuse collector might, in a given case, be considered to go too far, since there were other ways of acquiring an appropriate qualification which had been pursued successfully by the applicant in question.

Given the appropriate qualifications it might be considered not unreasonable to reject an applicant who had been expelled for an offence under the union rules, or for persistent failure to maintain payment of union dues. Whether such rejection would be considered to be reasonable at any time during the whole of the remainder of the working life of the applicant is open to question. It must also be questionable whether it would be reasonable to reject an applicant on the ground that he had left another union able and willing to bargain for him, or that he had left another union with unpaid arrears of union dues (that is to say, to continue to adhere to the Bridlington agreement). Certainly it would never be reasonable to reject an applicant on the ground that he had obtained his appropriate qualifications after a given age, which was a provision to be found in a number of the rule books of craft unions before 1972.

It is interesting to observe, however, that an applicant who wishes to enter a skilled union so that he can work in its closed shops in order to obtain the necessary qualifications can be excluded on the ground that he is not appropriately qualified for employment. Such an argument will, however, not normally be available because skilled unions usually permit membership of apprentices and others learning the trade and, of course, the applicant could be appropriately qualified as a worker of *that* description.

Save in the case of registered unions, no statutory or other legal requirements exist as to the form of admission procedure. An organization which had no procedures, or an inadequate procedure, would, however, run more risk of a successful challenge based on unreasonable exclusion of a qualified applicant.

DISCIPLINE – SUBSTANTIVE OFFENCES

The common law imposed no restriction on the type of offence which a union might specify in its rules. It consistently took the view, formulated in the nineteenth century, that members of a voluntary association could choose with whom they associated. Lord Denning had suggested in cases which came before the Court of Appeal that the law ought not to permit the specification of unreasonable offences, but he had been unable to secure any obvious support from his fellow judges. As a matter of fact it was very difficult to find unreasonable offences in the rule books of any union, but some of the more widely phrased rules might have been applied unreasonably. This applies particularly to what is often referred to as the 'blanket offence': 'Any member acting contrary to the best interests of the union . . .'; 'any member whose conduct is liable to bring the union into discredit . . .'; 'any member guilty of unbrotherly conduct . . .' The qualification 'which in the opinion of the national executive is . . .' is very frequently added to this type of offence. The danger is that, though the courts always insist that because the rules are the terms of a contract, it is, in the last resort, for the courts to say what they mean, it is very difficult for anyone to declare positively that a particular action is not within such a broad rule. The addition of the qualifying phrase will not preclude the courts, although they might be more inclined to say that the interpretation was permissible so long as it was not unreasonable.

It is probably fair to say, however, that no set of rules can comprehend all acts which may properly be considered reprehensible. Some such sweeping-up provision is necessary. It must be clearly understood that once admitted, a member then possesses a contract. Such a contract can be terminated by agreement, but if one party wishes to terminate the contract against the will of the other he can only do so as permitted by the contract. Sometimes such a right is implied, as was formerly the case with termination of the contract of employment by notice and as is the case where a member wishes to resign from a union. But in the case of discipline no such implications are made and no discipline is, therefore, permitted unless it is provided for in the rules. If this is so, objection to the reasonableness of the rules can only be taken when the rule book uses the blanket offence to include all undesirable conduct, with no attempt, or only an inadequate attempt, to set out such specific offences as can reasonably be visualized. In such a case the member has inadequate information of the boundaries of permissible conduct. The situation would then be similar to the position that would exist if it were a crime to do anything which the High Court considered undesirable.

The Industrial Relations Act 1971, however, did not seek to attack the existence of particular rules, but rather struck at particular application of the rules. This it did in very broad terms by providing that no member of any organization should be subjected, by or on behalf of the organization, to any unfair or unreasonable disciplinary action. It then went on to prohibit particularly (but without detracting from the application of the general rule) disciplinary action against a member by reason of his refusing or failing:

(a) to take any action which would constitute an unfair industrial practice on his part;

(b) to take part in any strike called, or in any strike or irregular industrial action short of a strike organized, procured or financed by any person otherwise than in contemplation or furtherance of an industrial dispute;

(c) to take part in any such action in such circumstances that the action would constitute an unfair industrial practice on the part of the organization or of the person concerned.

These prohibitions on internal discipline, particularly the general ones, are as was said in the preceding chapter, probably the most serious legislative restriction on the freedom of a trade union to regulate its own affairs which has ever been imposed. It may be thought that, in refusing to impose such a restriction, the common law has displayed a greater appreciation of reality than the legislature. In attempting to enforce a personal relationship like trade union membership the law has always trodden close to a line, drawn by itself, between feasibility and impracticality. While courts could point to a clear breach of union rules as their justification, the organization itself proved ready to accept a decision forcing upon it a member it did not desire. If such a member has broken not only the rules of the union but the solidity of industrial action upon which trade unionism depends, expulsion will tend to be considered justified whatever the external justice of that breach. Insult may be added to injury by an attempt to reinstate the offender.* In the past it has always been possible for a reinstated

(*NB. To obtain a reinstatement order the complaint would have to be made to the NIRC.)

member to be expelled for some established offence or by the correct procedure, thus putting right the error which invalidated the original action. Such was the respect for the law that such retributive action was almost never taken. It is possible that such acceptance will break down in face of the new approach.

Apart from this, as we have seen, a registered trade union is required to specify any descriptions of conduct in respect of which disciplinary action can be taken by or on behalf of the organization against any of its members. The effect of this provision depends largely on what is meant by 'specify'. It is a very open question whether the blanket offence can be said to *specify* any conduct. On the other hand, it will be difficult for the organization to do without it, if only for the reason already indicated, that no rule book can comprehend specifically all reprehensible conduct.

DISCIPLINARY PROCEDURE

Almost all trade union rule books have, in the past, contained a procedure which was below the standard required by the rules established by common law. From what has been said it might have been thought that, as the right to discipline arose out of the provisions of the rules alone, so also the procedure for discipline was governed solely by the rules and that a trade union might, at common law, have adopted what procedures it chose. Having adopted a procedure, however, it was, and is so far as it conforms with legislative requirements, bound to adhere rigidly to it. This is because unlike the applicant, the disciplined member has a contract containing that procedure. Unless the court in its discretion was prepared to overlook the defect, the most minor slip would invalidate the proceedings. In addition, however, the procedure had to conform to certain minimum standards often referred to as 'the rules of natural justice'. In fact there was only one rule. A person liable to be deprived of a property right is entitled to a fair hearing after proper notice before an impartial tribunal. The detail of what conforms to this requirement varies from situation to situation so that what is natural justice in a town planning application may differ in detail from natural justice in a trade union case. The right is implied in what the courts call 'quasi-judicial proceedings', but the better view seems now to be that such a proceeding will be considered to exist whenever the result of any action may be deprivation of property, including the imposition of a penalty, whether or not any actual procedure is prescribed. To the surprise of most people the common law never accepted that anyone had a property right in his job, holding that it was merely a matter of whatever rights the contract provided. A trade union member was always considered, however, to have a property right in membership of the trade union for reasons which often appeared far less substantial than might have been advanced for employment.

The rules of natural justice are almost certainly now comprehended within the guiding principles applicable to the conduct of all industrial organizations laid down in Section 65 of the Industrial Relations Act 1971. Indeed more has been added. To depart from these requirements will constitute an unfair industrial practice actionable at the suit of the person against whom the action was taken. This is in addition to an alternative action at common law on the former basis of failure to comply with natural justice. The procedural requirements in the Act are that the person to be subjected to disciplinary action (except in respect of non-payment of union dues):

(a) has written notice of the charges brought against him and is given a reasonable time to prepare his defence;

(b) is afforded a full and fair hearing;

(c) is given a written statement of the findings resulting from the hearing;

(d) has either exhausted his internal appeals (if any), or allowed the right to appeal to expire.

In the case of discipline for non-payment of dues all that is required is that reasonable notice of intention to terminate membership and the reason for it is given. This requirement applies to all forms of termination apart from disciplinary termination. A registered trade union must have rules setting out its disciplinary procedure, and providing for appeal. The Registrar must see that these should be adequate to satisfy the above requirements. An unregistered organization need have no such rules but will then run the risk of offending against the guiding principles if it merely observes inadequate rules. The absence of an appeal procedure would, however, offend no such principles.

The rules of a registered union must contain a procedure by which a member may complain of any breach of union rules.

Presumably, however, this applies to administrative rather than disciplinary rules since appeal is already provided for in the latter case.

At least for some years the earlier cases on what amounted to notice and what amounted to a full and fair hearing will continue to influence the NIRC in deciding whether the procedural requirements have been satisfied. What will alter is that it will no longer be possible to argue as to whether natural justice applies in the circumstances or whether it can be expressly excluded by the contract of membership stating, for instance, that summary discipline may be imposed without a hearing. Any such provision would be void as an attempt to exclude the statutory requirements. Notice must now always be written, whereas in the past it was theoretically possible that oral notice would have been sufficient. The principles only state that the notice shall be of the charge. The common law had established that the notice should make plain the essential facts from which the charge arises. A notice which did not allude to such facts would plainly be inadequate to enable preparation of a proper defence. The courts have said categorically that a member is not to be left to guess at the charges, however inspired his guess may be. It ought to follow that he should not be left to guess what facts they allude to and that a knowledge of those facts is impliedly required by the clear intent of the principle which is to enable him to prepare his defence.

The question of how much time he should be given depends entirely on the complexity of the facts and, probably, the seriousness of the charges. It is impossible to give any better guide-line than to ask what is 'reasonable'. The court will not be astute to take too strict a view. An official acting honestly should be able to decide what would be reasonable. He should probably be prepared to grant a request for an extension of time if it appears to have support and he would be wise to attempt to err on the side of exceeding the limits. One obvious aspect which is sometimes overlooked must not be forgotten. If fresh facts emerge during the hearing which materially affect the charge, whether or not they lead to fresh charges, the person charged should be given an opportunity to consider whether he requires more time to prepare his defence and should be given that time if he asks for it. It is suggested that whenever fresh charges are made fresh notice and a new date for hearing should be given.

The new statutory provisions omit one matter upon which the

common law, though often overlooked, is quite clear. Not only is the person charged entitled to notice, but so also is each member of the committee hearing the case. The intention is that he may decide whether or not to attend. No account will be taken of the fact that, as it turns out, his vote would not have altered the decision, because the courts take the view that it cannot be said what influence he would have had had he attended. So the courts have held that, unless it is physically impossible to notify the member, a person tried by a committee, a member of which has not been given notice of the meeting, may have the decision declared void. Since such a failure does not fall within the terms of the Act, and would probably not be a breach of the union's rules as such, it would appear that a complaint of it would have to be brought in the ordinary courts and not before the Registrar, the industrial tribunals or the NIRC.

The expression 'a full and fair hearing' is obviously imprecise and the statutory provision certainly adds nothing to the common law, save, perhaps, a more efficient procedure for enforcement of the obligation. The common law, theoretically, did not insist on an oral hearing if a fair trial could be had in writing. Such a possibility was, however, unlikely in practice. It may be assumed that it would be unwise to conduct a written hearing if either side objected or if the case was of any significant complexity, either as to its facts or to the law. Generally provision of a fair hearing would require opportunity to call, examine and cross-examine an adequate number of witnesses. Rule books which artificially restrict the number of witnesses cannot safely be followed on this point. The common law had never clearly settled whether the right to a hearing extended to afford a right to be heard on the penalty to be imposed as well as on the substantial question whether the accused had committed the offence. It seems unlikely that courts operating under the 1971 legislation would deny such a right.

Of much greater importance than any other aspect of the requirement of a fair hearing is the requirement that the tribunal should be free from bias. This was well established in the common law and the decided cases upon it will undoubtedly guide tribunals in interpreting the provisions of the 1971 legislation. It is probable that there are many degrees of permissible bias, depending on the type of tribunal under consideration. Little help can be obtained from discussing whether disqualification will arise if

there is a 'reasonable suspicion of bias' or if the judge concerned 'can be suspected of bias' or whether there is 'a real likelihood of bias'. Of greater value is the warning of an American
judge:

> 'If, however, "bias" and "partiality" be defined to mean the
> total absence of preconceptions in the mind of the judge, then no
> one has ever had a fair trial, and no one ever will. The human
> mind, even at infancy, is no blank piece of paper. We are born
> with predispositions; and the process of education, formal and
> informal, creates attitudes which precede reasoning in particular
> instances and which, therefore, by definition are prejudices.'

The question becomes, therefore, one of how much prejudice the
courts will permit of a trade union tribunal before it passes the
boundary into disqualification. There are, however, certain situations in which in practice it would be impossible to discount a
presumption of disabling bias. The common law has always dis-
tinguished financial advantage and, in effect, held that where
a member of a tribunal or court stands directly to gain financially
from a decision one way or another that person is disqualified.
The courts have not been astute to find such a gain. If, for instance, a
trade union member is accused of default in payment of his dues, a
decision to this effect will tend to induce him to pay and the union
will be that much better off. The nominal share of all the members
in the funds will increase and, in the event of dissolution of the
union, they might receive fractionally more money as representing
this share. All this would be considered too indirect to count. The
same position was held to exist where licensing justices, all of
whom were members of the local co-operative society, had granted
an 'off-licence' to a department of that society. They would stand
to gain from any rise in the amount or rate of dividend on pur-
chases made as a result of the off-licence rules, but it was held that
this did not disqualify them. Plainly, however, if an official of a
trade union were accused of improperly refusing payment of
benefit to members, a member who had claimed such benefit
would be disqualified. So long as the financial advantage is direct
it will act as a disqualification however small it may be.

In the case of other alleged causes of bias the decision in the
case of trade union matters is likely to rest on one of the less strict
tests, such as that of a real likelihood of bias. In turn 'bias' is likely

to be construed narrowly so as to mean either a mind closed to argument or a mind affected by a special circumstance so as to be likely to come to one decision rather than another. Most of the cases have revealed something very closely approaching a closed mind, probably because where bias has existed trade union tribunals have not been careful to conceal it. The existence of special circumstances, such as relationship with the prosecutor, being the subject of an attack by the member charged, or having actively taken sides against the member charged, would almost always lead common law courts to conclude that bias existed. It should be noted that the participation of one biased member will disqualify the entire tribunal so as to render its decision void. This would be so even if the biased member did not vote. It is more doubtful whether the non-participatory presence of such a person would have the same effect. The courts would probably consider in such a case the extent of any evidence that such presence might have influenced other members.

A disciplined member can complain of an unfair industrial practice unless he receives a written statement of the findings resulting from the hearing. He is under no prior obligation to ask for this, but it would seem that the notice need only be a bare statement of findings and need contain no reasons. The intention behind this statutory requirement was almost certainly to facilitate an appeal but, if this view of its extent is correct, it will serve little purpose.

APPEAL PROCEDURES

In recent years common law courts had devoted some considerable thought to the question of the extent to which an accused member, found guilty of the offence charged, was bound to exhaust internal appeals before he appealed to the ordinary courts on the ground of procedural or substantive defect. Generally speaking, the courts would not allow their ultimate right to ascertain whether the contract of membership had been complied with to be excluded. To put it another way, internal tribunals could conclusively determine the facts but could not finally decide on the application of the law to these facts. The courts would, however, permit an express term of the contract to require the member first to resort to internal appeals procedures. The question was whether such an obligation could be implied from the mere provision of such machinery. The final position reached before the passage of the 1971 Act was that even an express requirement of exhaustion could be ignored if the plaintiff could show cause why the contractual obligation should be set aside. In the absence of such express requirement the courts would more readily intervene, but might require the plaintiff to resort to his internal appeals. Finally it was pointed out that an explicit attempt entirely to exclude the courts, which many rule books contained, was entirely void. It could not be read as a permissible requirement that the member should first exhaust internal remedies.

Much can be argued on either side of this formulation. The common law did not preclude the imposition of the penalty pending appeal. It could hardly do so since the ordinary criminal law normally operates on the same basis. So it might be said that there would be cases where speedy resort to the courts would be the only effective means of securing justice. On the other hand, it could be contended that an organization was entitled to be saved from the expense (and, indeed, the bad publicity) of legal proceedings by providing its own means of remedying initial errors.

The Industrial Relations Act 1971 cuts through this uncertainty by providing that it will be an unfair industrial practice to impose upon a member of any organization of workers a restriction in respect of his instituting, prosecuting or defending proceedings before any court or tribunal or giving evidence in any such proceedings. This must apply to prohibit even a temporary restriction pending exhaustion of internal remedies. Such a prohibition is less explicable in the light of the prohibition, already noted, upon the imposition of a penalty before exhaustion of internal appeals (or the expiration of the time for them to be taken). The effect of the two provisions is that an organization which provides internal appeals will not necessarily afford itself an opportunity to rectify errors without resort to the courts, but will compel itself to delay the imposition of any penalty. In view of the desirability of internal appeals procedures the obvious effect of this is to be regretted. For a registered trade union, however, there is an advantage in that where a member complains to the Registrar of an unfair industrial practice or a breach of the rules by the association, the Registrar may refer the matter to the union's own internal procedures if it appears to him, in accordance with the rules of the organization, that these procedures are adequate and that the matter could be, but has not been, referred to them. The procedures referred to are obviously appeal procedures, so that without them there can be no chance of the reference back of a complaint.

COMPLAINTS BY MEMBERS

We have seen in the previous chapter that the rules of a registered trade union must specify procedures for discipline, which must include an appeals procedure, and a procedure for inquiring into any complaint by a member of breach of the rules of the trade union. Apart from this there is now a very wide range of action that can be taken against registered or unregistered organizations of workers. It may be set out in tabular form as shown overleaf.

Statutory requirements imposed by the Industrial Relations Act 1971 can be divided, as has been seen, into general precepts governing all industrial organizations and into those which directly control the content of the rules of registered trade unions. Breach of the first group – the 'guiding principles' contained, so far as organization of workers are concerned, in section 65 of the Act – gives rise to an unfair industrial practice. With the exception of those unfair industrial practices relating to the employment of individuals, all unfair industrial practices can be complained of before the NIRC. In practice it is unlikely that a member would incur the extra expense of making a complaint to this court and the normal action will lie to an industrial tribunal. A tribunal is, however, only entitled to declare the rights of the complainant and award him compensation; whereas the NIRC has power, in addition, to make an order directing the organization to refrain from continuing the unfair practice and from taking any other action of a like nature in relation to the complainant. In this context that amounts to an order of reinstatement. A member who felt that such a positive order was the only means by which the organization would be induced to follow the legal requirements would, therefore, be obliged to take action in the court. This may be thought an inexplicable defect in the jurisdiction of industrial tribunals. On the other hand, such tribunals include an employer representative. Unions are not likely to be happy about reinstatement orders supported by him and the chairman and opposed by the third member. It should be observed that the action before the

Complainant	Cause	Defendant	Court
1. Any person against whom the action was taken	Unfair industrial practice constituted by breach of the guiding principles in the 1971 Act	Any organization of workers or employers*	NIRC (6 months' limit)
2. Individual member, involuntarily removed member applicant for membership	Unfair industrial practice constituted by breach of the guiding principles or breach of rules of the organization	Registered organizations*	(a) Registrar. Thence to industrial tribunal (four weeks' limit) (b) Direct to industrial tribunal (four weeks' limit) (at option of complainant)
3. As 2	As 2	Any organization of workers or employers*	As 2(b)
4. Member or expelled member	Breach of rules	Any organization	Common law courts (there is no power for these courts to stay this action on the ground that it might be litigated elsewhere)
5. Registrar upon failure to pursue claim under 2(a)	As 2	As 2*	(a) Industrial tribunal (b) NIRC (at option of registrar)
6. Registrar on his own initiative	Serious or persistent breach of rules or guiding principles	Registered organizations	As 5(b)

*Actions against organizations of employers under these heads are not available to corporate members of employers' organizations.

court is not limited to those who are or have been members or applicants for membership; although in the normal way it would be unlikely that any other person could show that he was a person 'against whom' this type of action 'had been taken'.

The other two statutory procedures are limited to persons, other than corporate persons, who either:

(a) are members of organizations of workers or employers (other than federations);

(b) were members of such organizations and have ceased to be so, other than by voluntary resignation;

(c) have sought to become members of such organizations and been refused, or prevented, by the organization, or someone acting on its behalf, from obtaining admission.

The exclusion of corporate persons from these procedures means that the companies which generally make up the membership of employers' associations are unable to make use of them.

If the organization is registered on the ordinary, or the special, register any such person may complain to the Registrar that action specified in the application constituted an unfair industrial practice as being in breach of the 'guiding principles'; or was a breach of the rules of the organization, other than political fund rules or rules for taking a vote on a resolution to approve an instrument of amalgamation or transfer of engagement. The application must be made *within four weeks* of the latest date on which the actions complained of occurred, or came to the knowledge of the applicant, or, alternatively, within four weeks of a final determination of the complaint by the internal machinery of the organization, if that machinery was resorted to. If the matter could be, but has not been, referred to an internal procedure, established by the rules of the organization and appearing to the Registrar to be adequate, the Registrar may defer consideration of the matter until it is resubmitted to him within four weeks of a final determination by that procedure or after a reasonable time has been allowed after reference to such procedure for determination. The effect is to force the complainant to use internal appeal machinery and to throw on him the burden of a fresh application. Whether or not this is done, however, is entirely at the discretion of an administrative official.

If the matter is initially, or secondarily, referred to the Registrar he is required to investigate it and give notice of his conclusions both to the applicant and to the organization. If it appears to him that the complaint is well founded, he must then endeavour to promote a settlement without reference to an industrial tribunal. Anything communicated to the Registrar in connection with this conciliation stage is privileged from use in evidence before the industrial court or a tribunal without the consent of the person making the communication.

There is nothing to prevent any complainant bypassing this procedure, without resort to it at all, by making application direct to an industrial tribunal. In the case of an unregistered organization, such direct application is all that is available. The same is true if the Registrar's attempt to conciliate has failed, but in that case the Registrar might himself refer the complaint, even if the complainant did not wish to pursue it. Once an application to the Registrar has been made, however, it must be proceeded with until the point where the Registrar has communicated the findings of his investigation. An application to an industrial tribunal on such a matter must be made within four weeks of the facts giving rise to the cause of action, or of the Registrar's report, whichever is longer.

Somewhat surprisingly, we find that if a well-founded application is made to the Registrar and no reasonable settlement is reached, the Registrar may, if he is of the opinion that the matter is sufficiently serious, present a case on his own initiative to the NIRC. In less serious matters where, none the less, he feels that a complaint ought to be presented and that the applicant has not and does not intend to present it, he may present the application to an industrial tribunal. No doubt neither the court nor a tribunal would award compensation to a former complainant who did not desire to pursue his claim, but the procedure which can take the matter out of the hands of a complainant and pursue it is a far-reaching form of supervision. It should be noted that though some justification might be found for the existence of such a procedure in the fact that a complainant might have been intimidated from pursuing his claim, the power is neither confined to such situations nor cast in such terms as to suggest that it should be so confined in practice. In any event no such protection from the effects of intimidation is afforded in the case of the applicant who does not pursue his claim after reference to internal machinery.

Member
Involuntarily removed member

Applicant for membership

Breach of rules

Common Law Courts

Damages
Declaration
Injunction (order to reinstate)

If organization is registered

Breach of rules
Breach of guiding principles

If applicant does not pursue

Industrial tribunal

Compensation
Declaration of rights

Organization's own machinery

Registrar

Applicant

Conciliation

Registrar

Applicant

Transfer of action by NIRC

Registrar

If applicant does not pursue claim

If undertakings are not complied with

Serious or persistent breach of rules or of guiding principles

Consultation to secure compliance

Any person against whom action is taken

Breach of guiding principles

National Industrial Relations Court

Compensation
Declaration of rights
Order to cease practices

Order to take such action as would be appropriate to remedy or mitigate consequences and or prevent continuance or repetition

Finally, the Registrar may institute an investigation entirely on his own initiative if he has reason to suspect that there has been serious or persistent breach of the rules of a registered organization (other than relating to the political fund or the taking of a ballot on amalgamation or transfer of engagements), or that there has been serious or persistent breach, by or on behalf of the organization, of the 'guiding principles'. If as a result of such an investigation it appears that one (which seems odd if the supposition is of persistent breach) or more breaches have occurred, or that the guiding principles have been contravened, he must give notice of these conclusions to the organization and endeavour to secure such action or undertaking on its part as in his opinion would remedy or mitigate the consequences, and/or prevent continuance or repetition of the breach. If no such satisfactory action or undertaking is obtained, or one obtained is not fulfilled, the Registrar may present a complaint to the Industrial Court after notifying the organization of this effect. The court may order the organization to take such action as in its opinion would be appropriate to remedy or mitigate the consequences, and/or prevent continuance or repetition of the breach.

There can be little doubt that these procedures, coupled with the statutory requirements which they enforce, amount to the most complete supervisory control over the organization and functioning of industrial organizations outside those countries which are either Communist or Fascist dominated. The history of British trade unions produces no evidence whatsoever that such a degree of control is necessary to ensure that standards are observed. It is true that those who derive their information only from certain sections of the Press are apt to cite the ETU (ballot rigging) case, or any one or more of a few reported cases (such as *Edwards* v. *SOGAT*) where clear and deliberate malpractice in admission or expulsion procedures took place. It would be incredible if, in a movement of 10 million persons over a period of, say, twenty-five years, no such cases should occur. It is highly surprising, even allowing for the good sense of local officials, that so few examples exist. The common law had found it easy to control wrongful expulsion. It could do little about deliberate ballot rigging, but one case in 150 years of trade unionism scarcely justifies such complex quintuplication of control.

Chapter 4
Internal Government

FUNDS, PROPERTY AND ACCOUNTS

Until 1971 all trade unions were obliged to vest their funds in trustees who, however, normally acted upon the instructions of the governing body of the organization. This requirement still applies to the funds of unregistered organizations. A registered organization is, however, given corporate status by the Industrial Relations Act 1971. As it thereby acquires a separate existence in law it can directly own its property. There is no reason, however, why, like any other person, it should not, if it so wishes, place its own property in trust for itself. So registered trade unions may continue to vest funds in trustees. No great advantage will be obtained by doing this, however, save in the case of a fund for a particular purpose which can be established as charitable. It might be expected that the trust system will gradually be dispensed with by registered unions; but this does not inevitably follow since trade unions tend to adhere to long-established practices.

The rules of a registered union must make provision as to the purposes for which and the manner in which any property or funds of the organization are authorized to be applied or invested. In the case of an unregistered organization which had no such rules, or rules which did not relate to the entirety of its funds, funds not specifically dealt with would be treated as general funds applicable to all its purposes and open to investment within the normal powers of trustees. The ordinary statutory powers of investment (contained in the Trustee Investment Act 1961) are complex. It is suggested that all organizations with trustees should have a rule such as that:

> Trustees are empowered to invest the funds of the union in any securities whatsoever as if they were the beneficial owners

thereof, subject, however, to the directions of the National Executive Committee.

The rules of a registered organization must also make provision as to the amounts of benefit payable to members and the circumstances in which the benefits are to be payable. A registered organization which maintained a members' superannuation scheme when the Industrial Relations Act came into force must secure the report of a qualified actuary upon the scheme within two years; sending the report to the Registrar before the end of the third year. (If, upon its application to register, a union can show that the scheme was examined by a certified actuary not more than two years before the Act came into force, the Registrar may exempt it from further report for five years.) In the case of any scheme commenced after the date of the Act the report must be made and sent to the Registrar before the scheme comes into operation. The Registrar can revocably exempt an organization from these requirements if he is satisfied that, because of the small number of members to whom it would apply, or for some other special reason, it is unnecessary for the examination to be made. Where the report is required on an existing scheme it must include a valuation of the assets and liabilities of the fund. In the case of both new and old funds the actuary must state whether in his opinion the premium or contribution rates are adequate, whether the accounting or funding arrangements are suitable and whether, if a separate fund is provided, it is adequate. Separate funds must be provided immediately for all new schemes, and for all existing schemes within five years of the coming into force of the Act.

Thereafter, the organization must arrange for further examination at intervals of not more than five years, or such shorter periods as the Registrar may direct. In each case the report must be sent to the Registrar within one year of its being made. This is, no doubt, a series of very proper requirements, but it will have the effect of restricting funds, which in some cases may be considerable, to a specific purpose. Previously, in times of stress, superannuation funds have, no doubt, been pressed into general service.

The rules of all registered organizations must make provision for the keeping of proper accounting records and for the preparation and auditing of accounts. The organization must cause such proper records to be kept and establish and maintain a satisfactory system of control of its accounting records, cash holdings and receipts and remittances and the rights of members to inspect the accounting records. This requirement will, in practice, cause most unions considerable trouble, since few union accounts are well audited.

The rules must contain provision for the appointment and removal of auditors who must be qualified in accordinace with Schedule 5, paragraphs 6–10, of the Industrial Relations Act 1971. No auditor may be removed save by a resolution passed at a general or delegate meeting of members. He must be reappointed unless it is expressly resolved at a general meeting that he shall not be reappointed, or such meeting appoints someone else, or he gives written notice of his desire not to be reappointed, or he is ineligible or incapable of acting.

Every auditor has a right of access at all times to the accounting records of the registered organization and to all other documents relating to its affairs. He is also entitled to require from its officers or branch officers any information and explanations which he thinks necessary to enable him to perform his duties as auditor. He is entitled to attend all general or delegate meetings of members and to receive the normal notices of, and other communications of, such meetings. *He has a right to be heard at any meeting he attends on any matter in the business of the meeting which concerns him as auditor.*

The auditors must report to the organization on the accounts audited by them and contained in the organization's annual return to the Registrar. In preparing the report the auditors must carry out such investigations as enable them to form an opinion on whether the organization has fulfilled the general statutory duty, imposed on registered organizations, to keep proper records and to establish and maintain a satisfactory system of control of its finances, and whether the accounts agree with the records. If the auditor does not obtain all necessary information and explanations, his report must state that fact.

Before 1 June of each year (unless otherwise specified by the Registrar) every registered organization must send to the Registrar an annual return relating to the immediately preceding calendar year (unless the Registrar specifies some other period).

The return must be in the form required by the Registrar and must contain:

(a) income and expenditure accounts for the period;
(b) a balance sheet at the end of the period;
(c) any other accounts required by the Registrar;
(d) a copy of the auditors' report.

This annual return must be reproduced in the next following annual report of the registered organization. The report must be supplied free to every member, or included in a journal relating to its affairs and available to all members, and made available to any non-member on request at a prescribed charge. The Registrar may exempt small trade unions from the requirement to produce such an annual report if, having regard to the small number of members, the requirement would, in his opinion, be onerous. If such an exemption is granted, however, a copy of the annual return to the Registrar must be supplied free of charge to each member.

OTHER ADMINISTRATIVE REQUIREMENTS

Every registered organization must keep a register of its members in a form required by the Registrar, and the rules of the organization must make provision as to the rights of members to inspect the register. Every registered organization must supply a copy of its rules, either free or at a reasonable charge, to any person on request. A copy of all changes in rules, a note of changes in officers, and any change of address of the principal office must be sent to the Registrar within one month of the change. In the case of changes of rule, a registration fee of £10 must also be paid.

OFFENCES AND PENALTIES

Failure to satisfy any of these statutory obligations as regards audit, accounts or returns, or the provision of information to members, constitutes an offence on the part of the officer bound by the rules of the organization to perform the obligation. He has a defence if he can prove that he believed, on reasonable grounds, that some other competent and reliable person was authorized to perform the duty instead, and would perform it. The maximum penalty for this offence is a fine of £100.

Any person who wilfully alters, or causes to be altered, any document required to satisfy these provisions, with intent to falsify it or enable the organization to evade any of the provisions, commits an offence for which the maximum penalty is a fine of £400.

LIABILITY OF FUNDS

The funds of all industrial organizations, whether registered or not, are liable to satisfy an award of damages, compensation or costs in an action brought against the organization as a corporate entity, or, if not incorporated, in its own name as if it were a corporate entity; unless the property in question is, or has been, part of a fund which is precluded from being used for financing strikes, lock-outs or other industrial action. This appears to mean that the exclusion must apply to all industrial action and not merely that within the somewhat confined definitions of strikes or irregular industrial action in the Industrial Relations Act 1971.

The most effective method, therefore, of protecting the funds of such organizations would be expressly to provide that none of its funds were to be available for the financing of industrial action. It would seem that this would still leave the organization free to administer the action and pay those taking part in that administration. It would, of course, prohibit the payment of any strike benefit, but many unions now do not have strike funds or pay benefit. Even where strike benefit is paid it is relatively little. It is, however, true to say that though its non-payment would make little material difference it would probably make considerable psychological difference. Unions already worried about the need to maintain authority over their members might well be reluctant to take what would thus be a major, rather than a minor, step.

More probably, organizations will divide their funds in more detail for particular purposes, immunizing funds such as those for education, research and administration. There is no reason why the land and buildings of the organization should not be treated in the same way, so long as any income derived from letting, or other use, of them is not to be used for financing of industrial action. If the organization does derive substantial income from its real property which it cannot afford to deny to a strike fund, then the only way to save that property from liability to satisfy judgments would be to provide a covering fund expressly only for the payment of damages, compensation or costs. This would always ensure that money was available to meet such awards. This has no great value, however, because once that fund is exhausted the property becomes liable. The fund has to be constantly primed and so only serves to ensure that less money can be made available for financing strike action.

It is important to appreciate that a last-resort statutory power is given to the Registrar which might be used to bypass even the protective immunization of special funds. Strangely, whereas the right to immunize funds is available both to registered and un-registered organizations, the right of the Registrar to petition the High Court for a winding-up order is available only against a registered organization believed to be insolvent. Presumably a union faced with a large sum to pay by way of compensation can-not be believed to be insolvent if its immune funds exceed that amount; but it would be otherwise if they did not exceed it. It is probable that the procedure was only intended to deal with ob-viously financially insecure organizations and that it would not in practice be utilized to bring into account protected funds. The attempt to wind up any large-sized trade union would be almost as interesting to watch as the gaoling of shop stewards for contempt of court.

If the Registrar did take action under this provision he would be required to appoint an inspector to inquire into the affairs of the organization. The inspector may require production of all or any of the books and documents of the organization and may examine on oath any of its officers, members or employees with respect to the conduct of its affairs. If the inspector's report confirms the belief in insolvency the Registrar may petition the appropriate court for a winding-up in accordance with the Companies Act 1948.

THE POLITICAL FUND

At the beginning of the century the House of Lords accepted the argument that the use of the general funds of a trade union for political purposes was beyond the powers of the union, which it considered to be exhaustively defined by statute. It is now accepted that this view must be regarded as incorrect and the Trade Union Act 1913, which appeared as a permissive measure, is now in fact a restrictive measure in that it prevents use of anything but a specific political fund for certain specified political purposes. These purposes are:

(*a*) payment of any expenses incurred directly or indirectly by a candidate or prospective candidate for election to Parliament or to any public office before, during or after the election, in connection with his candidature or election;

(*b*) expenditure on the holding of any meeting or the distribution of any literature or documents in support of any such candidate or prospective candidate;

(*c*) expenditure for the maintenance of any member of parliament or holder of a public office;

(*d*) expenditure in connection with the registration of electors or the selection of a candidate for Parliament or any public office;

(*e*) expenditure on the holding of any kind of political meeting, or on the distribution of political literature or political documents; unless the main purpose of these is the furtherance of the union's statutory objects.

Any organization of workers may set up a political fund for these purposes if the adoption of political fund rules is approved by a majority of those voting in a ballot for the purpose, conducted by the organization, by a procedure approved by the Registrar. In practice, the Registrar has so far (that is to say, under the pre-1971 system of registration) required a second ballot, after the vote for adoption, in order to approve the actual rules, a copy of which should be sent to every member before this second ballot. After a positive second ballot the organization may amend its rule book to include the political fund rules. If the organization is registered, this amendment must be registered like any other amendment. The Registrar must then consider whether the rules satisfy the requirements of the 1913 Act, although in practice that has usually been assured already; up to this time normally by the adoption of one of the sets of model rules issued by the Registrar.

Once it has political fund rules the union may impose upon its members a political levy. It is under no obligation to do so, unless the particular rules impose such an obligation. So a union could selectively impose the levy. In the past the registrar has taken the view that the rules themselves could provide that certain classes of members should not be subject to the levy, but since 1971 the union would have to be careful that selection did not appear as discrimination against applicants. Apart from this, all members will, prima facie, contribute, in the case of new members one month after they have been supplied with a copy of the political fund rules (which is required in the Registrar's model rules), in the case of existing members one month after publication of notice of the right not to contribute. A member who does not give notice to contract out of payment within that month is liable to pay until the first day of January next after he has given notice of his wish to contract out. Such a notice cannot validly be given before an applicant has been accepted for membership.

A member who is exempt from the obligation to contribute to the political fund must not be excluded from any benefits, or placed, directly or indirectly, under any disability or at any disadvantage as compared with other members of the union by reason of exemption, save in relation to the control or management of the political fund. It is not proper to exclude a non-contributor from the whole of an office because that office involves some management of the political fund. In such a case he can only be excluded from those aspects of management. It might be right to exclude entirely a non-contributor if the office substantially involves such control and management.

Only an existing member of a union can complain of discrimination under the 1913 Act. An applicant who was refused membership because he indicated that he would not contribute to the political fund could now, however, complain of an unfair industrial practice arising from breach of the guiding principles relating to admission in section 65 of the Industrial Relations Act 1971.

It is impossible here to look in detail into the question of what activities fall within the list of those which must be supported only from the political fund, but one or two major points may be made. It should be noted that the general description 'political' is misleading. No political overtones are necessary for the support of a candidate to come within the Act. On the other hand, payment of money to members of parliament, or the holder of a public office, is only within the Act if it is referable to that post rather than, for instance, to his retention of an office in the union. Rather strangely, this position is reversed when the Act deals with expenditure on political meetings or the distribution of political literature.

Here the word 'political' is expressly used. The Registrar has held that in this case the meetings and literature referred to are of a party political nature. This would, of course, still bring within the Act a meeting called, for instance, to support a plan for state takeover of a private airline. Some of these strictly political objects may, however, fall within the general statutory purposes of a worker's organization. Such, for instance, would be support or opposition to a government's prices and income policy. Where expenditure is for a mixed object the proper course would appear to be to have regard to the major purpose.

The Registrar has power to decide the meaning of political fund rules and to decide whether they satisfy the requirements of the 1913 Act. There is now an appeal for his decision to the National Industrial Relations Court. The interpretation of the Act itself is not, however, a matter for the Registrar but for the High Court. Despite the transfer by the Industrial Relations Act 1971 of other High Court jurisdiction to the NIRC, this matter has not been so transferred.

ELECTIONS

It is provided, in the case of all industrial organizations, as a guiding principle, that no member of the organization, or of any branch or section of it, shall, by way of any arbitrary or unreasonable discrimination, be excluded from:

(a) being a candidate for or holding any office in the organization or in a branch or section of it;

(b) nominating candidates for any such office;

(c) voting in any election for any such office or in any ballot of members of the organization or of a branch or section of it; or

(d) attending and taking part in meetings of the organization or of any branch or section of the organization.

The voting in any ballot (but apparently not in an election) must be kept secret and every member shall have a fair and reasonable opportunity of voting without interference or restraint. Failure to comply with any of these requirements constitutes an unfair industrial practice which can be made the subject of complaint before either the NIRC, an industrial tribunal, or (if the organization is registered) the Registrar, according to the procedures examined under the heading of 'discipline' in the preceding chapter.

Trade unionists will, no doubt, be puzzled by some of these requirements, at least until some judicial decisions are available to clarify the matter. It is not uncommon to restrict the higher offices in a trade union, either to those who have held lower office or to those who have been members for a specified minimum period. Presumably this would be held not to constitute arbitrary and unreasonable discrimination. Exclusion, for instance, of Communists, equally clearly, would infringe the requirement. The problem of nomination is more difficult to understand since it is, more often than not, the union branch which nominates persons for office. Whether this is an exclusion of the right of the individual member to nominate is an open and difficult question. If it is, it would seem to require some special reason to prevent it from being regarded as arbitrary and unreasonable.

It should be noted that the statutory provisions make quite clear the intention to distinguish between a ballot and an election. Neither term is defined, but the first seems to be regarded as a vote upon a proposal or issue, whilst the second is a vote for a candidate for office. The first, but not the second, is required to be secret. It will, therefore, still be permissible for an organization to conduct elections by a show of hands at a branch meeting. The same distinction, inexplicably, applies to the fair and reasonable opportunity to vote without intereference or restraint, although some forms of interference or restraint would obviously amount to a denial of the right to vote at all. The term 'interference or restraint' is imprecise and, probably, wide. If it had applied to elections it could have been argued that it would preclude the present general rule of forbidding or restricting the issue of election addresses. As it is only applicable to ballots it is likely that examples of malpractice will, in practice, be clear in law, even if factual proof is not always easy to obtain.

So far as registered organizations are concerned, we have already noted in Chapter 2 that the rules must provide for the governing body to be elected at reasonable intervals, and for the election and appointment of all officers and officials (including shop stewards). The rules must also define the manner in which elections are to be held, or ballots taken. This must include eligibility to vote, preparatory procedure, procedure for counting and sorting and for disclosing, or notifying, the result. Determination of the detail needed to satisfy these rather general requirements is obviously largely in the hands of the Registrar. On the whole, unions desiring registration should not find it too difficult to bring rules on this subject up to standard, but most will find that it is necessary to produce rules relating to shop stewards. Electoral practice in respect of them often exists, but is rarely contained in formal union rules.

Although an unregistered union is not required to amend its rules, it should certainly re-examine them to see that they are not likely to lead to infringement of the guiding principles. It is probably true to say that even if the rules are put in order many breaches will occur and some of them will involve breach of these principles. Certainly in the past, elections were the area in which most infringement of rules, as distinct from malpractice, occurred; although little of it was serious. Branch elections frequently more closely resembled appointment by the branch secretary; but that was normally because the branch was fortunate to have even one candidate, let alone a contest. It was not unknown for a branch secretary to forget to distribute voting papers for a national election, but the omission was very rarely more than an oversight, nor likely to affect the result. No doubt in future, with the development of more complex rules, technical deviation will become more common. It is unlikely to be made the subject of action unless it is injurious to some member's interest. Such action is, however, more likely to be brought now that the judicial procedure is more readily available. In the past the inhibitive factors of reluctance to go to the courts and the uncertainty of any head under which an action could be brought were stronger. One will run into the difficulty facing all law, namely, that technical infringement is usually very common and a lot of give and take is practised behind which the law operates in practice only in serious cases. If one over-encourages litigation, as may well be the case with the large number of cheap courses open to a complainant of minor grievance, the resultant rigid regulation may serve to hinder the administrative processes the law is trying to impose.

DISSOLUTION AND AMALGAMATION

An unincorporated organization with no special provisions for dissolution may dissolve itself by a majority vote of its members. A registered industrial organization acquires corporate status so that this procedure would not be applicable. Such an organization is, however, required to have rules which specify the circumstances, and the manner, in which the organization can be dissolved. Presumably, it is free to adopt whatever rules it wishes, provided that the Registrar considers them to be adequate. The only other method of dissolution is that upon a bankruptcy petition by the Registrar, which we have already noted.

The number of organizations of workers in the United Kingdom is declining. The pace of amalagamation has considerably increased in the past three or four years and the machinery of bargaining agents provided in the Industrial Relations Act 1971 is likely to produce an even higher rate of decline in future. The current theory appears to be that the larger the union the more efficient it will be. This is not true, however, and large unions are much more likely than smaller craft unions to be out of touch with the views and interests of specialized sections of their membership. Nor does the record of the large unions in the provision of central services bear out in practice the theoretically unchallengeable assertion that they are better equipped for this purpose. The small craft union is often blamed for the perpetuation of sectional interests and demarcations long after industrial circumstances have ceased to provide a justification for them. The history, however, of such restrictions among dockers, for example, does not justify the conclusion that they inevitably tend to break down when a well-defined group is included within a general union. It may be that sectional interests derive little support from the existence of sectional unions. It is undeniable that difficulties arise in industrial relations merely because of the need to deal with numerous unions rather than one representing the labour force. It is not clear that equal, though different, difficulties will not arise where a single union attempts to represent a number of diverse interests. Illogical combinations of work groups in conglomerate but sectionalized unions may very well produce a serious problem for the future.

Whatever the objections to blind acceptance of the desirability of increasing amalgamation, the theory is at present strongly entrenched and the legislature, in the Trade Union (Amalgamations, etc.) Act 1964, sought to make the procedure for such merger more workable than had been the case under the preceding legislation. Apart from the ordinary method of direct amalgamation of two organizations to form a new organization or, alternatively, of one organization with another continuing organization, a method of amalgamation exists known as 'transfer of engagements' whereby both organizations nominally continue to exist but one transfers all its rights and obligations, including its membership contracts, to the other.

The organizations of workers concerned must draft an agreed instrument of Amalgamation or Transfer of Engagements and submit it to the Registrar for approval. Certain matters must be covered in the instrument and the Registrar issues guidance on its terms.

The issue of merger in the terms of the instrument must then be put to the members of each amalgamating union. If transfer of engagement is in issue only the members of the transferring union are required to vote. Every member must be entitled to vote without interference or constraint (now a general requirement in all ballots and elections). All reasonable steps must be taken by each voting union to ensure that, not less than seven days before voting begins, every member of the union is supplied with a notice in writing approved by the Registrar. The notice is designed to inform members of the proposals and must contain either the complete instrument or an account of it sufficient to enable those receiving it to form a reasonable judgment on the main effects of the proposal. If this alternative course is adopted the notice must state where copies of the instrument may be inspected.

The manner of conducting the ballot, subject now to the general requirements affecting all ballots and contained in the Industrial Relations Act 1971, is a matter for the governing body of the union. The decision, however, will be made by a simple majority unless the union rules expressly, *and with reference to the Act*, provide that the statutory requirement shall not apply and that a different majority shall be required. All rules as to the required majority made before the Act are, therefore, replaced by the statutory requirement. This was not intended as a restriction on union self-government but was necessary because a number of union rules had incorporated the requirement of larger majorities, contained in earlier Acts, which had in practice made merger almost impossible.

When the proposals have been approved by the requisite majority an application for registration of the instrument must be made to the Registrar. It must be accompanied by two copies of the instrument, the proposed rules of the amalgamated, or transferee union (in the case of a transfer of engagements the instrument itself must state whether the rules of the transferee union are to be changed and, if so, the effect of the alterations), and by a statutory declaration of compliance with the ballot requirements and verification of voting figures. A registered transferee union or a registered union with which another was amalgamated would, of course, have to register any alteration of rules consequent upon the merger. If a new union was to be formed following amalgamation it would be necessary to register it as such if this was desired.

For *six weeks* from the date when the application for registration of the merger is sent to the Registrar any member of a union involved in the voting has a right to complain to the Registrar on any of the following grounds:

(a) that every member of the union was not entitled to vote;
(b) that there was interference with or constraint in the voting, or that a fair opportunity to vote was otherwise lacking;
(c) that the ballot did not, as required, involve the marking of a ballot paper;
(d) that the arrangements for voting were otherwise contrary to the union rules or the procedure laid down by its governing body;
(e) that the requisite majority was not obtained.

If the Registrar finds the complaint justified he may, at his discretion, declare it to be so but take no further action, or make an order specifying the steps to be taken before he will consider the application for registration. He must give reasons for his decision, orally or in writing, and he may order either the complainant or the union to pay the costs. He may vary his order.

He may not use the processes of the Industrial Relations Act 1971 to deal with the matter, nor may an aggrieved member refer such a matter to him under that Act. It is, however, not clear that an aggrieved member could not complain direct to an industrial tribunal or the NIRC of an unfair industrial practice involving breach of the guiding principles and arising, for instance, out of conduct of the ballot. If this were intended no problem would arise as to time limits in the case of an industrial tribunal, where the limit is four weeks. In the case of proceedings before the NIRC, however, the limit is six months and it is unlikely, therefore, that the court could hold such an action to be available in view of the clear intention to settle disputes as to merger complaints quickly, and certainly before the merger has become effective. Alternatively, the court might, at its discretion, decline any remedy. This conclusion is reinforced by the fact that, under the 1964 Act, when the six-week complaint period has expired without complaint, or when a complaint has been satisfactorily settled, the Registrar may register the merger unless the Registrar has been requested by the complainant or the organization to which the complaint related to state a case on a point of law for the opinion of the NIRC.

It seems that merger is treated as a contract so that if one of the parties failed to carry out the terms of the instrument, as for instance by stopping payment of dues to the combined fund, the other could repudiate the agreement.

GOVERNMENT

A registered union must have rules specifying the powers and duties of the governing body of the organization and of each of its officers and officials. Such rules must always make provision as to the manner in which meetings for transacting any business of the organization are to be convened and conducted. In practice virtually all union rule books contain such provisions (although some of them are rather inadequate).

As a matter of contract such rules must be adhered to and an injunction has been issued against the National Executive of a union which purported to reverse the policy decision of the annual conference. Alternatively, an aggrieved member could either resort to the internal machinery of the union or present a complaint to the Registrar (if the union was registered), or an industrial tribunal.

In addition, any organization, whether registered or not, would commit an unfair industrial practice of breach of the guiding principles if, by way of any arbitrary or unreasonable discrimination, it excluded a member from attending and taking part in meetings of the organization or of any branch or section of the organization.

Part II
Industrial Action

Chapter 5
Definitions

STRIKES

We are only concerned with those matters relevant to the application of the law and so shall not deal with popular or sociological subdivisions of industrial action. Until 1971 many important elements in the definition of strike action were unclear. It was, for instance, not certain whether there could be a 'strike' by one person. Much argument had recently been devoted to, but little light shed upon, the problem of the extent to which strikers might be in breach of their individual contracts of employment. More than these, however, the problem lay in the relevance of legal distinctions based on breach of contract to what was considered the fundamental economic problem. The unofficial strike possessed no points of legal distinction from strikes in general.

The definition of a strike contained in the Industrial Relations Act 1971 is intended solely for the purposes of that Act, and not in any way as an exhaustive definition of the phenomenon for any other purposes. That Act, however, now contains all the practically important law on the subject so that we may safely say that the legal definition is:

'... a *concerted* stoppage of work by a group of workers *in contemplation or furtherance of an industrial dispute*, whether they are parties to the dispute or not, whether (in the case of all or any of those workers) the stoppage is or is not in breach of their terms and conditions of employment, and whether it is

carried out during, or on the termination of, their employment.'
(Author's italics.)

So a concerted stoppage is a strike even if those taking part give notice terminating their employment. On the other hand, for legal purposes, there is no such thing as a 'political strike' since either the stoppage is in contemplation or furtherance of an industrial dispute, and so not primarily political, or it is primarily political and so not a 'strike'. As we shall see, the definition of an industrial dispute only includes a situation in which an employer is in dispute with workers. If two rival unions were engaged in a demarcation (or jurisdictional) dispute in which the employer had taken no part and one of the unions withdrew the labour of its members to seek to persuade the employer to make a decision in its favour, the withdrawal would not, for legal purposes, constitute a 'strike'. An employer with a single employee cannot be faced with a 'strike'.

The same Act, for the first time, also makes a significant distinction between official and unofficial, and constitutional and unconstitutional, strikes, to which we will return more fully later. Suffice it to say here that the key unfair industrial practice, contained in section 96, of inducing a breach of contract cannot be applied to official strikes authorized by registered trade unions (although it can be freely applied if a strike is called on the authority of an unregistered organization). The section provides that complaint of an unfair practice arising under it cannot be made if the inducement to breach of contract (whatever form it may take) is committed by a registered trade union (or employers' association), or a person acting within the scope of his authority on behalf of a registered trade union (or employers' association). The scope of the prohibition contained in section 96 is otherwise very wide, and some forms of the unofficial strike are, as we shall see, substantially within it.

Unconstitutional strikes (that is, those in breach of a procedure agreement) are particularly struck at only if the agreement is contractually enforceable. In such a case it would be an unfair industrial practice for a party to the agreement to institute such action. More significantly, if this action were taken by its officials' or members' authority, but without its own authority, the party would commit an unfair industrial practice if it failed to take all reasonably practicable steps to prevent the commission, continuation or repetition of such breach. The view as to implied authority taken by the NIRC means that it does not follow that unofficial strikes are unauthorized so as to be within section 96.

The legislature has sought to bring legal prohibition into line with the types of strike considered as most damaging or reprehensible. It may be that the effect will merely be that another, permitted, type takes on the economic role of one of the prohibited forms, or that successful efforts to bypass the illegal elements are made. At least it can now be seen, however, that there are legally meaningful distinctions between the various forms.

'IRREGULAR INDUSTRIAL ACTION SHORT OF A STRIKE'

It is well known that there exist a number of other forms of industrial action, designed to bring pressure upon an employer, but falling short of withdrawal of labour. Some of these, before 1971, involved at least a technical breach of the contract of employment or some other illegality on the part of those taking part. Such were the 'go-slow', a ban on *obligatory* overtime and the various forms of sit-in. Other forms were thought to have no such illegal element; although sometimes, as with the 'work to rule', this immunity only applied if the activity was carefully controlled. Little significance attached to the distinction because employer's, with the notable exception of the National Coal Board, rarely brought actions against individual workers arising out of such practices. The 1971 Act, however, makes the distinction all important because the definitition of 'irregular industrial action short of a strike', which governs many of the prohibitions applicable to strikes, rests upon it.

'In this Act "irregular industrial action short of a strike" means any concerted course of conduct (other than a strike) which, in *contemplation of furtherance of an industrial dispute,* –

(a) is carried on by a group of workers with the intention of preventing, reducing or otherwise interfering with the production of goods or the provision of services, and

(b) in the case *of some or all of them,* is carried on *in breach of their contracts of employment* or (where they are not employees) in breach of their terms and conditions of service.'

It is difficult to see how the condition in sub-paragraph (a) would ever fail to be satisfied by industrial action; although something turns on what the courts decide to construe as 'intention'. The condition in sub-paragraph (b) at first sight appears to have an oddly limiting effect on liability, actually appearing to encourage greater use of devices like the work-to-rule, which had tended not to be considered a breach of contract. In practice this may well not be so since it should be noted that a breach of the contract of employment by some or all of those taking part will suffice to make the action of all participants irregular. The NIRC has said, however, that 'some' should be taken to mean a substantial number. In some industries, such as chemical manufacture and oil-refining, it would be easy to produce very serious restriction on production by a strict adherence to works rules. In other cases such restriction is usually increased by practices going beyond such adherence. It is safe to say that in a large proportion of cases of work-to-rule a number of breaches of the contract of employment could be detected.

The question has, however, already been the subject of considerable judicial discussion in a case where the emergency procedures, which can only be used to deal with strikes, lock-outs or irregular industrial action, were invoked to control a work-to-rule on the railways. Sir John Donaldson, in the NIRC, made a number of points:

(a) If normal working is not regarded as a breach of the rule book an instruction to interpret the rules in a way other than usual looks as if it does constitute a breach.

(b) In a work-to-rule any rule actually requiring normal working is not intended to be observed.

(c) The intention of a work-to-rule is to interpret the rules unreasonably and then work to that incorrect interpretation.

(d) The object of a work-to-rule is to render the railways unworkable. That is 'a breach of the fundamental obligation of every employee to behave fairly to his employer and to do a fair day's work'.

Lord Denning confirmed that in his view it was a breach of contract to construe the rules unreasonably and then apply the unreasonable construction. He indicated that breach of one rule would make 'irregular' the entire course of conduct. Lawful conduct could not be separated from unlawful conduct when both were part of the same activity. He also confirmed the view that intentional disruption was necessarily a breach of contract, although he laid emphasis on the need for 'wilful' disruption. What, therefore, primarily made a work-to-rule a breach of contract was the intention behind it. The other two members of the Court of Appeal took much the same view and Lord Justice Roskill added support for the first of the NIRC's points. He also took the view that a long-established construction of the rules whereby the railways operated smoothly would imply such a construction into the contract. The courts should accept the construction the parties have accepted.

THE LOCK-OUT

The third type of activity, at which the provisions of the Industrial Relations Act are aimed, is the lock-out. This is presented as if it were the employer action correlative to strikes and other action by labour. This, of course, is not so. The employer does not normally, in modern times, use the lock-out as a bargaining weapon because he has no need to. He may use it as a form of retaliation to a strike or a work-to-rule or some similar labour activity, but he has to hand far more effective pressures; most notably the simple prerogative of management to make the changes desired, leaving labour to take the initiative to reverse them. Although the definition of a lock-out is wide, it is, therefore, unlikely to produce any widespread libability.

> ' "Lock-out" means action which, in contemplation or furtherance of an industrial dispute, is taken by one or more employers, whether parties to the dispute or not, and which consists of the exclusion of workers from one or more factories, offices or other places of employment or of the suspension of work in one or more such places or of the collective, simultaneous or otherwise connected termination or suspension of employment of a group of workers.'

It seems, therefore, that a short suspension of two or more workers for their activities during an industrial dispute would constitute a lock-out as much as the more widespread and concerted activities that normally are so regarded. The crucial distinction between lock-out and lay-off or suspension is, therefore, the existence of contemplation or furtherance of an industrial dispute.

INDUSTRIAL DISPUTES

Virtually all the classes of conduct prohibited by the Industrial Relations Act 1971 depend on this requirement that the conduct should have been undertaken in contemplation or furtherance of an industrial dispute. This is sensible enough, since what is desired is a code of conduct regulating action in such disputes. It appears, however, as an odd reversal of policy, since previous legislation had granted *protection* from general legal liability precisely upon that basis. The 1971 Act, indeed, continues that protection from common law liability for tort (i.e. for civil wrongs established by the common law). There is produced a situation where conduct not in contemplation of an industrial dispute (e.g. a political strike or a purely inter-union dispute) is not within the new field of liability, but is fully open to the law of tort; whilst conduct in contemplation of an industrial dispute is within the new liability, but protected, to some extent, from the law of tort.

The term 'industrial dispute' replaces the term 'trade dispute' which previously governed the availability of protection from the law. It is both wider and narrower:

' "Industrial dispute" means a dispute between one or more employers or organizations of employers and one or more workers or organizations of workers, where the dispute relates wholly or mainly to any one of the following, that is to say:

(a) terms and conditions of employment, or the physical conditions in which any workers are required to work;

(b) engagement or non-engagement or termination or suspension of employment, of one or more workers;

(c) allocation of work as between workers or groups of workers;

(d) a procedure agreement, or any matter to which . . . a procedure agreement can relate,

. . . that is to say:

(i) machinery for consultation with regard to, or for, the settlement by negotiation or arbitration of terms and conditions of employment;

     (ii) machinery for consultation with regard to, or for the settlement by negotiation or arbitration of other questions arising between employers and workers;
    (iii) negotiating rights;
    (iv) facilities for officials of trade unions or other organizations of workers;
    (v) procedures relating to dismissal;
    (vi) procedures relating to matters of discipline other than dismissal;
    (vii) procedures relating to grievances of individual workers.'

A dispute between a Minister of the Crown and one or more workers or organizations of workers counts as an industrial disput (even though the Minister is not an employer) if the matter is referred for consideration by a joint body on which, by virtue of statutory provision, the Minister is represented, or if no settlement of the matter can take place without the exercise by the Minister of a power conferred on him by statute.

Any commentary would be purely speculative in the absence of judicial statements on the definition. The NIRC will not rely on previous decisions on the meaning of 'trade dispute' which it sees as devised for another system. Some general point are of interest. As already noted, the dispute must involve employers on the one side, and workers on the other, so that an inter-union dispute in which the employer took no part would not constitute an industrial dispute. It would previously have constituted a trade dispute. On the other hand, the term 'workers' in the 1971 Act includes any 'person who works or normally works or seeks work under a contract of employment or any other contract . . . whereby he undertakes to perform personally any work or services for another party to the contract who is not a professional client of his.' It also includes anyone employed under, or for the purposes of, a government department who would not otherwise come within the definition. This eliminates the long-standing controversy, arising from the former definition of a person employed in trade or industry, as to whether disputes relating, for instance, to local authority employers could be said to be trade disputes. It also includes, for the first time, disputes relating to self-employed workers.

It should be borne in mind that there must be a dispute. Mere involvement in a claim is not necessarily sufficient, and an employer who, for instance, agrees with a wage claim but says that he cannot meet it because of competition from employers not subject to the same claim has, under the early legislation, been held not in dispute. Similarly, a union which withdrew labour in order to force an employer to join an employers' association to which he had previously refused to adhere has been held merely to be supporting one side in a dispute between employers and employers; which was not, and is not now, within the definition.

The new definition talks of a dispute which 'relates to' the matters set out, whereas the former definition talked of one 'connected with' similar, but more generally defined, matters. This would seem to emphasize the tendency of the courts to seek the predominant purpose of the dispute rather than taking a wider view including anything which it concerned. It some cases this narrow view is clearly justified. A purely disruptive activity should not have enjoyed the statutory protection which then went with a trade dispute because of some incidental connection with the defined purposes. On the other hand, a dispute about employment of a particular person was held not to be a trade dispute because it arose from a personal quarrel. This would seem more questionable if applied beyond the particular facts of the case in which it arose.

The courts had been prepared to hold that a recognition dispute was 'connected with terms and conditions of employment', which was then the prerequisite of a trade dispute. This type of dispute is clearly within the new definition; but one leading case involving such a dispute a member of the House of Lords had taken the view that the matter was merely a dispute between two trade unions as to their respective status. It should be observed, however, that other efforts to narrow the scope of the definitions were made in the light of the special statutory *protection* to which it gave rise. It will be interesting to see what attitude prevails now that its main purpose is to define the scope of statutory *liability*.

Under both the old and the new definitions the effect depends on the activity being 'in contemplation or furtherance' of the dispute. It has been held that though there need be no dispute in existence, one must be imminent or impending. In some cases the courts have considered that this stage may be reached long before there is a combat. In the case just referred to, however, some members of the House of Lords considered that the fact that the employer had not been contacted, since the original request a year before, meant that the dispute had lapsed. Apparently the gathering of information preparatory to the submission of a claim which may well lead to a dispute is not normally to be considered in contemplation or furtherance of the dispute.

It is worth reiterating, in conclusion, the warning that all previous authority has been based on the trade dispute as a defence. It is highly probable that a different approach will be taken to the industrial dispute as a basis for liability.

Chapter 6

Unfair Industrial Practices

'SUPPORTING' PRACTICES

Unfair industrial practices are often divided into those applicable to employers and their organizations and those applicable to workers and their organizations. This is a useful division which will be adopted in this chapter in respect of one category of such practices. It is suggested, however, that a better understanding of the nature of unfair industrial practices will be obtained if a different classification is also used. The Industrial Relations Act 1971, in which the unfair industrial practice is solely contained, provides certain basic rights for workers (in respect of trade union freedoms), for employees (in respect of dismissal), and for members of industrial organizations. It also provides machinery connected with trade union recognition and collective bargaining. We have already discussed the statutory concepts of agency and closed shops. The point to make here is that all this machinery, and the results of using the statutory machinery, are supported by sanctions for breach available by way of complaint of an unfair industrial practice. This type we might call 'supporting' unfair practices. So it is an unfair practice to dismiss an employee unfairly. It is also an unfair practice to take industrial action to secure an unfair dismissal. It is an unfair industrial practice to take industrial action to support a claim for a bargaining agency once application for such an agency has been made under the statutory machinery. If an order to enter into a sole bargaining agreement is made it is an unfair industrial practice for anyone except the designated agent to take industrial action to obtain bargaining rights in respect of the same unit of workers.

The most important thing to notice about these supporting unfair practices is that most of them are only committed if industrial action is taken; so, for instance, it is only an unfair industrial practice to seek to compel a worker to become a member of a particular organization of workers if that compulsion is applied by way of industrial action. Other methods, such as refusal to speak to non-unionists, are not prohibited. This acquires an additional aspect when applied to employers' activities since, as previously pointed out, the corresponding prohibition is upon the lock-out and this will rarely be the method an employer seeks to adopt to achieve his purpose. Specifically, the activities mentioned in this type of unfair practice are to call a strike, or to organize, procure, or finance a strike or any other irregular industrial action short of a strike, or to threaten to do so. On the employer's side the 'corresponding' activities are the institution, carrying on, organization, procurement or financing of a lock-out, or threat thereof.

The full list of such practices is as follows:

(a) By strikes and irregular industrial action or threat thereof for any person:

Agency shop agreements

(i) knowingly to induce or attempt to induce an employer not to take all requisite steps to make and comply with an agency shop agreement following a successful ballot;

(ii) knowingly to induce or attempt to induce an employer to enter into an agency shop agreement after an application relating to the workers involved in such an attempt has been made; except in accordance with the result of a ballot conducted under the statutory procedure;

(iii) knowingly to induce or attempt to induce an employer to refrain from making an application in respect of the establishment of any agency shop;

Individual 'trade union' and job rights

(iv) for the *principal purpose* of knowingly inducing an employer, or a person acting on behalf of an employer, to take any action which would constitute an unfair industrial practice by the employer or any person acting on his behalf, to infringe the rights of a worker in respect of union membership or activities under section 5 of the Act, or, as regards an employee, in respect of unfair dismissal;

Closed shop agreements

(v) for the *principal purpose* of knowingly inducing an employer to comply with a void pre-entry closed shop agreement or to enter into one, whether or not such agreement has been declared to be void;

(vi) for the *principal purpose* of knowingly inducing an employer, or an employers' association, to join in making an application for special permission to operate a post-entry closed shop;

Sole bargaining agencies

(vii) to further any dispute relating to the establishment of a sole bargaining agency while a statutory reference on the matter is pending and for six months following the report of the Commission for Industrial Relations on the reference;

(viii) where a sole bargaining agency order is in force, knowingly to induce or attempt to induce an employer either to bargain with another organization or not to take all such action with a view to bargaining with the agents as might reasonably be expected;

(ix) at any time within two years of the report of the CIR on an application for a sole agency, knowingly to induce or attempt to induce an employer to recognize as a sole agent for the unit in question an organization not recommended by the report (whether the report recommended recognition of any organization or not), or to carry on any collective bargaining with such a non-recommended organization. (It is not clear whether this last prohibition is meant to apply if the report recommended no recognition of a sole agent);

(x) knowingly to induce or attempt to induce an employer to whom the order relates not to comply with an order of the NIRC to terminate a sole bargaining agency.

NB. It should be noted that no statutory prohibition is imposed on industrial action where only a voluntarily agreed sole bargaining agency exists.

(b) By means of a lock-out or threat thereof for an employer:

Sole bargaining agency

(i) knowingly to induce, or attempt to induce, any person to refrain from applying for the establishment of a sole bargaining agency, or the revocation of such an agreement;

(ii) to act in furtherance of a dispute concerning the grant of a sole bargaining agency while an application is pending, or within six months of the date of the report of the CIR on the reference;

(iii) knowingly to induce or attempt to induce a trade union, joint negotiating panel or any other person, not to apply for an agency shop, or not to apply for the revocation of an agency shop agreement.

(c) Other supporting unfair practices likely to be committed by workers or their organizations, not dependent on the use of industrial action:

Contractually enforceable collective agreements

(i) breach of any part of a collective agreement which is contractually enforceable;

(ii) if a party to such an agreement, to fail to take all such steps as are reasonably practicable to prevent a breach of the agreement or the enforceable part of it, or to prevent continuation or repetition of such a breach by any person acting or purporting to act on its behalf, or by any of its members;

Breach of 'guiding principles' relating to organizations of workers (either before NIRC or ITs)

(iii) for any organization of workers, or any official, or person acting on behalf of such an organization, to take, or threaten to take, any action in breach of the guiding principles applicable to such organizations and contained in section 65 of the Act.

(d) Other supporting unfair practices likely to be committed by employers or persons acting on their behalf, not dependent on the use of industrial action:

Contractually enforceable collective agreements

(i) and (ii) those actions set out in (i) and (ii) of section (c) above.

Individual 'trade union' and job rights (Industrial Tribunals)

(iii) prevention or deterrence of a worker from exercising

his rights in respect of trade union membership or trade union activites contained in section 5 of the Act; except that an employer may seek to encourage the worker to join a registered trade union that the employer recognizes as having negotiating rights in respect of the worker;

NB. Many forms of encouragement would in any event not be an infringement of the right, so that the exception is not exhaustive.

   (iv) dismissal, penalization or other discrimination against a worker by reason of the exercise of those rights;
   (v) refusal to engage a worker on the ground that he is a member of a registered trade union, or is not a member of a workers' organization or a particular organization of workers.

NB. (iv) and (v) do not apply where any agency shop, or specially permitted closed shop agreement, is in existence and the worker has refused, or failed, to become a member of the trade union, or one of the trade unions, party to the agreement or to pay his dues as permitted.)

   (vi) unfair dismissal of an employee;

Sole bargaining agency
(special procedure for complaints)

   (vii) if an employer to whom a sole bargaining order applies, to bargain with any other than the designated organizations, or not to take all such action by way of or with a view to carrying on collective bargaining with the agent as might reasonably be expected to be taken by an employer ready and willing to carry on such collective bargaining;

Breach of 'guiding principles' applicable to organizations
(either NIRC or ITs)

   (viii) as an organization of employers, or any official or person acting on behalf of such an organization to take or threaten to take any action constituting breach of the guiding principles contained in sections 65 and 69.

OTHER UNFAIR INDUSTRIAL PRACTICES

This innocuous heading is used by the draftsmen of the Industrial Relations Act 1971 to describe a series of three major unfair industrial practices having nothing in common with the type so far described. It is indeed difficult to know what description to apply to them. We might say that the type so far discussed *primarily* prohibit the attainment of certain purposes, whilst the type here under discussion prohibit the use of certain methods, whatever the purpose. So long as too much reliance is not attached to this distinction it seems well enough. If we wanted a correlative to 'support', we might say that these are the main 'attack' weapons. This would give rise to the objection, largely from employers, that they are in no sense an attack weapon but merely a defence against non-permissible forms of industrial pressure. The analogy has, however, some validity if we accept that these forms of pressure are the normal last-resort measures of the worker, as distinct from the employer, so that the neutralization of them necessarily strengthens the position of the employers.

INDUCEMENT TO BREACH OF CONTRACT

It is an unfar industrial practice, under section 96 of the Act, for any person, in contemplation or furtherance of an industrial dispute, knowingly to induce or threaten to induce another person to break any kind of contract (other than a contractually enforceable collective agreement) unless the inducer or threatener is a registered, or provisionally registered, trade union or employers' association, or someone acting within the scope of his authority on behalf of such an organization.

This is unquestionably the most important unfair practice defined in the Act and it is probably true to say that the principal advantage of registration is that the authority of the organization will then protect it and those acting on its behalf, within their authority, from liability. An unregistered organization cannot give such effective authority, and an official acting without authority will be personally liable. An official of an unregistered organization acting on its behalf within his authority would make both himself and the organization liable. Determination of the existence of authority has proved a key issue when fixing liability on a union for the actions of its officials. A registered organization must have rules specifying the powers and duties of its officers and officials and the bodies and officials who can give instructions to members on its behalf for any kind of industrial action, and the circumstances in which such instructions may be given. As remarked in Chapter 2, however, comprehensive rules of this nature will be extremely difficult to draft and it is likely that any formulation will leave large areas of uncertainty. Within the scope of it, certainly, however, such a rule would serve as a protection since there would be no room to imply additional authority. It is likely to be more difficult to decide whether an official, acting within his authority, was acting on behalf of the organization as distinct from a local group of its members. The NIRC, supported by a unanimous House of Lords, has taken the view that an official, within rules, has an implied authority to organize industrial action, and that this can only be altered by specific rejection of his actions by the union demonstrated, for instance, by disciplinary action, or by removal from office.

The most important question to determine is that relating to the situations when, in contemplation or furtherance of an industrial dispute, a breach of contract is most likely to occur. The Act itself attempts to clarify the effect of a strike upon the contracts of employment of those taking part. It provides that where an employee gives due notice of his intention to strike his action shall not be considered to be a breach of his contract of employment for the purpose of this action, or of any action against anyone for tort, or for the purpose of the criminal liability arising from a breach of contract involving injury (dealt with in the next chapter). The right of the employer to dismiss a striker for breach of contract is, however, protected. There is one major exception to this in that if the contract of employment contains, expressly or impliedly, a restriction on the individual's right to take part in a strike, a breach of that restriction will be considered to be a breach of contract. 'Due notice' for this purpose is, prima facie, notice of at least the same period as would be required to terminate the contract. A longer (but not a shorter) period could be required to constitute due notice of a strike. The minimum period of notice required of an employee of more than thirteen weeks' standing to terminate his contract is laid down as one week by the Contracts of Employment Act 1972. White-collar workers, in particular, are frequently required to give at least a month's notice. The proper period of notice of a strike will, of course, be the longest period required of any participant in the strike.

Even if proper notice is given, a breach of contract may still be involved if the contract contains a restriction on the right to strike. Such restrictions will normally arise by way of implication into the individual contract from a restrictive clause in a collective agreement. In the past this type of clause has had little effect, save as an expression of good-will. Its introduction into a collective agreement in future will be a matter over which the trade union concerned should devote considerable thought. As a matter of fact, the law at present is unclear on the answer to the question when such a clause will be implied from a collective agreement into an individual contract, although it is clear that the answer does not depend in any way on whether the collective agreement itself is contractually enforceable. The clear assumption of the draftsmen of the Act is that such implication will, in future, be regarded as normal. It is probably safe to say that the NIRC will tend to take the same view.

So we have a situation in which a strike without the authority of a registered union, and either without proper notice or contrary to any agreement, for instance, not to strike until exhaustion of procedure, will render the leaders of the strike liable to action for an unfair industrial practice, without more.

Even if these barriers are avoided the strike may, of course, knowingly produce a breach of a commercial contract, such as a contract of supply, between the struck employer and another.

It is to be noted that, though an employer could sue the individual strikers for damages for breach of contract, he could not obtain an order for them to return to work. It must be assumed, therefore, that, as in the past, such actions will be very rare. The sanction in the 1971 Act is not directed against the individual strike but against the strike leader – the inducer or threatener. In consequence, supporters of the Act tend to assert that it in no way infringes the right to strike. The courts will probably take over from the common law the view of virtually any leader as an inducer. It has been established that one can 'induce' a willing group, or even a group which is making the running, provided that one advances, rather than retards, its efforts. The alleged 'inducer' must seek to show, therefore, that he is either a mere onlooker or has actually and consistently discouraged the activity. The views of management vary according to industry on the extent to which it is possible for a strike leader to conceal the fact. The answer seems to depend on the extent of experience of such conduct and the conclusion must be, therefore, that, with practice, it is possible in many instances to make such activity appear spontaneous. In the past there has been little real incentive for such practice save the fear of victimization, but now very real advantages are to be derived from it. On the other hand, the idea of implied authority will serve to make the organization liable for inducement if it is clear that the inducement must have come from some one or more of its officials acting within their normal scope as such. This form of 'vicarious liability' will, therefore, go a long way to destroy the value of the allegation of spontaneous inducement.

SYMPATHETIC ACTION

Section 97 provides that a person himself commits an unfair industrial practice if, in contemplation or furtherance of an industrial dispute, he calls a strike, organizes, procures or finances a strike or an irregular industrial action short of a strike, or institutes, carries on, organizes, procures or finances a lock-out; or threatens any such action; if his principal or only purpose in so doing is to further any action already taken by him or anyone else which is itself an unfair industrial practice. The main application of this section will probably be to prevent sympathetic financing, although it should be noted that such financing could also be brought under one of the 'supporting' unfair practices if the purpose sought fell within those prohibitions. The real value of the provision lies in the fact that, whereas an employer may be reluctant to proceed against organizations with which he has to negotiate, he may be more willing to take action to prevent support from outside organizations.

It seems hardly necessary to have extended the provision to include support for the supporters' own unfair practices since almost inevitably that support would be comprehended within the original prohibition.

Some concern has been expressed as to how wide the term 'to further' might be. Particularly, it has been suggested, it might apply to the journalist who wrote an article in support. It is submitted that this type of extension is unlikely. Firstly, the journalist's principal purpose is to further his job as a journalist. Secondly, for the same reason, his action is in contemplation and furtherance of that job and not of an industrial dispute. Thirdly, he would have to go to considerable lengths before he could be said to be furthering the initial unfair practice. There is no reason, of course, why the journalist should not overstep these bounds. One writing in a trade union journal might readily do so. Even then, it is submitted, there is little to fear in practice. It is not characteristic of the civil law that those with rights of action indiscriminately use them. Few would go to the trouble of bringing an action against a journalist unless his support had become a substantial factor in the furtherance of the dispute. Certainly, fears that were expressed about actions against teachers and lecturers who expressed support for unfair industrial practices in the course of teaching are not well founded.

It was correctly suggested that the section as originally drafted could be applied to a situation in which unofficial action had, by reason of its lack of authorization, constituted the unfair industrial practice of inducement to breach of contract but had been authorized by a registered organization so as to immunize it from the effect of section 96. Such a union would then be said to be financing, or at least organizing, the action and could have been held thereby to be furthering it by seeking to remove its illegality. This possibility, but no more than this, was expressly removed in the final draft of the Act. (See section 97(3).)

SECONDARY ACTION
The third of this type of unfair industrial practice is aimed at secondary boycotts and similar pressures. It is provided, in section 98, that it is an unfair industrial practice for any person, in contemplation or furtherance of an industrial dispute, to call a strike or organize, procure or finance a strike or any irregular industrial action short of a strike, or institute, carry on, organize, procure or finance a lock-out, or to threaten any of these, knowing, or having reasonable ground to believe, that another 'extraneous' person had entered into a contract (other than a contract of employment) with a party to an industrial dispute, if the principal purpose of the industrial action was knowingly to induce the extraneous party to break that contract, or prevent him from performing it. A person is extraneous to the dispute, within the meaning of this provision, if he is not a party to it and had not, in contemplation

or furtherance of that dispute, taken any action in material support of a party to it. It is provided that a person does not become a party to, or support a party to, a dispute merely because:

(a) he is an associated employer in relation to an employer who is a party; or

(b) he is a member of an employers' organization of which a party to the dispute is also a member; or

(c) he has contributed to a fund which may be available by way of relief of loss incurred in consequence of the dispute, so long as the fund was established, and his contribution paid, without specific reference to that dispute; or

(d) he supplies goods to, or provides services for, a party to a dispute in pursuance of a contract entered into before the dispute began, or is a party to such a contract under which he is, or may be, required to supply goods or provide services.

Either the extraneous party, or the party to the dispute with whom the contract was made, can complain of an unfair industrial practice under this section. The section is, again, of vast scope, not only because of the number of ties which it eliminates in considering the secondary nature of the pressure but also because it is enough that the pressure should *prevent the performance* of an existing contract. It does not have to produce a breach. One guilty of such action cannot, therefore, protect himself from liability by relying on a clause in the contract permitting failure to perform it in the event of, say, impossibility to perform by reason of industrial action.

If workers employed by A. Ltd, which is a separate company within a group of associated companies including B. Ltd, are members of a union in dispute with B. Ltd, and decline to load goods which A. Ltd is under contract to supply to B. Ltd, they will inevitably commit this unfair industrial practice, providing that A. Ltd instructs them to load and they refuse. They will then be acting in breach of their contracts to restrict supply and so will be committing an irregular industrial action. It will not affect this issue that A. Ltd has excluded its liability to B. Ltd for non-performance in such circumstances.

The only large exception to the scope of the prohibition is that, on the face of it, such boycotts can be imposed by picketing which is not an irregular industrial action. It would, however, not be difficult to bring this effect of picketing under some other prohibition. A driver who refused to cross a picket line to deliver goods, for instance, might well commit a breach of his contract of employment. The pickets, or the organizers of the picket, would then have committed the unfair practice of inducing a breach of contract unless they acted with the authority of a registered trade union. Several cases of picketing inducing a breach of contract have already been dealt with under section 96.

An interesting point arises in connection with the fourth group of persons expressly declared not to be parties to a dispute. Some unions, possibly in anticipation of this section of the Act, have entered into agreements with employers that union members will not be asked to work on behalf of an employer with whom the union is in dispute. If an order were given in breach of this agreement it would seem that any action taken would be in furtherance of an industrial dispute directly with the supplying employer who had given the order, rather than secondarily against the employer initially in dispute. It does not appear that the fourth group of extraneous parties prevents this conclusion since it only refers to a relationship between supplier and supplied.

COMPLAINTS PROCEDURES

BEFORE INDUSTRIAL TRIBUNALS

Complaints against an employer in respect of infringement of trade union rights, or unfair dismissal, must initially be taken before an industrial tribunal. Complaints against an industrial organization of infringement of its rules or breach of the guiding principles will normally also go before these tribunals, but in the latter case the complainant may, if he wishes, take his case directly to the NIRC. In the case of complaints to an industrial tribunal of the first two practices by an employer it is provided that a conciliation officer shall endeavour to promote a settlement without determination of the complaint by a tribunal. He is to do so either if he is so requested by both parties, or if he considers that he could act with a reasonable prospect of success. Even if no complaint is presented to a tribunal one or other of the parties in either of these situations may *at any time after the employee* (apparently therefore a self-employed worker who alleged infringement of his trade union rights may not use this procedure) *has ceased to be employed,* ask for the services of the conciliation officer. In the case of a dismissal the particular function of the conciliation officer is to seek to promote re-engagement on terms appearing to him to be equitable or, failing that, if the parties so desire, to seek to promote agreement as to the amount of compensation to be paid.

If a claim goes to an industrial tribunal, the tribunal may make an order determining the rights of the parties, and/or award compensation of such amount as it considers just and equitable having regard to the loss sustained in consequence of the matters to which the complaint relates. It may not make an order that something should be done or should not be done. The nearest it can come to this is in a dismissal claim when it can *recommend* reinstatement, and increase compensation if an employer does not comply with the recommendation, or decrease compensation if an employee does not agree to reinstatement. As already pointed out, in the case of complaints against organizations for infringement of the guiding principles applicable to them, the power of the NIRC to make a coercive order may well induce complainants to use that court rather than an industrial tribunal.

BEFORE THE NIRC

All other instances of unfair industrial practices may be complained of only through the NIRC. That court also is required so to arrange its work that parties to a complaint have opportunities for conciliation. The only provision so far appearing in the court rules to this effect is as follows:

' . . . the court shall, whether by adjourning any proceedings or otherwise, use its best endeavours to ensure that, in any case in which it appears to the court that there is a reasonable prospect of agreement being reached between the parties, they are enabled to avail themselves of the services of conciliation officers or of other opportunities for conciliation.'

The court is under a statutory duty to avoid formality in proceedings so far as it appears to the court to be appropriate to do so and generally it is not bound by the rules of law relating to admissible evidence. This is necessary partly because any person, whether or not he is a lawyer, may appear before the court to represent any party (the same is true of an industrial tribunal). It should not be imagined, however, that procedural rules are in-

NATIONAL INDUSTRIAL RELATIONS COURT

FORM NO. 21

Notice of Complaint of Unfair Industrial
Practice Under Section 101 (1).

Name and address of complainant	1. This complaint is presented by **(i)**
Here complainant's address for service, *including* telephone number if any	2. Any communication for the complainant relating to this complaint may be sent to **(ii)**
Delete as appropriate	3. The name(s) and address(es) of the organization(s) person(s) **(iii)** against whom the complaint is made are **(iv)**
Here name(s) and address(es) of proposed respondent(s) including telephone numbers if known.	
Here summarise the facts and matters relied on in support of the complaint	4. The grounds on which this complaint is presented are **(v)**:

Dated.............................. Signed..

Continued on page 2 [where space
for the statement of claim is found]

1. This form should be sent or delivered to the Secretary, National Industrial Relations Court, at 5-7 Chancery Lane, London WC2A 1LX, or in Scotland to 44 Palmerstone Place, Edinburgh EH12 5BJ.

2. This form or statement written in the same layout on several sheets of this size paper (A4) should be used together with any necessary continuation sheets.

3. The offices of the Court are situate at 5-7 Chancery Lane, and in Scotland at 44 Palmerston Place, Edinburgh, and will be open to the public between the hours of 10 a.m. and 4.30 p.m.

NATIONAL INDUSTRIAL RELATIONS COURT

Form of Answer to
Application (Complaint/Appeal) (iii)

Application No.:.................................

Reference No: /   /   /

(i) Enter full
name

(ii) Respondent's
address for
service,
including tele-
phone number if
any

(iii) Delete as
appropriate

1. I (i).....................................have received
the above-mentioned form.

2. My address for service is (ii) ....

....

3. My answer to the
complaint (iii)
application   reference   /   /   /
Appeal
is as follows:

     (a) I [agree] [dispute] [admit] (iii) the facts
         as alleged

                 complaint (iii)
       in the application
                 appeal

            OR

Dated..   Signed..

                         Continued on page 2 [where space
                         for the answer is to be found]

1. This form should be sent or delivered to the Secretary, National
Industrial Relations Court, at 5-7 Chancery Lane, London WC2A
1LX, or in Scotland to 44, Palmerstone Place, Edinburgh EH12 5BJ.

2. This form or statement written in the same layout on several sheets
of this size paper (A4) should be used together with any unnecessary
continuation sheets.

3. The offices of the Court are situate at 5-7 Chancery Lane, and in
Scotland at 44 Palmerston Place, Edinburgh and will be open to the
public between the hours of 10 a.m. and 4.30 p.m.

vented in order to assist lawyers to maintain a closed shop for themselves. The less formal and controlled the fact-finding process, the more likely it is not so much that errors of fact will occur, but that relevant facts will be omitted, only to be discovered to be relevant on appeal when it is too late to admit them. This has undoubtedly emerged in the activities of industrial tribunals. This is not to infer that there is anything wrong with these tribunals. Inevitably one is compromising between high degrees of precision on the one hand and cheapness and simplicity on the other. It is also fair to say that, in practice, the procedure of the NIRC is not as informal as it might be presumed to have been the intention of the Act to make it.

Certainly the initial intention is to keep forms of application to the court as simple as possible and to exclude the science of what lawyers call 'pleadings'. The two principal forms connected with complaints of unfair industrial practices are set out on pages 104 and 105. On the second page of each is space for a statement of the claim, or of the answer to the claim. No doubt lawyers will tend to use more formal language, but it is plain that informal statements will not give rise to rejection of the claim on some technical ground of pleading.

REMEDIES

The remedies available in the NIRC are:

(a) an order determining the rights of the complainant and of the respondent in relation to the action specified in the complaint (that is to say a mere declaration of the position);

(b) an award of compensation of such amount as the court consider just and equitable in all the circumstances having regard to the loss sustained by the aggrieved party;

(c) an order directing the respondent to refrain from continuing to take the action complained of and to refrain from taking any other action of a like nature in relation to the complainant;

(d) in cases only of those actions of an employer failing properly to bargain with the designated sole bargaining agent, or in failing to provide information relevant to collective bargaining under section 56 authorization to present a claim to the Arbitration Board. In the case of the first of these offences this is the only remedy which can be given by the court.

(*e*) proceedings for contempt of court if an order is not obeyed or compensation not paid. This arises because the NIRC has a position similar to other branches of the High Court.

In the past, where the law has been involved at all, the remedy most often sought against industrial action was the injunction – the equivalent of (*c*) above. Damages could not be obtained in an action in tort against a trade union from the passing of the Trade Disputes Act 1906 until its repeal in 1971. There was little point in seeking damages against individuals involved in industrial action. The injunction, until the passage of the 1971 Act, had one very great advantage in that an interim injunction could be obtained *ex parte*. That is to say, an injunction pending trial of the action could be obtained simply on the basis of sworn statements by the parties and without the safeguards provided by the opportunity to examine witnesses and the presence of the parties. Such an injunction could be obtained, usually within twenty-four hours, merely by making out a prima facie case. Within five days or so there would be a hearing in the presence of the parties, and with witnesses, to consider whether the interim injunction should be continued. Even then it was only necessary for the complainant to establish a prima facie case and show that continuation of the injunction would not unduly damage the other party. So it was possible to obtain an order to cease an industrial action on a comparatively flimsy case with a minimum of delay. The injunction, or its counterpart, now loses some of this advantage, for the NIRC rules, following the provisions of the Act, forbid the grant of such an order unless reasonable steps have been taken to enable both parties the opportunity of making representations. This could be construed so as to allow the requirement to be satisfied by opportunity to submit a written affidavit but the rules of the NIRC make it clear that oral hearings are required in all complaints of unfair industrial practice. If this is so, then the grant of an interim order may be delayed for four or five days at least. Even without this the injunction is not an ideal remedy. Presumably it would now lie against a registered organization as such or against an unregistered organization since that can be sued in its own name, so that it loses the disadvantage that the individuals bound by it could simply be replaced by others to whom it did not apply. It suffers, however, from the major defect that the sanction for non-observance is imprisonment for contempt of court. This is a sanction many trade union officials would be prepared to incur in what they considered to be a good cause. The injunction, therefore, is apt to be disobeyed in heated situations. The first example of imprisonment of individuals was not exactly a success. On the other hand, to fine an organization for contempt in failing to discipline officials guilty of forbidden practices is clearly a more effective deterrent.

It is possible that an action for compensation, or more often the threat of such an action, will replace the injunction as the principal remedy where the respondent is an organization the funds of which can be attached. So long as there are funds available it will be almost impossible for the organization to refuse to pay, since if an application to enforce the judgment were made the court could hardly refuse to make an order attaching the organization's property to secure that payment. Theoretically an order for attachment could be made against the goods of an individual. This might be ruinous for the individual but it would usually not produce a high proportion of the damages awarded.

The assessment of damages on the basis of what is just and equitable will not be an easy matter for the court. It is provided that this assessment shall include:

(a) any expenses reasonably incurred by the aggrieved party in consequence of the matters to which the complaint relates;

(b) loss of any benefit which he might reasonably be expected to have had but for these matters.

The aggrieved party, however, remains under the common law duty to mitigate his loss. That is to say, for instance, that if dismissed from his job he must take reasonable steps to find another job. If his supplies are cut off he must take reasonable steps to secure others. None of these considerations produce much precision since the element of reasonableness introduced into each obviously allows considerable discretion in the assessment.

Four further provisions of importance are contained in the Industrial Relations Act as to compensation. Firstly, where complaint is made against an official of a registered organization in respect of action taken by him in that capacity and it is shown that he took that action 'within the scope of his authority on behalf of the trade union or employers' association' no award of compensation, nor by way of the equivalent of an injunction, shall be made against him. Both may be made against the organization. Officials of unregistered organizations and those not acting within their authority are not so protected. It was initially thought that it would be very difficult to lay down any precise guide-lines to determine the existence of action 'within the scope of authority' and 'on behalf of a trade union'. The principle of implied authority supported by the House of Lords in the Heaton case considerably enhances the difficulty of such determination. Secondly, where an employer commits the unfair industrial practices of unfair dismissal, or interference with the trade union rights of a worker, he is liable to pay compensation in full notwithstanding that he may himself have a right to complain of an unfair practice by someone else arising from pressure brought upon him to commit the wrong. The employer's remedy in that case is to join the third party in the action and seek contribution (which may be up to the full amount) towards the compensation he is ordered to pay.

Thirdly, limits are imposed on the amount of compensation that may be ordered against a *registered* trade union or federation. These are:

(a) £5,000 where the union has less than 5,000 members;
(b) £25,000 where the union has 5,000 or more members but less than 25,000;
(c) £50,000 where the union has 25,000 members or more but less than 100,000;
(d) £100,000 where the union has a membership of 100,000 or more.

(The limit in a claim for unfair dismissal is £4,160 or 104 weeks' pay, whichever is less. To this a claim for damages at common law for wrongful dismissal might be added.)

Finally, and most significantly, it is provided that:

'Where the Industrial Court or industrial tribunal finds that the matters to which the complaint relates were to any extent caused or contributed to by any action of the aggrieved party in connection with those matters (whether that action constituted an unfair industrial practice on his part, or not), the Court or tribunal shall reduce its assessment of his loss to such extent as, having regard to that finding, the Court or tribunal considers just and equitable.'

This apparently means that where, for instance, a worker's organization was sued or threatened with action, for an unfair industrial practice, it could respond that its activities had been provoked by the employer's bad management. Not only might this reduce the amount of compensation paid but the warning of such a counterclaim, if likely to succeed, would act as a major deterrent to an employer's decision to bring the action.

The prohibition order cannot make the organization or person against whom it is directed seek to stop the actions of others. The question is, however, as to the extent of activities which will be considered to be its own. The NIRC has taken the view that once an organization has held out an official as possessing authority on its behalf it must take steps to prevent him continuing the prohibited action or dissociate itself from him by repudiating his authority. Such repudiation, it has been said, would, in the case of a shop steward, require withdrawal of his credentials. The House of Lords has confirmed this. This decision means, therefore, that the organization will normally be able to be made liable for industrial action called by accredited officials until it positively disowns those officials.

EFFECTIVENESS OF THE 'UNFAIR PRACTICE' SANCTION

As experience of the operation of the new legal provisions examined in this chapter develops, it will be possible increasingly to replace speculation as to their practical effect with reality. At this stage, however, it is thought advisable to offer a tenable counter to the widely held view that they are all a dead letter because they will never be used or, if used, will greatly decrease the chances of a settlement being reached.

The purpose of the legislation is primarily inhibitive. This is true of most legal sanctions. The idea is not that everyone should rush to the courts but that people should regulate their conduct within permitted boundaries. Infringement of these boundaries in civil matters occurs quite frequently and is frequently overlooked, for a wide variety of reasons. None the less, almost all such boundaries do tend to inspire in the majority of people efforts to keep within them. Many reasons for this tendency to observance exist. We will only look at three:

(a) a natural tendency to observe the law simply because it is the law;

(b) the risk that penalties will be incurred if those boundaries are overstepped;

(c) the severity of the penalty if it is exacted.

It is often said that employers have not been very ready to invoke the law in the past, so they will not do so in the future. This is an unsafe analogy. In the past there was almost no specific legal provision against industrial action. Such law as there was was mostly developed in other contexts and widely thought to be either incomprehensible or irrelevant and to have been artificially found to fit into the industrial context. So the first inhibitive factor was weak. The chances of enforcement action were small largely because trade unions as such could not be sued and individuals were not worth suing, bearing in mind the bad effect this would have on industrial relations. The principal sanction was the injunction, again, normally only obtainable against individuals and so relatively easily capable of circumvention.

Two of these factors are now unquestionably changed. A purpose-built law, rightly or wrongly, will tend to produce obedience. The sanctions if applied could be ruinous, certainly to the individual and probably in the long term to an organization which persistently ignored the law. The doubt lies with the chances of legal action being taken.

It must be admitted that an employer would be reluctant to threaten action against his own shop stewards or the unions with which he had to negotiate, much less to take it. It is equally true that this reluctance will steadily decline as the employer tends to the view that they are acting unreasonably, to the point where he decides that not only could they not become more unreasonable but that they might become less unreasonable if shown that he meant business.

Even then he might be reluctant to take them before the NIRC, but he might be prepared to warn them that he was thinking of it. The inhibitive effect would then, as it were, be publicly invoked. The limitation on the effectiveness of the factor of likeliness of invocation would thereby be lessened and the other two factors would increase in effect. This, it is suggested, is precisely what was intended by the legislature. No one intends the employer faced with his first strike to go to court. When it is the sixth in six weeks he might do so. His threat to do so will, of course, gain or lose in weight according to what is seen of the operation of the Act.

This element in the inhibitive process will be enormously enhanced if we do not rely on the employer having to sue his own unions and stewards. By the time this book is published the answer may have been supplied to the most intriguing doubt in the whole Industrial Relations Act – the question of how far a third party to a dispute can bring an action if he suffers damage as a result of an unfair industrial practice. The Act provides that the complainant must be 'the person against whom the action was taken'. Use of the definite article might suggest that in each situation there is only one such person, but this is manifestly incorrect. If a strike is called against employer A because he refuses to cease to engage the services of employer B, some of whose employees are not union members, the action has been taken against both A and B. If we can read 'the persons' instead of 'the person', we are nearer to the conclusion that if action is taken against employer A, who supplies employers B and C with goods in the clear knowledge, but without the primary intention, that this will force employers B and C to close down, then B and C are persons against whom the action is taken. If employer C negotiates with a different set of unions than those taking the action against employer A he might well consider bringing an action. If this barrier is surmounted in this way the scope of the unfair industrial practice is very considerable indeed.

There is one statutory answer. The employer who warns his unions of legal action, and can reasonably be met with the reply that if he takes it they will successfully allege that he is substantially to blame for their conduct, will have produced an ineffective sanction. The intention is that the best weapons should be in the hands of parties who are in the clear.

No legislation can achieve good industrial relations. That is a matter for the people involved. Legislation can, however, make it more expensive to resort to undesirable methods and ends arising from the existence of poor relations or machinery. Greater expense should produce greater effort to avoid that expense. If everyone is already working as hard as possible to achieve good industrial relations, the sanction of the unfair industrial practice will produce irritation and no improvement. If they are not, then the philosophy behind the Act is that they will be inspired to make more effort. Since patently some, however few, are not, the sanctions must have some inhibitive effect. The question is whether it will be enough or, conversely, whether a sledgehammer has not been taken to crack a nut.

We have already seen that the risk of union funds being liable for heavy damages cannot readily be avoided by allegations that the conduct in question was unofficial. The doctrine of implied authority forces unions positively to disavow their shop stewards. In theory they might do so. If they did then the sanction is called in question because action would have to be brought against the shop steward himself. Again, in theory, his goods might be attached to satisfy a fine for contempt. In practice, however, the High Court does not attach the goods of individuals for contempt. Imprisonment for contempt has been shown, if evidence was needed, to produce a godlike aura around the person concerned. (This is usually called martyrdom, but it is much more than that.) So it might be thought that the whole of this counter-argument falls at the last hurdle because there is no effective sanction that can be invoked.

In practice this is not so. The courts, by requiring positive disavowal of authority, have forced the unions into an impossible position. In contra-distinction to the situation in the United States of America, from which the idea of legal sanctions of this type was borrowed, this country has uniquely strong workshop organization and relatively weak central union control. Although it is an over-generalization, it is broadly true that the unions regulate and direct workshop organization but do not give it its authority. Its authority is inherent. If union recognition is withdrawn, workshop organization will continue to operate of its own volition. All that will happen will be fragmentation and loss of any central directional agency.

One of two things will happen. The foregoing argument will hold good, the law will triumph and the unions will seek to achieve the impossible by reversing the current trend and controlling workshop organization. To force them to do this, however, it is necessary to counteract arguments that the law is disastrous to them and to industrial relations and should be disobeyed. In fact, the arguments to this effect seem quite strong. The other course (apart, of course, from sitting back and paying the damages) is to prove that the whole of the foregoing argument is untenable in this situation. To put it another way, the limits of the possible operation of the law to induce obedience have been so strained by the methods used and the type of observance required that they have collapsed and the law is no longer capable of inducing observance. Rather it induces opposition. In that situation, the law itself collapses.

Chapter 7

The Common Law Residue

The law has acquired a new machine which its operators allege is capable of producing a necessary incentive to good industrial relations. Trade unions allege that this is irrelevant because no one will buy the product. The government allege that that does not matter much because in order not to buy it they will have to produce a substitute of their own. Employers and individual workers take various views, according to their experience or fancy, or keep quiet. But the law, like most employers, having acquired a new machine, has not thrown the old one away. If the unfair industrial practice does not offer a solution, the law of tort may still be resorted to. This resort is, in practice, not very likely. The value of knowledge of that old law lies elsewhere. The law of tort has contributed to the unfair industrial practice its most effective concept: that of liability for inducement to breach of contract. Much of the way in which sections 96 and 98 of the Industrial Relations Act operate will depend on the interpretation the courts in the past have given to this tort.

In this chapter, therefore, we shall examine some of the elements of this tort in detail, and the remaining relevant torts, and the defences to them, more generally. Before we do so, however, it must be pointed out that the complainant will not have a free choice of resort to an allegation of an unfair practice or a tort as he sees fit. As we have already said, the unfair industrial practice generally arises only where action is taken in contemplation of furtherance of an industrial dispute. It is provided that if proceedings are brought in tort on a matter which has been or could be the subject of action before the NIRC, or an industrial tribunal, the common law court may stay the proceedings. This presumably means that it will do so. Indeed in one early case of picketing the High Court revealed itself as anxious not to become involved. In any event, where action is taken in contemplation or furtherance of an industrial dispute, actions in tort are subject to fairly extensive statutory defences, and are not likely to be attractive. The main value of the tort action as a weapon, in itself, therefore, lies in its unprotected availability against action which is not in contemplation or furtherance of an industrial dispute. But the law of tort has lent to the unfair industrial practice much of its inspiration.

INDUCEMENT TO BREACH OF CONTRACT

This type of liability has two forms. It might be incurred directly by the defendant approaching A and inducing him to break his contract with B. B might choose to sue A for breach of contract; but he may, for many reasons, prefer to seek compensation from the person most directly responsible or, better still, obtain an injunction to prevent the continuation of the defendant's inducement. The important reason for making this form of inducement a separate category is that the courts consider it to be actionable whether or not the means of inducement used are themselves unlawful. The second form of the tort arises, for instance, where the defendant induces others to act in such a fashion as to force A into a position where he is induced to break his contract with B. In this form the inducement must be by unlawful means. It seems that the illegality must occur at the point of inducement. That is to say; if X threatens to beat up Y unless Y withdraws his labour in order to force A, who employs Y, to break a contract to supply B; and Y properly and without illegality withdraws his labour no action by either A or B lies against X. Diagramatically the position is shown opposite.

If illegal pressure occurs along both lines X–Y and Y–A, then B can sue either or both of X and Y. The same is true if no illegality occurs between X–Y but X contemplates that illegality will occur, and it does occur, between Y–A. If, however, illegality occurs between X–Y but not between Y–A, then B has no action against X. The chain is, as it were, broken. The pressure on A being such as Y is entitled to bring neither A nor B has any complaint save as regards each other or against Y who in our example has produced direct inducement over and above the indirect inducement of X.

It must be observed that only a party to the contract which is broken can sue. The idea of the action in tort is to protect existing contracts. So, if the whole purpose of the pressure in the last example is to persuade B Ltd to dismiss P, a non-unionist, and B does so without breach of contract, P cannot sue in this tort. (This example is based only on the strict form of the tort. We shall deal in due course with a suggested extension of the tort which would permit mere interference with contract to produce liability.)

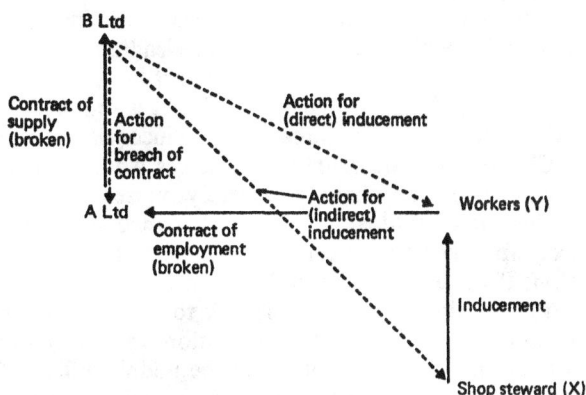

B Ltd

Contract of supply (broken)

Action for breach of contract

Action for (direct) inducement

A Ltd

Contract of employment (broken)

Action for (indirect) inducement

Workers (Y)

Inducement

Shop steward (X)

Liability also depends on the inducer having a measure of knowledge of the contract. The courts have whittled down the required extent of this knowledge. Detailed knowledge has never been required. Recently it has been considered sufficient to know that the action would produce a breach of contract. The courts have even gone further to include a situation where the inducer is 'knowingly, or recklessly, indifferent' whether there is a breach or not. So a careless failure to discover the facts would suffice to produce liability. Given such knowledge, the most difficult point of all is to decide what degree of intention, if any, to produce the breach is required. Obviously an extensive chain of breach may flow from one induced breach. There may be sufficient knowledge of all the contracts involved but the defendant has been only interested in one of them. No case has ever considered a situation concerning a contract other than the one directly aimed at. As a normal rule, once knowledge of the contract is established intention to produce the breach will be presumed. This presumption has only been successfully rejected in one case where an initial intention to produce lawful termination was established. It will not suffice as a defence to establish that this was the primary intention, but the defendant did not object to a breach if termination could not be brought about in any other way. It seems to have been assumed, however, that the defendant is not liable for the incidental consequences of his inducement however much he was able to anticipate that they would occur.

The normal description of the tort speaks of 'inducement', though some judgments refer to interference leading to a breach. There is no doubt, however, that the contract-breaker may be a willing party and judges have said that all that is required is that the alleged 'inducer' knows his pressure to be inconsistent with the contract. Clearly there are examples of actors who, though they have participated in the chain, are merely messengers or other intermediaries. It is unlikely now that an intended inducement could successfully be concealed behind a façade of conveyance of information. If the alleged 'inducer' had an interest in procuring the breach he would have a difficult task to persuade the court that he was merely a conveyor of information. Inactivity is, however, a different matter and it might not be unduly difficult for a shop steward to appear to have taken no part in furthering an apparently spontaneous act. Note, however, that an NIRC order to a shop steward to desist from a course of action illegal under section 96 would probably be taken to require the shop steward to take positive steps to dissociate himself from the actions of those he represented.

It will be appreciated that much of the law discussed here could be applied to section 96 of the Industrial Relations Act 1971. The meaning of inducement is obviously relevant. Use there (and indeed in other places in the Act) of the word 'knowingly' brings up the question of the extent of the knowledge that is necessary, especially because section 98 might be thought to spell out a requirement of more precise knowledge than use of the word by itself implies. The element of intention is mainly dealt with by the provision that the complainant must be a person against whom the action was taken. The uncertainty of this requirement has already been discussed.

It will have been observed that in section 98 the concept of inducing a breach of contract is extended to cover also prevention of performance of a contract. This extension derives from the growing modern tendency in commercial contracts for the parties expressly to exclude liability for non-performance of the contract. The obvious problem of whether there can be said to be a contract at all if there is no liability for not performing it need not trouble us here. What is relevant is the difficulty of saying that there has been a breach of contract if no liability for breach arises. It is possible, of course, to say that there has been a breach; only *liability* is excluded – but there is a certain artificiality about such an argument. The courts have dealt with this situation in several ways, the most effective of which appears to be to state that liability should extend to mere interference with contract falling short of inducing a breach of contract. It is not clear whether it is intended that this tort should have both direct and indirect aspects (although such authority as there is suggests that it would seem to have), or whether its direct aspect should require the use of illegal means. It is apparently established, if we accept that it has an indirect aspect, that liability for that can only stem from the use of illegal means. It has been said that the interference must be 'deliberate', but this is said to include turning a blind eye to the breach. The formulation in section 98 is, of course, narrower than interference since it only extends to prevention of performance. It is not established that 'interference' could not cover other effects. It is, however, alarming that such speedy legislative recognition should have been given to what was thought to be a largely unwarranted extension of the common law.

OTHER 'ECONOMIC' TORTS

Two other heads of tort liability have been used to restrict industrial action. One of them – the tort of intimidation – has been absorbed into almost all unfair industrial practices by way of provision that a threat of prohibited action is actionable as such. Not only can the threatened action be the subject of a preventive order but an order can be made to terminate the threats. Compensation can be awarded to someone damaged as a result of the threat, so long as he was a person against whom the action was taken. This is the essence of the tort of intimidation which could be defined as a threat of action, which would be illegal if taken, intended to be acted upon and in fact acted upon to the detriment of the plaintiff. In the tort of inducement the plaintiff has to be someone with a contractual right to protect. In intimidation the plaintiff need have no connection with the threatened illegality. This produces a rather unexpected effect upon the diagram used to explain the tort of inducement.

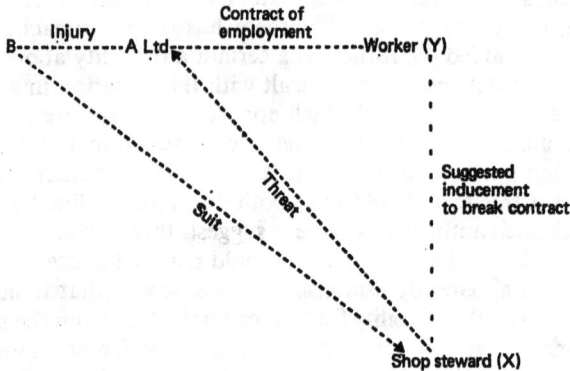

In this example both torts are involved for the sake of indicating the distinction, although it must be remembered that the threat could be of any illegal action. The illegal action threatened could be directly against the party threatened rather than, as here, by way of a third party. If A–Y involves a breach of contract then X–Y also involves illegality because X would commit the tort of inducement to breach of contract. If, instead of inducing such breach Y threatens to induce it, X–A is a threat of unlawful action since, as between X and A, X has no right to induce A's workers to break their contracts and A could sue X if he did so induce them. If the purpose is to persuade A Ltd to take action, whether lawful or not, which injures B then, whether there is any legal or other tie between A Ltd and B or not, B can sue X. He could not have done so if the inducement had occurred without the prior threat because he has no contract to protect.

It must be emphasized that there is no illegality in threatening to do what one has a right to do, however injurious that threat may be.

No one can sue for intimidation if no one has been coerced, i.e.

if the threat has been rejected. This has led to the suggestion that, since it is only the threat of illegal action that constitutes the tort, if the illegality is so insignificant that it has no coercive effect no action will lie. For example, if, in order to secure the dismissal of a worker, other employees threaten to strike in three weeks' time whereas, to be lawful, the strike should have been preceded by four weeks' notice, there may be no right of action because the employer would be just as affected by a threat preceded by four weeks' notice as by what actually occurred. This possible defence has not been translated into the Industrial Relations Act 1971. A threat of industrial action which would constitute an unfair industrial practice if carried out will itself constitute an unfair industrial practice however technical the illegality. No doubt, a claim for compensation could be reduced if it could be shown that something other than the threat had produced the coercion, but it seems that the NIRC could still make an order forbidding continuation of the threat.

Finally, we meet the same problem of identification as was encountered in inducement to breach of contract. Just as it may be difficult to show that a particular individual produced sufficient leadership to be said to have 'induced' the action, so it may be difficult to show that an individual who communicated a threat was more than a messenger. Similarly, potential intimidators may remain silent as to the purpose of their action, knowing that the object of it will put two and two together and act accordingly. If that knowledge can be proved it will, presumably, suffice, but such proof may be difficult.

The second tort involves the, now well-established, liability for conspiracy. Both in criminal and civil law the courts have long felt that, of its very nature, a combination calls forth special protective measures for the benefit of those against whom it is directed. Gradually during this century they have formulated two forms of liability for civil conspiracy arising from:

(a) a combination to achieve its purpose by unlawful means; or,
(b) a combination intended, whether by lawful or unlawful means, primarily to injure someone, rather than primarily to benefit those combining.

In the first type, if the combination is carried through, those combining become liable both for conspiracy and for whatever other wrongs they may commit. But even if it is not carried through, but produces injury merely because it exists, it will be actionable. So also, if some of those combining commit no illegality themselves they will still be liable for conspiring. Suppose, for instance, two shop stewards and a district official agree to call a strike in breach of the contracts of employment of those taking part, including the shop stewards. All will have induced a breach of contracts of employment and would be liable for a conspiracy to do so (save that, as we shall see, the Industrial Relations Act 1971 (Section 132) in this situation provides protection from the inducement and so destroys the essential illegal element necessary to constitute an actionable conspiracy to induce). But the two shop stewards have also broken their own contracts and would be liable for conspiring so to do. The district official has no contract to break, but will be equally liable for conspiring to break contracts of employment.

It might be supposed that the second type of conspiracy, which is constituted solely by the existence of a primary intent to injure another, would have been used by the courts to impose considerable restrictions on trade unions which sought, for instance, to impose a closed-shop agreement in the days when such an agreement would itself have been lawful. In fact, and quite apart from any special statutory protection from liability, this was not so. The courts (rather uncharacteristically, it may be felt) took a broad view of the scope of objective which a union could be said to pursue primarily in its own interest. The closed shop was, before 1971, always considered to be so justified. It followed that to seek to maintain it by securing the dismissal of a non-unionist would be primarily in the interest of those combining. (Without the special protection of section 132(3) such an agreement would now have been a conspiracy to use unlawful means of an unfair practice.) It was, of course, possible to pass the boundary. In one case branch officials rejected the advice of their National Executive to reinstate a member of the union whom the branch had expelled. Thereafter they could hardly be said to be acting in the interests of the union. The officials then pursued the expelled member to a number of successive actual or potential places of employment and secured his dismissal or rejection ostensibly because he was not a union member. The court found that they were at that time primarily motivated by a desire to injure him in pursuit of a personal vendetta, rather than to benefit themselves.

The reader may think it strange that pure self-interest operates to justify a combination. It may be easier to regard the matter from the other end as the existence of injurious intent operating to make a combination unlawful. Either way it is apparent that liability, or the absence of it, owes a great deal to concepts of the right of freedom of trade which are not now so strongly held as they were. The industrialist may point out, for instance, that his combinations may be justified from the point of view of the tort of conspiracy but fall foul of the Restrictive Trade Practices Act. The trade unionist will now have an equal if not greater complaint concerning the numerous unfair industrial practices specified in the Industrial Relations Act 1971. By contrast the tort of conspiracy was particularly liberal. On the one hand it did not prevent the members of a shipping combine agreeing together to undercut the carriage charges of a newcomer to the trade so as to force him out of business. On the other it did not prohibit a trade union requiring its members who were dock-workers to refuse to handle imported yarn which had been woven and exported at lower prices than the entirely local cloth. The object of the union was to enable the local producers to raise their prices so that they could pay its members higher wages.

The concept of liability for conspiring (that is to say, of liability or extra liability arising where none would otherwise exist, merely from the fact of combined action) is not taken over into the specification of liability in the Industrial Relations Act 1971. Because of the reasonably extensive statutory protection available for tort liability it is not likely to form any significant part of the law relating to workers organizations in the future, despite its major influence in the last century.

STATUTORY PROTECTION

The civil liability we have examined in this chapter did not initially develop to deal with the industrial action that might be undertaken by trade unions. Nor were its major principles designed primarily to relate to the characteristics of that action. Indeed, it could fairly be said to be somewhat irrelevant for the court to be trying to find an induced breach of contract, when it really desired to regulate a strike in breach of a procedure agreement which was itself not recognized as a contract. None the less there was felt to be a considerable potential for restriction of industrial action in the torts of conspiracy and inducement and, much later, in the tort of intimidation. Before 1900 it had been assumed that this potential would not be realized, because trade union funds were thought not to be open to action on the grounds that trade unions had no separate existence in law, and because individual workers were not worth suing. In 1901, however, the Amalgamated Society of Railway Servants was successfully sued for damages arising from picketing, and in the few years before statutory protection was afforded a considerable drain was imposed on trade union funds. In 1906 a Liberal Government afforded to industrial action the greatest statutory protection it has had, or is ever likely to enjoy. Trade unions themselves were entirely exempt from all action in tort. Individuals, if acting in contemplation or furtherance of a trade dispute, were protected from inducement to breach of contracts of employment, conspiracy to injure (if it did not involve other unlawful means) and 'interference with trade' in case, as appeared possible, that became a tort in itself. In 1964 the House of Lords for the first time opened up a substantial hole in this protection and, as we have seen, extended the tort of intimidation so as to produce a substantial liability for threatened industrial action. The hole was partially stopped by legislation in 1965, although it had become clear that there was no statutory protection for a conspiracy to used unlawful means (so that a combination to threaten unlawful action might still be actionable), or for inducement to breach of contracts other than contracts of employment. It is therefore surprising to find this policy of special statutory protection from general aspects of tort which bore especially harshly on industrial activity completely reversed in 1971. The general protection from all tort liability previously offered to trade union funds is completely withdrawn. Only those funds which are expressly rendered unavailable for financing industrial action are now protected, although there is, as we have seen, an upper limit on each claim for damages against a registered trade union. The principles of the torts of inducement to breach of contract and intimidation are incorporated into purpose-built heads of liability aimed specifically at industrial activity. The test of contemplation and furtherance of a trade (industrial) dispute, which formerly defined protected activities, is now used to define the area of liability for the new 'unfair industrial practices'.

The ultimate cynicism, however, is achieved by the provision which maintains and even extends all the former statutory protection from the law of tort. The end result is to render the law of tort as such virtually unusable, but to replace it with a new form of liability founded on the most extensive of its principles and infinitely more efficient as a method of control.

The major exception to the general re-enactment of immunity from tort actions is, as we have seen, the absence of the general immunity afforded to all trade unions whether registered or not. In theory, therefore, actions in tort, unless subject to specific immunity, can be brought against any organization of workers; provided, of course, that it is responsible for the activity constituting the tort, as, for instance, by failing to withdraw the normal authority of its officials to undertake that activity. In practice it is unlikely that many such actions will arise from industrial activity. This is partly because the action for an unfair industrial practice has such a wide scope and is more likely to succeed. Partly it is because of the express provision in the Industrial Relations Act that where complaint is made in tort in the ordinary courts of a matter which is, or could be, the subject of complaint in the industrial courts or tribunals as constituting an unfair industrial practice, the common law courts may (presumably will) stay the proceedings. In the case of conspiracy the court has no discretion because section 132 (4) says that it 'will' stay the action.

Because of the limitation of the definition of an 'industrial dispute', particularly so as to exclude disputes between workers and workers, and political issues, there may be a few examples of industrial action in future which cannot be made the subject of complaint as constituting an unfair industrial practice. Action against them would have to be, if at all, in tort. It may be that an action in tort will have one significant advantage over the action for an unfair industrial practice. The rules of the National Industrial Relations Court, following the wording of Schedule 3 of the 1971 Act, provide that:

'Before making an interim order [that is an order forbidding further action pending the full trial of the action] . . . the court shall take all reasonable steps to secure that notice, whether or not in writing, of the application for the interim order has been given to the person against whom it is sought and that he is given an opportunity of making representations to the court in regard to it.'

Although it is not entirely clear that this is so, it would appear that the court should interpret this so as to exclude the common law practice of making an *ex parte* interim order if the party against whom the complaint is made indicates a desire to appear to defend himself. An *ex parte* order is one made merely on the sworn written statements of the parties as the facts, without any chance to cross-examine to ascertain the truth or to sort out conflicts. Its whole object is speed and *ex parte* orders are normally sought within twenty-four hours or so. In urgent matters some High Court judges assert that they would issue such an order by telephone. The value to a complainant against industrial activity of such an order is, of course, that once the activity stops, even for a few days, it is difficult to start it again. So a party unsure of how his case will stand up to trial might still achieve his purpose of stopping the activity because all he has to do is present a prima facie case, that is to say one that reasonably looks as if it may have substance. The order will then normally be granted unless the other can show that it would do him more damage to grant the order than it would do the plaintiff if it was refused. If this continues to be so, an employer might in some situations prefer the common law *ex parte* injunction order to that of the NIRC.

Specific protection from some of the tort liability dealt with in this chapter continues to be provided whenever an act is done by a person in contemplation or furtherance of an industrial dispute. It must be noted, therefore, that if action in tort was brought because the industrial action complained of was not part of an industrial dispute, and so not normally subject to complaint of an unfair industrial practice, no statutory protection would be available. Otherwise action in tort will not lie on the ground only that the activity complained of:

(a) induces another person to break any contract to which that other person is a party, or prevents performance of such a contract;

(b) consists in threatening that a contract (whether one to which the threatener is a party or not) will be broken or prevented from being performed, or in threatening inducement of breach, or prevention of performance, by a party to such a contract;

(c) is an interference with the trade, business or employment of another person, or with the right of another person to dispose of his capital or his labour as he wills;

(d) is an agreement or combination which would not be actionable in tort without the element of combination.

The last heading is interesting. It will be observed that in order to destroy the protection it does not merely have to be shown that the combination employed some other actionable means, but that these means were actionable in tort. So it is not possible to allege that a conspiracy to commit unfair industrial practices is actionable as such. This seems to be designed as a form of second line defence against common law courts assuming jurisdiction over unfair industrial practices by treating them as tortious conspiracies to commit unfair industrial practices.

PICKETING – CIVIL LIABILITY

The law relating to picketing appears to be largely unknown even to people otherwise reasonably well informed. It is not surprising, therefore, to find many misapprehensions as to the legality of this practice.

It must first be clearly appreciated that the police possess power to terminate most forms of picketing, whether peaceful or not. The police have certain duties such as the removal of obstruction on the highway and the prevention of a reasonably anticipated breach of the peace. If hindered in the execution of these duties they are entitled to arrest persons for obstruction of the police in the execution of their duty. There are numerous situations in which peaceful picketing none the less may give the constable on the spot reasonable cause to believe that in due course a breach of the peace is likely. The courts reserve to themselves the right to say, in the last resort, whether such anticipation is reasonable, but they accept that the person on the spot is in a better position than they to judge. In practice they will not lightly upset his decision. It is accordingly common and well advised for the organizers of pickets to inform the police of their intentions and projected method. Police 'permission' is, of course, no guarantee against reversal of the decision, particularly if the notified information turns out to be incorrect, nor, of course, can the police 'permit' illegality. But it is at least an indication of the initial attitude which will be adopted.

Picketing may produce direct liability either in civil law, permitting the object of the activity to sue for damages or an injunction, or in criminal law. We will first consider the civil aspect. Prima facie, and without consideration of the existence of any statutory protection, the following causes of action may easily arise:

(a) trespass, if the picketing is on private property;

(b) public nuisance, if the picketing is on the highway and causes an obstruction. This is generally so even if the pickets keep moving. This may be actionable by an individual but only if he has suffered injury over and above that to the general public;

(c) assault and battery, if the picketing has violent aspects;

(d) intimidation, if the picketing is threatening violence or other illegality;

(e) inducement to breach of contract, either as a tort or as an unfair industrial practice under section 96 of the Industrial Relations Act 1971;

(f) breach of a contractually enforceable collective agreement under section 34 of the Industrial Relations Act 1971;

(g) an unfair industrial practice under any other section of that Act which is not confined to strikes and irregular industrial action (e.g. section 33).

It is provided, however, in section 134 of the Industrial Relations Act, that picketing of any place where a person happens to be, other than his residence, in contemplation or furtherance of an industrial dispute, shall not constitute an offence under any statute or rule of law, or a tort, if it is done only for the purpose of peacefully obtaining from, or communicating to, him any information, or peacefully persuading him to work or not to work. It is clear from decided cases on the similar provisions of section 2 of the Trade Disputes Act 1906 that this protection is only available:

(a) where communication, or obtaining, of information, or persuasion to work or not to work is all that is done; and,

(b) where the only illegality committed is such as is necessary for those purposes.

It is arguable, therefore, that an obstruction of a lorry is necessary in order to communicate with the driver. But this will not be so if the object of the obstruction is not such communication but prevention of the lorry proceeding. In the same way, since persuasion not to work is permitted, inducement to breach of contract of employment may be allowed if, for instance, a breach of section 96 can be avoided by authorization of the action by a registered union. Even if the object is communication or persuasion, the protection will only be available where no more obstruction than is necessary for that purpose is used. So it is probably true to say that the presence of four pickets at a narrow gateway through which only one person at a time can pass is outside the protection of the section even if they only seek to communicate or persuade. It follows that liability for assault, intimidation, riot and inducement to break contracts other than contracts of employment is unprotected.

Doubt must centre on some of the words used in section 134. The word 'offence' could be read as applying only to a criminal offence. This, indeed, is the better view. If that is so, no protection whatsoever is afforded to those who commit unfair industrial practices so that peaceful persuasion not to work in breach of contract of employment will constitute an actionable inducement to breach of contract within section 96.

The conclusion has been reached by the NIRC in one of the container blacking cases. The Court said:

'Parliament did not, however, say that these activities were permissible for all purposes. They were permissible so far as the criminal law and the general civil law were concerned. But when it came to the new industrial framework it all depended upon why the picketing was being undertaken. ... If the action was taken for a purpose forbidden by the Act – for example, calling a strike without notice—it was no less wrong because it happened to take the form of picketing.'

It is submitted that this line of reasoning to support the conclusion that picketing to induce a breach of contract is not protected is similar to that based on use of the word 'offence' in the section. One way or another, however, the conclusion must be assumed to be established.

The Court of Appeal had, however, indicated at an earlier hearing that one must not be astute to assume that communication has necessarily intimidated a person and thereby itself induced a breach of contract. Shouting abuse at people who were breaking a picket line did not constitute a breach of an order not to commit an unfair industrial practice. It is true that these remarks were made in contempt proceedings when the standard of proof is required to be higher than in a civil action for damages, but it is suggested that the principle should be the same in judging the legality of picketing.

The section has also inserted the words 'to him' and 'from him' to limit the communication or obtaining of information. This could be taken to mean that those picketing premises and conveying information to the public who might resort to those premises were outside the protection, since they were not picketing the place where the public happened to be and so were not entitled to communicate information to the public. The 1906 Act did not contain these qualifying words.

It is probably not too much to say that in practice very little protection is afforded to pickets, but that some of the liability they incur is purely technical or, at least, is unlikely to be made the subject of action. Certainly in the past it has not been common to bring civil actions against pickets. There is no reason why this practical immunity should continue.

It may be observed that if a 'cooling-off' order is made under the emergency provisions to be considered in the next chapter it prohibits only strikes and irregular industrial action and does not include picketing. Picketing is not of itself an 'irregular industrial action' within the definition in the 1971 Act and so does not constitute any one of the relatively numerous unfair industrial practices which, as seen in the previous chapter, can only be committed by strikes, lock-outs or irregular industrial action. But it must be emphasized again that where the prohibition on the means used is not confined in this way (and this is particularly so in the case of section 96 dealing with inducement to breach of contract), picketing as a means of inducement will be considered to have constituted the unfair practice charged.

CRIMINAL LIABILITY

Pickets, unless protected within section 134 of the 1971 Act, may incur criminal liability as any other persons. There is a group of crimes which, though of general application, bear particularly on pickets. These are contained in section 7 of the Conspiracy and Protection of Property Act 1875 which provides that:

'Every person who, with a view to compel any other person to abstain from doing or to do any act which such other person has a legal right to do or abstain from doing, wrongfully and without legal authority,

(1) Uses violence to or intimidates such other person or his wife or children, or interferes with his property; or
(2) Persistently follows such other person about from place to place; or
(3) Hides any tools, clothes, or other property owned or used by such other person, or deprives him of, or hinders in the use thereof; or
(4) Watches or besets the house or other place where such other person resides or works, or carries on business, or happens to be, or the approach to such house or place; or
(5) Follows such other person with two or more other persons in a disorderly manner in or through any street or road,

shall on conviction thereof by a court of summary jurisdiction, or on indictment as hereinafter mentioned, be liable to pay a penalty not exceeding twenty pounds, or to be imprisoned for a term not exceeding three months . . .'

It is important to note that these crimes do not occur unless the activity is, apart from this section, unlawful in some other respect. Thus a 'watching and besetting' is only criminal if it is, for instance, otherwise a nuisance. Possibly a hiding of tools or clothes would have to constitute some wrong other than the very technical aspect of trespass involved in touching the property.

Strike action may also, in rare cases, amount to a criminal offence. It is an offence punishable on indictment with two years imprisonment, or on summary conviction with three months' imprisonment and/or a fine of fifty pounds (and if the offender is a policeman, to loss of pension rights and disqualification for any police force):

> 'If any person causes, or attempts to cause, or does any act calculated to cause disaffection amongst the members of any police force, or induces or attempts to induce, or does any act calculated to induce any member of a police force to withhold his services or to commit breaches of discipline.'

Criminal sanctions are available against merchant seamen who strike at sea, although these do not now apply to a strike proceeded by forty-eight hours notice after the ship has reached a safe berth in the United Kingdom.

Finally a general provision of section 5 of the Conspiracy and Protection of Property Act 1875, which is still in force, provides that where any person wilfully and maliciously breaks a contract of service or of hiring, knowing or having reasonable cause to believe that the probable consequences of his so doing, either alone or in combination with others, will be to endanger human life, or cause serious bodily injury or to expose valuable property to destruction or serious injury he shall be liable to a fine up to £20 or to imprisonment not exceeding three months.

The introduction of legislation to control rises in incomes has been, and is apparently again to be, accompanied by prohibition of strikes designed to induce breach of the policy. A criminal sanction has been considered appropriate although it is difficult to see how it will operate in practice.

Chapter 8

Emergency Procedures

Most industrial countries possess some form of emergency powers which can be used when industrial action produces a shortage of goods or a threat to essential services. In this country, with the exception of Northern Ireland, there was, immediately before 1972, only the Emergency Powers Act 1920, as amended. Under this Act the Government, by way of the Queen in Council, may declare a state of emergency if it appears that:

'there have occurred, or are about to occur, events of such a nature as to be calculated, by interfering with the supply and distribution of food, water, fuel or light, or with the means of locomotion, to deprive the community or any substantial portion of the community, of the essentials of life.'

Upon the declaration of a state of emergency, Parliament, if not in session or due to re-convene within five days, must be recalled and the proclamation communicated to it. The state of emergency may last for one month, although none of the seven so far declared has done so. If necessary, the same procedure would be used to continue the state of emergency beyond the end of this time. During the existence of a state of emergency Orders in Council may be made as deemed

'. . . necessary for the preservation of the peace, for securing and regulating the supply and distribution of food, water, fuel, light and other necessities, for maintaining the means of transport, or locomotion, and for any other purposes essential to the public safety and the life of the community.'

Any such order must be laid before Parliament as soon as may be, and will last for seven days without renewal. Such orders may not forbid strikes or peaceful picketing, or introduce compulsory military service, or order persons to return to work. Existing criminal procedure may not be altered by this method, nor may fines or imprisonment be imposed without trial.

An amendment was introduced in 1964 which could have considerable significance. Without a declaration of a state of emergency:

> 'The Admiralty, the Army or the Air Council may, by order authorize officers and men of Her Majesty's naval, military or air forces under their respective control to be temporarily employed in agricultural work or such other work as may be approved in accordance with instructions issued [by the appropriate authority] as being urgent work of national importance, and thereupon it shall be the duty of every person subject to [the discipline of such forces] to obey any command given by his superior officer in relation to such employment.'

This latter device may seem more inflammatory than the former. In practice neither is ever used save in extreme circumstances and seem generally to be intended more as a way of persuading workers to resume work pending settlement than anything else. In all but one case (the seamen's strike of 1966) work was quickly resumed following a declaration of a state of emergency. Nothing in this country approaches the device of Presidential seizure of the industrial unit, which is used more frequently in the United States. It is clear that the purpose is not to interfere directly with the industrial action which has been the cause of the emergency.

The Taft-Hartley Act had, in 1947, introduced into the United States a different form of control under which the President could declare a state of emergency whenever a strike threatened the national security. Strikers could then be ordered back to work for a ninety-day 'cooling-off' period. The order was by way of judicial injunction, so that refusal to obey it could be dealt with as a contempt of court. There is considerable evidence that the order for return to work is not very effective in the United States and might be no more so here. Nevertheless, the Labour government in 1969–70 proposed to introduce a twenty-eight-day cooling-off period, and the succeeding Conservative government did introduce a sixty-day cooling-off period, with the sanction lying against the strike leader rather than the striker.

Alternatively or indeed in addition to such an order, the NIRC can order a ballot to be held to ascertain the degree of support for strike action or irregular industrial action short of a strike. No prohibition order follows the outcome of such a ballot, but while the ballot is being taken the industrial action in question must be discontinued.

In the case of an application for either a 'cooling-off' order or a ballot order, three preconditions must 'appear to the Secretary of State', who alone can make the application, to be satisfied. They are:

(a) that strike action or irregular industrial action short of a strike, in contemplation or furtherance of an industrial dispute, has begun or is likely to begin;

(b) that *in the case of a cooling-off order*, having regard to all the circumstances, it would be conducive to a settlement of the dispute by negotiation, conciliation or arbitration to discontinue or defer the industrial action; or, *in the case of a ballot order* that there are reasons for doubting whether the workers who are taking part or are expected to take part in the strike or other industrial action are or would be taking part in it in accordance with their wishes, and whether they have had an adequate opportunity of indicating their wishes in this respect;

(c) that the industrial action in question has caused, or (as the case may be) would cause, an interruption in the supply of goods or in the provision of services of such a nature, or on such a scale, as to be likely:

  (i) to be grossly injurious to the national economy, to imperil national security or to create a serious risk of public disorder; or

  (ii) to endanger the lives of a substantial number of persons or expose a substantial number of persons to serious risk of disease or personal injury; or

  (iii) *in the case only of a ballot order*, that the effects of the industrial action in question on a particular industry are, or are likely to be, such as to be seriously injurious to the livelihood of a substantial number of workers employed in that industry.

In the case of conditions (a) and (b), the court has no power to examine the grounds of the Secretary of State's satisfaction that the situation so appears save to ascertain that he has acted in good faith and that he has not mistaken the legal meaning of the condition required, as distinct from the facts allegedly supporting its satisfaction. To contest the Secretary of State's application it would have to be shown that no reasonable man could reach such a conclusion or that there are *no* facts which could support it. The Secretary of State cannot be made to disclose his own reasons for thinking any of the conditions to be satisfied.

In the case of the third condition, however, it has been said both by the NIRC and the Court of Appeal that the court must be satisfied on the evidence presented to it that there are sufficient grounds for believing in the existence of the required situation. In the case in which this was decided, however, the facts indicated how little room there will normally be for the courts to disagree with the assertion of the executive in this respect.

The application by the Secretary of State to the National Industrial Relations Court for a cooling-off order must specify the persons appearing to him to be responsible for calling, organizing, procuring or financing the strike or other action, or for threatening to do so. On the face of it this looks as if it should exclude a 'general warrant' against e.g. 'such persons as shall be responsible'. In fact, since the application can specify any organization of workers (apparently even if it is unregistered and so not strictly a 'person' at all), unknown officials could at least be subjected to an order preventing continuation of union authorization for their actions. On the other hand, no order could be made, for instance, against a committee of shop stewards which would normally be regarded as failing to constitute any sort of entity for this or any other purpose.

The maximum total period of cooling-off in any dispute is sixty days. If the original order is for less than sixty days, the Secretary of State can make a fresh application before the end of the original period, for extension up to that maximum. The NIRC is free to specify the date when the order takes effect and has taken the view that it is free to do so by reference to a future event such as the date on which the calling-off of the industrial action takes effect. By the same process, other persons not mentioned in the original order may be added and any requirement which could have been contained in the initial order may be applied to such persons. The first such order made was for fourteen days from the date when the Secretary of State certified that the industrial action had ceased. No application for extension was made although the industrial action was renewed.

The order made must specify the area of employment in which it is to have effect by reference to one or more industries, undertakings or parts of undertakings or descriptions of workers, and must indicate the scope of the dispute so as to define the area of employment affected by it and the matters to which it relates. The persons bound by the order (i.e. those specified in the application) must not include any person who, in the opinion of the Industrial Court, has or would have no responsibility for the action beyond being included among the persons taking part, or who is only responsible in his capacity as an official of a registered trade union acting within the scope of his authority on behalf of the union. The order must direct those covered by it, within the specified area, not to call a strike or organize, procure or finance a strike or any irregular industrial action short of a strike or threaten to do so. It may also, and this is probably more significant, direct any such person, before the end of a given period, to take any specified steps for the purpose of securing that the industrial action to which the order related is discontinued or deferred during the period for which the order remains in force. This, and the corresponding provision to prevent industrial action while a ballot is being held, are two of only three provisions in the Act which permit an order positively to require a party to take steps to prevent others whose conduct he has not authorized to cease the offending action. (The third provision is section 36 dealing with breach of a contractually enforceable collective agreement.) In the course of an order to cease an ordinary unfair industrial practice, the prohibition can only be on the parties' own actions; although the concept of implied authority does introduce something like vicarious liability for officials acting in the area of their normal authorization.

Before applying to the NIRC to conduct a ballot, the Secretary of State must consult every employer, employer's association and trade union (but not necessarily an unregistered organization of workers) appearing to him to be party to the dispute.

The ballot (incorrectly called a 'strike ballot' because it may apply to any irregular industrial action) must be held among the workers involved in the industrial action and the order of the NIRC must include provisions for enabling the workers eligible to vote to be determined. It must also again specify the area of employment covered by relation to the scope of the dispute, and the extent of the matters to which the dispute relates. In the first ballot order to be made, the NIRC defined the area of employment as all employees of British Railways covered by the negotiations which were the subject of dispute.

The court may, if it wishes, call upon the assistance of the CIR in framing the order, that is to say, largely in formulating the question on which the ballot is to be taken. The first such question was: 'In the light of the [board's] pay offer (about which you are being informed by the [board]), do you wish to take part in further industrial action?' Provision was made for recording a vote for or against the proposal or returning the paper without such a vote, thus indicating abstention.

The court must also fix a period of time for the conduct of the ballot. The first example indicates that the choice will normally be for a postal ballot which takes time to organize and conduct. In that case, twenty-one days was allowed.

The ballot itself will be conducted by the Commission unless it exercises its power to ask a registered trade union with members eligible to vote in the ballot and which has negotiating rights in respect of workers involved in the dispute to do so. Such a request can only be made to a trade union the rules of which have been approved by the Registrar.

Save that the result of the ballot is to be reported to the court and published in such manner as it shall consider appropriate, no other provision is made for action following the ballot. The significance of the process lies in the fact that, from the date of the order for a ballot to the date of notification of the result, no organization or other person specified in the order shall, or shall threaten to, call, organize, procure or finance any strike or irregular industrial action short of a strike on the part of any of the workers eligible to vote in the ballot. The ballot order may also require steps to be taken by any person specified in the order to discontinue such action during the period of the order. Employers involved are also required not to institute, carry on, organize, procure or finance a lock-out of any of their workers or to threaten to do so. It appears that such an order will be made even though there is no indication that the employers had thought of doing so.

In neither a cooling-off order nor a ballot can there be any requirement that a particular employee, or particular employees, shall do any work or attend at any place for the purpose of doing any work.

Either of these types of procedure is most likely to be used in major disputes where industrial action has been continuing for some time and where the chance of settlement is relatively low. There is no obligation to use the procedure and there is indeed a warning (though it amounts to little more than that) to the Secretary of State that the procedures should only be used if there seems to be some industrial relations advantage to be gained. This seems a somewhat unreal hope. Compulsory termination of industrial action is only likely to entrench the opposition of those taking it. Certainly in the case of the only order so far made the action was resumed immediately the cooling-off period terminated. Experience in other countries reveals that a ballot will almost always produce a majority in favour of continuation of industrial action. It may reasonably be thought that this is more probable if the industrial action has meanwhile been compulsorily suspended. The result of using both procedures in the railway dispute of 1972 was to make it almost impossible to do anything but settle on the unions' terms. There is no doubt that in that case the procedures were invoked as a step in the dispute and at far too early a stage. There may be something to be said for using them after a prolonged stoppage when both public and participants are tired of the dispute and want a settlement. On the whole, however, little would seem to have been gained by adding to the emergency system provided by the Emergency Powers Act.

Part III

Industrial Relations

Chapter 9

Collective Bargaining

The characteristic of British collective bargaining before 1972 was its virtually complete voluntary character. Certain official machinery existed which we will examine at the end of this chapter, but the object of such machinery was invariably to encourage the development, or enhance the effectiveness, of voluntary procedures.

It is unnecessary to tell the trade unionist that, increasingly after 1945, the gap between national, or industry-wide, and local bargaining became apparent. Effective settlement of disputes and fixing of wages and conditions of work in large areas of industry, occurred only at local level. National agreements tended to establish a floor of wages or other conditions upon which local bargaining built. Superficially, in industries such as construction, the impression might be maintained of the existence of meaningful national wage negotiation, but throughout others (such as engineering) even this facade was not sustained. It remained, however, reasonably common to find nationally established disputes procedures and procedures to govern the negotiation of substantive agreements. Even here, however, there was growing evidence that national disputes procedures were avoided because of their delay or, if resorted to, did not produce any very satisfactory answer.

The Royal Commission on Trade Unions, reporting in 1965, strongly favoured emphasis on local bargaining. Again it is not necessary to point out the arguments in favour of one or the other system. It may generally be said that the Royal Commission considered that the further one was removed from the source of a dispute the more difficult became an effective settlement. This must be so, if only because one moves away from those with first-hand knowledge to those whose knowledge is indirectly acquired. One might argue that the dispute is settled in a more impartial atmosphere and that this may sometimes be an advantage. Against this, however, one must set the fact that at higher levels of bargaining, decisions are apt to constitute precedents of much more general significance. At a very simple level, for example, where a man who claims an extra 10p per hour for working standing in water, the matter can be dealt with at workshop level in the knowledge that the decision will at most only affect those employed in that industrial unit possibly no more than on one occasion a year. As the dispute progresses through a national procedure a decision will affect more and more people, until eventually it must be a decision to pay any worker in these conditions extra money. By that time it will have attached to it considerations of grading and differentials, classification of conditions, and so on, which will make settlement longer and more difficult and, at the end, probably less satisfactory.

The Royal Commission concluded that not only was the tide running in favour of local bargaining, but that this was a beneficial movement. To reach such a conclusion it had to overcome the fear that the shop steward, in whose hands local bargaining necessary was mostly concentrated, was neither the most efficient nor responsible person for such work. The attitude of the Royal Commission was strongly in favour of the shop steward as, on the whole, a moderating and valuable force in industry. In its opinion his main weakness lay in his isolation from the trade union organization, which often left him to his own devices, and his lack of central services, particularly of information.

In the Industrial Relations Act 1971, which we will now consider, the legislature, without necessarily agreeing with the Royal Commission's high opinion of the integrity of the mass of shop stewards, nevertheless accepted the fact of, and the need to advance, the primacy of local bargaining. At the same time it endeavoured to ensure that trade unions would exercise a higher degree of central supervision over it by copying the American system based on strong central organization. It thus placed British trade unions in an almost impossible position. In Britain, shop-floor organization is uniquely strong, whilst central union control is, relative to other heavily unionized countries, noticeably weak.

The legislation makes no attempt to affect the initial securing of bargaining rights, although it does make the possession of such rights a necessary prerequisite to an application for exclusive *organizing* rights among workers in a unit. This does not mean that some element of voluntary recognition is always essential. Application can be made for compulsory bargaining rights. These can then be followed by application for exclusive organizing rights.

The Code of Industrial Relations Practice lays down certain matters for consideration when non-exclusive recognition is sought. Some of them will also apply where management is approached for a voluntary agreement for exclusive rights. It is stated that management should take into account:

(a) the extent of support for the agent among the employees concerned, whether they are members of the union or not;
(b) the effect of granting recognition on any existing bargaining arrangement;
(c) whether or not recognition should be granted to the same union or section of a union in respect of supervisors and members of the work groups they supervise.

The Code states that management is entitled to know the number, but not the identity, of the employees who are members of the union making the claim and who will be covered by the bargaining recognition requested. Responsibility for avoiding disputes about which union should bargain for a group is said to lie with the unions, and, if unions are affiliated to it, with the TUC.

The Act concentrates its effect at the point where a union or a group of unions seek sole rights to bargain within a given unit of employment. That unit must be defined in terms of the employees of a single employer or a group of associated employers; so that the statutory machinery could only achieve a national sole bargaining agency by way of a number of industrial agreements with the same unions which then, as a matter of voluntary practice, conducted their negotiations simultaneously in the same place. Nothing prevents the voluntary formulation of exclusive bargaining agreements on a local or a national scale. It is plainly assumed that the statutory pattern will act as an example, even at the voluntary level so that recognition, whether voluntary or compulsory (and whether exclusive or not) of bargaining rights will tend always to be locally based.

SOLE BARGAINING AGENTS

The concept of the statutory sole bargaining agent is that of a defined group of employees (notice that no provision is made for groups of self-employed workers) negotiation of whose terms and conditions (or of a defined aspect of them) is exclusively in the hands of a single registered trade union, or a group of registered trade unions forming a joint negotiating panel. The voluntary counterpart does not materially differ from this save in that:

(a) any organization of workers can be included as agent;
(b) the sole right is not statutorily protected from industrial action by outside organizations seeking to set it aside; and
(c) a voluntary agreement is not so firmly protected from dissolution from within the unit.

The definition of the unit is, of course, of vital significance. Trade unions will tend to seek as large a unit as possible, without making the mistake of including too many groups of employees in which there is only minority support for them, so as not to destroy their overall majority. Employers will not necessarily oppose this move, but will be under pressure from groups of employees substantially opposed to the grant of exclusive right to negotiate for exclusion of such groups from the scope of the agency. The definition of the descriptions of employee to be covered will first be made in the application, but is ultimately to be decided by the Commission on Industrial Relations. The Act merely directs the Commission to have regard, in relation to each description of employees, to:

(a) the nature of the work which they are employed to do; and
(b) their training, experience and professional or other qualifications.

The Code of Industrial Relations Practice, issued under the Act, lays down some general guide lines:

(a) arrangements which are already working well should not be disturbed without good reason;
(b) the unit should cover as wide a group of employees as practicable, even if this has to be done by combining existing units with few unions into one large unit with many unions on the panel;
(c) there should be a substantial degree of common interest among the employees concerned, but the need to take into account the distinct interest of minority groups should be balanced against the need to avoid unduly small units;
(d) the following factors should be considered:

    (i) the nature of the work,
    (ii) the training, experience and professional or other qualifications of the employees,
    (iii) the extent of common interest,
    (iv) the general wishes of the employers,
    (v) the organization and location of the work,
    (vi) hours, working arrangements and payment systems,
    (vii) the matters to be bargained about,
    (viii) the need to fit the unit into the pattern of union and management organization,
    (ix) the need to avoid disruption of arrangements which are working well,
    (x) whether separate arrangements are needed for management categories of employees.

In the *Parsons* case the Court said that in the application the unit should be stated in terms of the whole area of employment (i.e. something like the factory – or at least clerical staff in the factory), leaving the CIR free to decide the more precise limitations in the light of the above provisions.

Any one of the following may make a statutory application for a sole bargaining agency, and is not precluded by the fact that the employees who it is sought should be covered are within a larger unit already recognized for this purpose:

(a) one or more *registered* trade unions;
(b) the employer, or one of the employers, concerned;

(c) any of the employers, jointly with any one or more registered trade unions;

(d) the Secretary of State.

Thus, a registered union whose members had formed a minority group and had been swept into a larger unit is free to invoke the statutory machinery on their behalf to seek to have the grouping redefined so that they form a separate unit. Before any of groups (a) to (c) make such an application, they must notify the Secretary of State. Before the Secretary of State makes an application on his own initiative he must consult the employers and the organizations of workers or the joint negotiating panel appearing to him to be directly concerned.

The immediate effect of the application is that it becomes an unfair industrial practice (UIP) for any employer concerned in a dispute regarding the bargaining rights sought to institute, carry on, organize, procure or finance a lock-out in furtherance thereof or to threaten to do so. It is also an unfair industrial practice for any organization of workers, official thereof, or other person, to call a strike or organize, procure, or finance a strike or other irregular industrial action, or threaten to do so. It is clear, therefore, that an application could be a way of securing industrial peace. If there were a genuine desire to seek a solution on the part of one of the parties, there is no reason why the application should not be made with such an object in mind. The NIRC, to which the application is made, however, has indicated that it will not entertain an application made only with such an object in mind, neither party wishing at the time to establish a bargaining agency.

The NIRC will hold preliminary private meetings with the parties, not only designed to secure a voluntary settlement of the entire issue, but also to narrow and define the issues. At these meetings guidance may be given on how to conduct the case at the public hearing. If confidential matters are disclosed during these, or conciliation, proceedings and it is desired to maintain confidentiality, the court will normally accept an application for future private proceedings to deal with these matters.

When the Secretary of State is notified of an impending application, he must offer such advice and assistance to all parties appearing to him to be directly concerned as he may consider appropriate with a view to promoting agreement between them. In the process he can, on his own initiative, refer any question relating thereto to the CIR. The parties are free to pursue the application during this period. The NIRC, however, cannot proceed to refer it to the CIR for consideration until the court is satisfied that the employers to whom the application relates, and the organizations having or seeking negotiating rights, have endeavoured to settle the questions proposed to be referred and, for that purpose, made use of facilities for conciliation available to them. The NIRC has indicated its desire to provide full opportunity for the operation of the conciliation services of the Department of Employment. These will include those made available by the Secretary of State. The NIRC must also be satisfied that reference of the application to the CIR is necessary with a view to promoting a satisfactory and lasting settlement of the matter in dispute.

It will be observed that considerable attention is paid to ensuring that, if possible, a dispute about sole bargaining rights is settled voluntarily. The NIRC has emphasized the importance it places on the introductory statement of statutory objectives, and, in this case, particularly on the recognition of the principle of freely conducted collective bargaining with due regard to the general interests of the community.

It seems, therefore, that if all parties were willing to have a sole agency, and merely wished to use the statutory procedure so as to gain the extra protection from outside industrial pressure which is afforded by an order of the NIRC, the court ought to reject their application; at least unless they could show a probability of such pressure so as to indicate that a voluntary settlement might not be 'satisfactory and lasting'. If efforts to promote a voluntary settlement have been unavailing over a period of time, the last-minute intervention of a new party will not mean that they must start all over again.

The efforts towards a voluntary settlement are clearly to continue to be pursued after the matter has been referred to the CIR, since it is provided that the Commission may apply to the Industrial Court to withdraw the reference if a satisfactory and lasting settlement has been reached.

It may be observed that the NIRC can bring in organizations of workers appearing to be seeking negotiating rights even if they have not been party to the application. Indeed, once the application has been made, the NIRC is free to choose the 'respondents'. It will often notify organizations on its own initiative and, indeed, an officer of the court is specially engaged to have expert knowledge of those who may be interested in an application. The CIR may also propose an extension of the reference to include other employees, or other organizations of workers, or other associated (but not unconnected) employers, if this appears to it to be necessary with a view to promoting a satisfactory and lasting settlement; of course there is no obligation on those brought in in these ways actively to pursue any claim. Appropriate notice must be given to persons who, in the opinion of the Commission, would be affected, and any person claiming to be affected may, within two weeks of the last date of such notice having been given, apply to the court to consider whether such proposals are necessary or expedient. If no such application is made, the court must confirm the extension. If such application is made the court may either confirm the extension, permit extension to a lesser degree, or direct that the scope shall remain unchanged.

The Commission must then consider the reference as it finally stands and report its recommendations to the NIRC and furnish copies of it to the Secretary of State, the employers comprised in the reference, and every organization of workers appearing to be directly concerned. The report may not recommend recognition of an organization of workers or a joint panel unless the organization, or every organization on the panel is 'an independent organization of workers'. The CIR must also be satisfied that such recognition would be in accordance with the general wishes of the employees in the unit and would promote a satisfactory and lasting settlement of the dispute. In any event, the Commission must *consider* whether the organization or the panel would have the support of a substantial proportion of employees in the unit, or of one or more descriptions thereof, and has, or would have, the resources and organization to enable it to be an effective representative. Some of these requirements are self-explanatory but a few general remarks may be made. The question of what is meant by independence is still an open one. The practice of the Registrar of trade unions, who has to consider the same point, has been not to object to organizations just because they are company unions, or even contain some element of employer initiation in their formation. Dependence on an employer, as by the employer paying the officers of the organization or contributing to its funds, would probably operate as a disqualification either for registration or statutory recommendation as an agent. It may be wondered why it is necessary for the Commission to consider the degree of support the agent has when, as we shall see, the ultimate test of recognition is a ballot vote of the employees in the unit. The answer seems to be that the ballot stage may never be reached. It is highly probable that in most cases the parties, even if they have refused a voluntary settlement previously, will accept the report of the CIR as a basis for voluntary negotiations. If this is so there would be a danger of voluntary recognition of bodies without substantial support, unless care was taken to see that the CIR considered that factor. Finally, the requirement of the possession of adequate resources is the only specific check contained in the Act upon the possibility that a small breakaway union will be formed in a particular unit, will register and successfully apply for sole bargaining status, so producing the type of fragmentation which it is hardly likely the legislature desired to encourage. This is a more substantial probability than might appear at first sight in view of the requirement that unions should discipline shop stewards if they wish to avoid liability for the actions of such officials. Disciplined shop stewards might well feel inclined to form breakaway unions.

The Commission may make its recommendation subject to any conditions it thinks fit. The Act particularly mentions a condition that the organization should make sufficient trained officials available for the purpose of collective bargaining. This again might be used as a way of ascertaining whether a newly created, or breakaway, union was more than a temporary organization. It is also provided that a condition may be attached that any organization of workers recommended as agent for one unit should not make or pursue any claim to be recognized as sole agent for any other unit which included employees of any employer to whom the recommendation relates. Once the report is transmitted to the NIRC it is an unfair industrial practice, within two years of the date of transmission of the report, by strike or irregular industrial action, knowingly to induce or attempt to induce an employer to recognize as sole agent, or carry on any bargaining with, an organization not recommended in the report. At this stage there is, of course, no objection to the employer doing either without such coercion.

The report of the Commission presented to the NIRC does not, of itself, produce any further consequence unless within a period of six months from its presentation any of the employers or organizations of workers or the joint negotiating panel who are party to the application, apply for a ballot.

It should be noted, firstly, that though the Secretary of State can commence the process he cannot take this final step, and secondly, that no application can be made at this stage if any one of the organizations of workers forming part of the agent recommended is unregistered. An unregistered organization of workers can enter into a voluntary sole bargaining agreement. It can also be included in the initial application under the statutory machinery but, in the latter case, it must have become registered before the statutory process is completed by application for a ballot on its behalf. It should also be noted that this is the fourth clear stage where voluntary negotiation may take over. To recapitulate, these stages are:

(a) initially, upon notification to the Secretary of State;

(b) in the introductory stage, by the NIRC;

(c) by withdrawal of the application before the CIR;

(d) following the report of the CIR, the recommendations of which will lapse if no formal application is made in six months.

If, however, application for a ballot is made, the only function of the court is to ascertain whether any conditions attached to the recommendation of the CIR have been complied with. If there are no such conditions, or they have been complied with, the court must request the Commission to arrange a ballot of employees in the proposed unit. The Commission itself may conduct the ballot, or arrange for some other body to do so, but it must ensure that it is secret. The result of the ballot is then communicated by the Commission to the court. If a majority of employees voting (note that on this occasion abstentions do not affect the result, whereas in an agency shop application they count against the proposal unless it is supported by two-thirds of those voting) support the establishment of the sole bargaining agency as proposed, the NIRC must make an order defining the unit, the employers covered and the trade union or panel which is to be the agent. The order takes effect two months after it is made and lasts until revoked, or until any one of the agency unions ceases to be registered. During this time it is an unfair industrial practice:

(a) for an employer to bargain with any other organization of workers on behalf of any of the employees in the unit;

(b) not to take all such action by way of, or with a view to, carrying on collective bargaining with the agent (or, by agreement, with any one or more of the unions forming a panel) as might reasonably be expected to be taken by an employer ready and willing to carry on such collective bargaining;

(c) for any person by industrial action knowingly to induce or attempt to induce a specified employer to commit any unfair practice mentioned in (a) and (b).

(*NB*. In the case of (b) above, or inducement or attempted inducement to commit (b) above, complaint is made in the normal way to the NIRC, but the normal remedies are not available. The NIRC can only refer the complaint to the Industrial Arbitration Board.)

Revocation or lapse of the order may occur in the following circumstances:

(a) by termination of registration of one of the organization of workers;

(b) by order of the court, where a fresh order is made covering the whole or part of the unit;

(c) (presumably) by agreement of all parties;

(d) by the statutory procedure for revocation set out below.

(The last two also apply to revocation of voluntary agreements.)

Any person claiming (whatever that may mean) to be an employee within the bargaining unit established by voluntary agreement may at any time make an application, supported in writing by 20 per cent of the employees in the unit as a whole, on the ground that the agent does not adequately represent the employees in the unit as a whole, or the section of the unit to which the applicant belongs. Where the establishment of the sole bargaining agency followed an order of the NIRC the revocation application can only be made after the end of a period of two years from the date of the order (twenty-two months after it took effect), and must be supported by 40 per cent of the employees in the unit. It is clear, therefore, as already said, that a small minority could not use this means to break out of such an agreement. It would have to rely on the support of a registered trade union prepared to make an application involving redefinition of the unit.

Once again, the application for revocation is the subject of discussion aimed at a voluntary resolution of the objection. These discussions are conducted, however, after the matter has been referred to the Commission. The NIRC must set aside 'sufficient time for the Commission to conduct these discussions'. If no settlement is reached the matter must be resolved by ballot. The Commission must decide whether to hold one ballot over the whole unit or if, in the light of the nature of their work, their training, experience and professional or other qualifications the different interests of various groups within the unit so suggest, separate ballots in different groups. Such a method would, of course, facilitate the eventual subdivision of the unit. The question on which the ballot is held must be whether the agent specified in the original application is to continue to be recognized as the sole bargaining agent for the unit or the part of it which the ballot is being held.

The result of the ballot is reported by the CIR to the NIRC. If it fails to produce a majority of those voting in favour of continuance of the sole agency the court must make an order directing the employers concerned to cease to accord the agent sole bargaining rights for the whole unit, or the appropriate group, and not to accord it such rights for two years from the date of the report. There is, of course, nothing to prevent the continuation of bargaining with a rejected agent. All that is prohibited is an agreement for the sole rights. No statutory application can be made by a rejected agent for the same period. The revocation order takes effect two months after it is made, and it is an unfair industrial practice, by industrial action, knowingly to induce or attempt to induce an employer not to comply with the revocation order. Strictly speaking there is no

[continued on page 159

STATUTORY PROCEDURE FOR SOLE BARGAINING AGENCY

FIRST APPLICATION BY:

Secretary of State or Registered trade union or Employer } Jointly or separately

→ Notification to Secretary of State

Consultation with those concerned

Advice and assistance towards agreement → **VOLUNTARY** (prohibition on **SETTLEMENT** industrial action would lapse)

Industrial action on dispute becomes unfair industrial practice

Application →

NATIONAL INDUSTRIAL RELATIONS COURT

Have conciliation facilities been used?
Is reference to CIR necessary to secure satisfactory lasting settlement?

Reference → **VOLUNTARY** (prohibition on **SETTLEMENT** industrial action would lapse)

Reference

COMMISSION ON INDUSTRIAL RELATIONS

Introduction of other: employees, organizations of workers, associated employers

Is every workers' organization independent?
Would recognition be in accordance with general wishes of employees?
Would recognition promote a satisfactory and lasting settlement?
Does organization or panel have support of substantial proportion of employees?
Does organization have sufficient reserves?

→ **VOLUNTARY** (prohibition on **SETTLEMENT** industrial action would lapse)

Report (with conditions) → **VOLUNTARY** (prohibition on **SETTLEMENT** industrial action would lapse)

NATIONAL INDUSTRIAL RELATIONS COURT

STATUTORY PROCEDURE FOR SOLE BARGAINING AGENCY (contd.)

SECOND APPLICATION IF FAVOURABLE REPORT BY:

Registered trade union
Employer
} Jointly or separately

↓

Application

NATIONAL INDUSTRIAL RELATIONS COURT
Are all organizations registered?
Have all conditions been satisfied?

Ballot Order

→ COMMISSION ON INDUSTRIAL RELATIONS

Report → ←

NATIONAL INDUSTRIAL RELATIONS COURT

Ballot ⟶

ORDER FOR SOLE BARGAINING AGREEMENT

Unfair industrial practices:
bargaining with other than agent;
failing properly to bargain with agent; knowing inducement by means of industrial action, to either of these ends.

COMPULSORY SETTLEMENT

FORMS OF APPLICATION IN CONNECTION WITH THE
FOREGOING PROCEDURE

Form 14 Rule 5

National Industrial Relations Court

NOTICE OF APPLICATION UNDER SECTION 45 (1) FOR
REFERENCE TO COMMISSION ON INDUSTRIAL RELATIONS
OF QUESTIONS AS TO RECOGNITION AS SOLE BARGAINING
AGENT

1. This application is made by (*name(s) and address(es) of applicant(s)*)

2. Any communication for the applicant(s) relating to this application
   may be sent to (*address(es) for service of applicant(s), including
   telephone number(s), if any*)

3. This application relates to the employees of (*name(s) and address(es)
   of employer(s) concerned*) and the (other) trade union(s) concerned
   are (*here give name(s) and address(es) of trade union(s) concerned
   other than the applicant(s) if trade union(s)*))

4. The applicant(s) [desires] [desire] the court to refer to the Commission the following questions:
   [*here set out questions which it is desired that the court should
   refer to the Commission*]

5. *The applicant(s) [has] [have] given the Secretary of State notice
   of [his] [their] proposal to make this application and a copy of the
   notice is attached.

6. The grounds on which the application is made are:
   [*here summarise the facts and matters relied on in support of
   the application*]

Date   *Signed*

* Delete in case of application made by the Secretary of State.

Form 15 Rule 5

National Industrial Relations Court

NOTICE OF APPLICATION UNDER SECTION 47 (4) FOR
CONSIDERATION OF PROPOSALS OF COMMISSION ON
INDUSTRIAL RELATIONS FOR EXTENSION OF REFERENCE
UNDER SECTION 46 RELATING TO RECOGNITION OF
SOLE BARGAINING AGENT

1. This application is made by (*name(s) and address(es) of applicant(s)*)

2. Any communication for the applicant(s) relating to this application
    may be sent to (*applicant(s) address(es) for service, including tele-
    phone number(s), if any*)

3. The applicant(s) [desires] [desire] the court to consider the follow-
    ing proposals made by the Commission:

    [*here give particulars identifying the proposals of the Commission
    to which the application relates*]

4. The applicant(s) [is] [are] affected by the Commission's proposals
    in that

    [*here state respects in which applicant(s) [is] [are] affected*]

5. The applicant(s) [desires] [desire] the court to [*here state the action
    in relation to the Commission's proposals which the applicant(s)
    [desires] [desire] the court to take*]

6. The grounds on which this application is made are:

    [*here summarise the facts and matters relied on in support of the
    application*].

Date   *Signed*

Form 16 Rule 5

National Industrial Relations Court

NOTICE OF APPLICATION UNDER SECTION 49 (1) FOR BALLOT AS TO RECOGNITION OF SOLE BARGAINING AGENT

1. This application is made by (*name(s) and address(es) of applicant(s)*)

2. Any communication for the applicant(s) relating to this application may be sent to (*address(es) for service of applicant(s), including telephone number(s) if any*)

3. This application relates to the report made on [*date of report*] by the Commission on Industrial Relations, recommending that [*here give particulars of Commission's recommendation for recognition of sole bargaining agent on which it is desired that a ballot be taken*]

4. The applicant(s) [desires] [desire] a ballot to be taken under section 49 of the Industrial Relations Act 1971 on the questions whether the recommendation referred to in paragraph 3 above should be made binding

5. The grounds on which the application is made are:

   [*here summarise the facts and matters relied on in support of the application*]

Date   *Signed*

Form 17 Rule 5

National Industrial Relations Court

NOTICE OF APPLICATION UNDER SECTION 51 (1) FOR BALLOT AS TO WITHDRAWAL OF RECOGNITION OF SOLE BARGAINING AGENT

1. This application is made by (*applicant(s) name(s) and address(es)*)

2. Any communication for the applicant(s) relating to this application may be sent to (*applicant(s) address(es) for service, including telephone number(s), if any*)

3. The applicant(s) [is] [are] employed by (*name(s) and address(es) of employer(s)*) and is [are] comprised in [*here specify bargaining unit in which applicant(s) [claims] [claim] to be compromised*], comprising in all [*here state number of employees comprised in the bargaining unit*]

4. The employer(s) [recognises] [recognise] [is] [are] required by an order of the court made on [date of order] [to recognise], as sole bargaining agent(s) for the unit referred to in paragraph 3 above, the (*name of organisation of workers or joint negotiating panel recognised or required to be recognised by employer*)

5. The applicant(s) [desires] [desire] the court to request the Commission on Industrial Relations to arrange for a ballot to be held on the question whether the (*name or organisation of workers or joint negotiating panel*) should cease to be the sole bargaining agent for the (*description of bargaining unit or section of bargaining unit concerned*)

6. The grounds on which the application is made are:
    [*here summarise the facts and matters relied on in support of the application*]

7. The written concurrence in this application of [*here state number of employees*] employees comprised in the (*description of bargaining unit*) [is attached] [has been obtained]

Date   *Signed*

Form 18 Rule 5

National Industrial Relations Court

NOTICE OF APPLICATION UNDER SECTION 112 FOR DECLARATION WITH RESPECT TO QUESTION RELATING TO COLLECTIVE AGREEMENT

1. This application is made by (*applicant(s) name(s) and address(es)*)

2. Any communication for the applicant(s) relating to this application may be sent to (*applicant(s) address(es) for service, including telephone number(s), if any*)

3. The applicant(s) [desires] [desire] the court to make a declaration with respect to the following question(s):

   [*here give particulars of collective agreement*].

4. The applicant(s) [desires] [desire] the court to make a declaration with respect to the following question(s):

   [*here set out each question in respect of which a declaration is sought and the provisions of the collective agreement to which the question relates*]

5. [A statement of the facts by reason of which the question(s) set out above [arises] [arise] is attached to this notice]

OR

   [The facts by reason of which the question(s) set out above [arises] [arise] are:

   [*here set out the facts by reason of which it is claimed that each question set out in paragraph 4 arises*]

6. The applicant(s) [desires] [desire] the court to make a declaration to the following effect:

   [*here set out the applicant(s) contentions as to the proper answer to each question to which the application refers*]

Date   *Signed*

bar to an organization which has not been an agent or part of a joint agent that has been rejected from immediately applying, on its own account, for either a voluntary agreement, or from following the statutory process towards a court order. The NIRC has, however, a discretion to reject any application through the statutory process if it is made within two years of a previous application, whether rejected or not. This discretionary rejection could therefore be applied to:

(a) an application to split up a newly created sole bargaining unit;
(b) an application following upon a previously unsuccessful application;
(c) an application following a revoked order, provided that the revocation and fresh application occurred within two years of the previous application.

CONTRACTUAL EFFECT OF COLLECTIVE AGREEMENTS

It is again unnecessary to point out to any trade union official that collective agreements come in all shapes and sizes; from the formal national (or large company) written agreement to the oral understanding between shop steward and foreman or line manager. In this country even the major agreements are characterized by loose expression laced with expressions of intent and, generally, bearing little similarity to a commercial contract. Occasionally, this characteristic pattern is not adhered to, usually in the case of national procedure agreements which may, though rarely, bear signs of an intention to produce a legal document. Academic arguments may be advanced to show that, logically, the courts ought to say that if two parties enter into an agreement in which each agrees to do something for the other (as lawyers would say 'supported by consideration'), it should be presumed that they intend that agreement to be open to legal enforcement by one party against the other. This would always be subject to a contrary indication in the agreement. Alternatively, the mere fact that it is a domestic agreement between husband and wife contradicts an assumption of legal enforceability.

Perhaps for no better reason than that it has always been so, it is better sense to say that collective agreements are, like domestic arrangements, in a class of their own where a presumption of non-contractual intention should apply. The fact is, as was pointed out in the only decision directly on the point, that trade unionists generally insist that they have no intention to make a legally binding agreement, most employers would entertain grave doubts (to put it no higher) whether a court would enforce such an agreement, and most legal writers admit that, whatever the logic of the argument, courts would generally act as if the agreement was not enforceable. If, therefore, everyone involved assumes there will be no enforcement, no one can have intended the agreement to be enforceable.

This was the common law position before 1971. It was alleged that this fact contributed to the informal nature of much of the language used and to the fact that agreements tended not to be expressed to be for a definite period of time. If the agreement was, in any event, unenforceable, why should a party, bound only in honour, declare that he was bound for a specific period? The Royal Commission concluded that there was little evidence to suggest that the unions which made major procedure agreements broke them. But, it agreed that individuals frequently departed from agreements to which, as individuals, they were not party, but which their unions had entered into intending that they should observe them. The Commission concluded, therefore, that as contractual enforceability would, in practice, only affect organizations which habitually observed unenforceable agreements, it would serve no purpose. This was thought to leave out of account the suggestion that a substantive agreement was renegotiated so frequently just because it was unenforceable. If it was enforceable, it was said, it would normally be made enforceable for two or three years (since that would be considered the maximum reasonable life of a substantive agreement) and, during that time, the parties would know their obligations, prices could be fixed with reasonable certainty and demands, backed by industrial action, for renegotiation would less frequently be made. It was also suggested that the very fact of contractual enforceability would induce the parties to be more careful in the formulation of the language of both substantive and procedural agreements, so that interpretation disputes would have a clearer answer.

In accordance, no doubt, with this reasoning the Industrial Relations Act 1971 introduced a presumption of contractual enforceability for all written collective agreements. A collective agreement, for this purpose, is defined as any agreement or arrangement for the time being in force, made in any form, by or on behalf of one or more organizations of workers and one or more employers or organizations of employers, or a combination of employers and their organizations, which either prescribes terms and conditions of employment, or is a procedure agreement, or is a combination of the two.

A procedure agreement is defined to include any of the following matters:

(a) machinery for consultation with regard to, or for the settlement by negotiation or arbitration of, terms and conditions of employment; or of any other questions arising between an employer or group of employers and one or more workers or organizations of workers;
(b) negotiating rights;
(c) facilities for officials (including shop stewards) of organizations of workers;
(d) procedures relating to dismissal;
(e) procedures relating to matters of discipline other than dismissal;
(f) procedures relating to grievances of individual workers.

Decisions reached by joint negotiating bodies on such matters are also to be considered as collective agreements.

The Act states that any collective agreement made in writing and not containing a statement that it, or part of it, is not intended to be legally enforceable shall be conclusively presumed by the parties to it, or the non-excluded part of it, to be a legally enforceable contract. The same presumption is applied to any 'decision' (including any award or resolution) recorded in writing by or on behalf of any joint body consisting of representatives of one or more organizations of workers and one or more employers, or organizations of employers, established by or under a collective agreement for any of the purposes which can be covered by the definition of a collective agreement. In this latter case it is not possible to dispose of the presumption of enforceability by a general statement that the body has no authority to enter into a binding settlement, because the Act states that such authority is conclusively presumed. It follows that an exclusion clause must be contained in each agreement and each record of proceedings if contractual enforceability is to be avoided. Any record from which the exclusion clause is omitted is bound to be presumed to carry the intention of contractual enforceability. Nevertheless, it should be noted that the presumption is only that the parties intend such enforceability, not that such enforceability exists. No court is able to enforce an agreement the meaning of which cannot be ascertained. Common law courts have consistently held uncertain provisions of a contract to be void for that reason. So the NIRC, to which is exclusively entrusted the interpretation and enforcement of collective agreements, is bound to say, in the event of such uncertainty, that however conclusively the intent of the parties is presumed, that intention fails for uncertainty. It so happens that much of the present wording of collective agreements, if continued in the same form in new agreements made after the coming into force of these provisions in 1971, would produce this effect.

Secondly, it must be borne in mind that minutes or notices on company notice-boards are sufficient to constitute the written record which, without express exclusion, will produce contractual effect for the agreements they record. Such minutes or notices to have that effect, however, must be written on behalf of the body, and not merely of one side. So, if management posted a notice without an exclusion clause, the notice would not produce a presumption of contractual intention unless the workers' side of the body had expressly or tacitly approved it. Presumably once a primary record of the decision is made which contains the exclusion clause, further written records will not be required also to contain an exclusion clause. Reference to the existence of a 'body' suggests some formal structure, so that it is suggested that an agreement between line manager and shop steward, within the terms of a collective agreement providing that as the first stage of a disputes negotiating procedure, written down on the back of a cigarette packet, would not have contractual effect.

Breach by the parties of a contractually enforceable collective agreement is an unfair industrial practice. The parties to a collective agreement are those employers, employers' organizations and organizations of workers on whose behalf it is made. All the language of the Act on this point, including the definition section, suggests that though the parties may include individual employers, they should not include the individual workers who negotiated the agreement but only the organization of workers on whose behalf the agreement was made. This may produce a procedural difficulty. A registered trade union is a legal person capable of being a party to an agreement. An unregistered organization of workers, though capable to being sued in its own name (judgment being enforceable against its property), is not, strictly speaking, a legal person and so ought to be incapable of being party to a contract. If this were held to be so, it would seem inescapably to follow that the parties to the agreement are the workers on whose behalf it is made or their representatives who made it. In practice it is likely that the court's would hold that any industrial organization within the two statutory definitions was sufficiently an entity to contract. A shop steward's committee, or some similar organization, would not be so considered.

In the case of breach of a contractually enforceable agreement, the parties bear not only the ordinary liability for themselves. It is also an unfair industrial practice for them to fail to take all reasonably practical steps in order to prevent any person acting or purporting to act on behalf of such a party, or, where the party is an organization, to prevent any member of the organization from breaking any undertaking in the agreement or the part of it which is enforceable, or from continuing or repeating actions in breach of the agreement. This is the same type of obligation as exists under the emergency procedures and is much wider than that under an order in respect of an unfair industrial practice. In this way the parties to an agreement are penalized if they do not reasonably police the activities of their employees, agents or members. Management, which permits a foreman to act in breach of agreement, will, no doubt, avoid liability on the first occasion by saying that as it could not have foreseen the breach no steps were then reasonably practicable. Thereafter it will be expected to do something. It will be no answer to say that the foreman had no authority, since he will have been *purporting* to act on behalf of his employer. What constitutes reasonably practicable steps is a question which can only be decided in each separate situation. There are no direct guide-lines as yet. But, by analogy with liability for other unfair practices, positive disciplinary action would seem to be necessary. An organization of workers faced with unconstitutional action by its local officials would probably be expected to discipline them even if it had no real hope that they would call off the activity. The suggestion that such organizations should appoint a 'reasonably practical steps' officer, who would visit the offending officials or members, has proved to be wishful thinking, since even in the case of the lesser obligation under an unfair industrial practice, the NIRC has required substantial steps to ensure compliance. Given this obligation, the reluctance of either side of industry, but particularly of trade unions, to enter into contractually enforceable agreements could be understood, even without any feelings of reaction to what is regarded as undesirable legal intervention.

The contractual enforceability of collective agreements has a further aspect in that provisions of a collective agreement may, perhaps normally will, be incorporated into the individual contract of employment so as to become binding between the individual worker and his employer. It is not at all clear what line the NIRC will eventually take on this; partly because it is by no means clear what conclusions the common law courts had reached previously. It has been suggested in some cases that the union or the bargaining representative could be considered as the agent of those on whose behalf it bargained. If this was accepted, the agreement reached by the agent would immediately bind its principals (the individual workers). Such a view would, however, raise difficult problems of the apparent and actual authority of the agent. If, for instance, an employer knew from the national press that the agent had clear instructions to bargain for a 10 per cent wage rise, could he reliably agree with it an 8 per cent rise, and if so would the workers be taken to have been committed to it or could they reject it?

Alternatively, of course, the collective agreement can be incorporated by express reference in the individual contract. Quite commonly the evidence for such incorporation would appear from the written statement which the Contracts of Employment Act 1963 requires to be given to every employee within thirteen weeks of the commencement of employment. This may state, for example: 'The terms and conditions of your employment are contained in the relevant national and local collective agreements, copies of which may be inspected in the .... office.' The 1963 Act makes it clear that this notice is not the contract itself, but is only evidence of it. Theoretically, therefore, such a statement as that above should pose, rather than solve, the question. In fact, however, failure to raise an objection upon the receipt of such a statement probably would be construed as acquiescence. A worker who accepted a rate of pay in a particular collective agreement could hardly be heard to say that he did not accept the burdensome elements of the agreement.

This consideration runs into the parallel consideration of implied incorporation of terms, which is the best known of the common law approaches. Under this doctrine, the terms of a collective agreement are considered to be incorporated into individual contracts of employment when (but only when) they can be said to have been accepted by both sides. An employer, therefore, will be bound to pay a newly negotiated rate once he indicates his acceptance of it by beginning to pay it. When, it may be asked, does an employee indicate that he has accepted a restriction on his freedom to strike? Certainly not by striking. Does one, therefore, have to wait for an occasion when the employees carefully exhaust procedure before striking? Probably the answer would lie again in the idea that acceptance of benefits, such as higher rates of pay, implied acceptance of the burdens that went with them. The answer is a vital one because, as we saw in Chapter 6, section 147 of the 1971 Act provides that a strike shall be considered in breach of the contract of employment of the individual striker, even if it is preceded by proper notice, if it is conducted contrary to a restriction on his freedom to strike incorporated either expressly or by implication into his contract. It may be assumed that most such restrictions derive originally from collective agreements, so that the matter of deciding their incorporation is likely to be an important one.

It should be observed that there are undoubtedly some terms of a collective agreement which are not proper to be implied into individual contracts. Presumably an individual employee, to whom a specially permitted closed shop agreement applied, could not sue his employer for breach of the individual contract of employment if the employer engaged another worker in breach of that agreement. These terms must be said to be intended solely to operate between the parties to the collective agreement.

It need hardly be added that this is a very simple picture of the problems raised by incorporation of collective agreements into individual contracts. In view of the growing importance of local collective bargaining, by which national or local agreements may give way to successive local agreements often confined to small points of detail, it may be difficult to arrive at any commonly accepted ground. Employers may allege adherence to local agreements, whilst workers assert the overriding effect of national agreements. It is not necessarily true that one can seek assistance from a previous pattern, revealing, for instance, regular adherence to successive local agreements, since court decisions differ as to the extent to which one should be said to have accepted a new agreement just because one has done so in the past. It is likely that, in sorting out these and many other problems, the courts will provide ample reason to support the complaint that too much time is being wasted on legal niceties and too little on the human relations that are the essence of industrial relations.

REMEDIAL PROCEDURE

The Donovan Commission had pointed to the well-known fact that many negotiating procedures, particularly at national level, were at best out of date and no longer in accordance with the requirements of the industry. It drew the obvious conclusion that there would be less action in breach of procedure agreements if they were modernized, quickened and made more efficient. If parties to a dispute were frustrated by previous experience, or hearsay information, of the fact that the procedure would not produce a suitable answer, or any answer at all, or an answer in time to be of any value, they were hardly likely to hesitate to achieve their purpose more effectively by industrial action. There is no doubt a great deal of truth in this and the legislature, in sections 37 to 43 of the Industrial Relations Act 1971, attempted to provide a method of improvement of procedure agreements, backed by compulsion if in the last resort the parties failed to reach a satisfactory agreement. Following the trend of thought favouring abandonment of national in favour of local bargaining, however, these provisions are confined to local procedures and cannot be utilized to improve national or industry-wide bargaining processes.

Either the Secretary of State, the employer, or any registered trade union recognized as having negotiating rights in relation to the unit concerned, or which is a party to an existing procedure agreement applicable to that unit, may apply to the NIRC alleging that a particular unit of employment suffers from an absence or unsuitability of procedure agreements for the prompt and fair settlement of disputes or grievances, and/or suffers from recourse to industrial action contrary to the terms or intentions of an existing procedure agreement. The 'unit' is defined as meaning an 'undertaking' or 'part of an undertaking'. It is not clear whether, and, if so, how far, this will differ from the unit consisting of 'descriptions of workers' for the purpose of agency shop and bargaining agency application. So far as the applicant is concerned, however, he will obviously select an existing unit rather than the broad general classification required by the Court in the other two situations. Before the Secretary of State makes such an application he must consult those appearing to him to be the parties just mentioned. Before the parties make such an application they must notify the Secretary of State, who must offer advice and assistance to all parties appearing to be directly concerned with a view to promoting agreement. He himself may refer any matter to the CIR for this purpose, but, during this procedure, the application may be pursued.

The task of the NIRC is merely to satisfy itself that it appears that the alleged disputes exist, and, by reason thereof, that the development or maintenance of orderly industrial relations in that unit has been seriously impeded, or there has been substantial and repeated losses of working time in the unit. The applicant has at this stage to make out, as it were, a prima facie case. The question whether the unit actually does suffer from one of the defects mentioned, and if so what remedy is appropriate, is then referred to the CIR.

As a first stage the CIR may consider whether, if the remedy would be to introduce new, or revise existing, procedure agreements, these alterations should apply to a wider unit of employment than that defined in the application. If so, and after consultation with those concerned, it may formulate such proposals, transmit them to the NIRC and give appropriate notice of them to persons affected. The extension may not go beyond units of employment of *associated* employers (section 43 (2) (c)).

If there is no objection to the extension within two weeks of the date of the notification of the proposal, the NIRC automatically confirms it. Otherwise it may either confirm or reject, but not vary, the proposal. It is by this means that organizations of workers (unregistered) may be introduced into the procedure. They may not apply or be considered parties to the initial application. But if (and only if) they are parties to an existing procedure agreement applicable to the original or larger unit, the CIR may add them if it considers it appropriate to do so. It may also add employers, employers' associations or registered trade unions as parties (whether or not they are already parties to an existing procedure agreement). It must be conceded that this is a clumsy way of bringing in unregistered organizations. If no procedure agreement previously existed they cannot be made parties at all, even though no procedure can possibly work without them. One is still tempted to think that the draftsman had become so used to conferring rights only on registered trade unions that he overlooked the fact that this procedure is more of an obligation than a right. In many cases it cannot be effective without the participation of all involved organizations of workers whether registered or not and whether or not they were already party to a procedure agreement. In other words, insertion of the distinction based on registration is totally irrelevant here on any view.

Having finally determined the unit and the appropriate parties, the CIR must then promote and assist discussions between them with a view to obtaining their agreement on revised provisions. This then is supposed to be primarily negotiation rather than an arbitration procedure. If satisfactory agreement is reached, the CIR may report the fact to the NIRC which, on the application of any of the parties, may then withdraw the reference. If the reference is not so withdrawn, the CIR must make a report on the new or revised procedure, incorporating any satisfactory agreements between the parties, but also containing any recommendations from the Commission itself. The most important requirement of this procedure, however, which also applied to a procedure agreement arrived at by negotiation at an earlier stage, is that it must be 'capable of having effect as a legally enforceable contract'. This will, in fact, make agreement on the part of the unions very difficult to obtain. One thing they will not accept is contractual enforceability. The odds are that the CIR will, therefore, have to try to impose 'agreement'. The subsequent order of the NIRC, which must be made unless the NIRC feels that an order is not necessary to secure acceptance and observance of the provisions, has effect as a legally enforceable contract. The order, however, will only be made following an application from one of the parties. That is to say that though the Secretary of State can initiate the procedure, he cannot take the final steps for ultimate implementation of the recommendations. It remains very difficult to see how, to the extent that the parties will not voluntarily accept the changes, 'agreement' can be imposed against the will of one of them.

Unless the NIRC is satisfied that there are special reasons, no further application under these provisions relating to the same or substantially the same unit may be entertained for two years following the date of transmission of the CIR report to the NIRC, whether or not an order is made as a result of that report. Once made, a procedure order will remain in force until revoked. It must be so revoked or varied if at any time all the parties to it make a joint application so to do. It must also be revoked on the application of one or more of the parties, but in this case only if the Court is satisfied that the order is no longer necessary to secure observance of the procedure it lays down. Thus the actual procedure must continue to be observed either compulsorily or voluntarily unless all the parties jointly decide otherwise.

It is reasonably plain that the entire remedial procedure is again designed to encourage, by the direct warning of ultimate compulsion, voluntary improvement. Like the emergency procedures considered in the last chapter there seems to be a danger of it being considered an inflammatory step leading, at least initially, to a greater degree of intransigence. Obviously, therefore, it will best be used during a peaceful period when no substantive issues exacerbate the procedural difficulties. Even then, as has been pointed out, it may be asked to what extent such procedure is necessary where the parties agree, and to what extent it will be effective when they do not agree.

INFORMATION

The efficiency of bargaining obviously depends upon the amount of information available to the parties, particularly to the workers. In the United States trade unions have built up far more efficient information services, both in collection and distribution, than exist in this country. In this country the Industrial Relations Act 1971 intervened for the first time to try to ensure the supply of vital information to workers' representatives, but it has proved more difficult to work out any meaningful details and the Code of Practice remained uncompleted on this aspect. The main effect of the provisions we are now to examine is likely to be simply the creation of acceptance of the need to supply information for the purpose of maintenance of good relations and the production of acceptable agreement.

It is provided that it is the duty of the employer to disclose to representatives of registered unions, that is to say, to officials of, or persons authorized by, the union with whom the bargaining is carried on, all such information relating to his undertaking as is in his possession or the possession of an associated employer. It must be shown that it is information without which those representatives would be to a material extent impeded in carrying on collective bargaining with the employer and is also information which it would be in accordance with good industrial relations practice that the employer should disclose for the purposes of collective bargaining. Such information must be supplied in writing if the trade union representatives so request. Failure to disclose such information may result in a complaint to the NIRC upon which the Court can make an order determining the rights of the trade union and of the employer and directing the employer to take such action as it would be within the power of the employer to take and which, in the circumstances, he ought to be required to take. Alternatively the Court can make an order authorizing presentation of a claim to the Industrial Arbitration Board.

At this point it might be thought that the employer could hardly refuse to disclose any information. He is, however, exempt from the duty in a great number of cases:

(a) he does not have to disclose information *about* associated companies when the negotiations are with him and not the associated company;

(b) it seems unlikely that associated companies only registered abroad can be required to furnish information to organizations in this country;

(c) he is expressly excused from producing, or allowing inspection of, or permitting copying any document or extract unless it is a document actually designed to convey or confirm required information;

(d) he need not undertake an amount of work or expense out of reasonable proportion to the value of the information for the purpose of collective bargaining.

(e) he cannot be required to disclose any information,

    (i) the disclosure of which would be against the interests of national security, or

    (ii) which he could not disclose without contravening a statutory prohibition, or

    (iii) which has been communicated to him in confidence or which he has obtained in consequence of confidence reposed in him, or

    (iv) relating specifically to an individual who has not consented to its disclosure, or

    (v) the disclosure of which would be seriously prejudicial to the interests of his undertaking for reasons other than its effect on collective bargaining, or

    (vi) was obtained by the employer for the purpose of bringing, prosecuting or defending any legal proceedings.

No information given by any person in evidence before the NIRC or an industrial tribunal in a private hearing may be disclosed without the consent of the person giving the information.

As they stand, these provisions are unlikely to produce an effective supply of information unless they produce the essential voluntary acceptance of the unions' right to receive it. Note that none of the statutory rights extends to representatives of unregistered trade unions.

Chapter 10

Official Instruments of Collective Bargaining

Even during the long period of voluntaryism which characterized British collective bargaining before 1971 there existed various official organs and devices, the ultimate aim of which was to foster and encourage the development of voluntary procedures. Some of them possessed aspects of compulsion, but compulsion was in all cases seen as an expendable means towards the more desirable end. This is the primary element of difference between the old and the new procedure. The new procedure accepts that a voluntary system is likely to be more effective, all other things being equal, but allows compulsion to take over, *not* because voluntaryism cannot operate but because one of the parties desires compulsion. We have already referred to much of the new machinery, but rarely to the old. Some of the old machinery still exists and has been absorbed, perhaps somewhat uncomfortably, into the new atmosphere. This we will deal with first.

THE WAGES COUNCIL

Wages councils, first set up as 'trade boards' under the Trade Boards Act 1919, were originally thought of as a substitute for voluntary collective bargaining in areas of industry where unions had found it difficult to attain any appreciable level of organization and where collective bargaining therefore did not operate and wages and conditions were accordingly bad. They were visualized as a temporary expedient to break down the obstacles to trade union growth and to provide bargaining experience to enable the development of an effective collective process. Not all subsequently created councils have fitted into this concept. There was, for instance, 60 per cent trade union organization in waterproof garment manufacture when the wages council for that industry was established. It is also true that the effect of the wages council system has not been that which was initially conceived. Trade unions were initially pleased with the recognition it provided, but have come to regard it as a discouragement to growth in membership. Workers, it is suggested, assume that it will achieve effective bargaining without any effort on their part. Wages governed by wages councils actually remain generally appreciably lower than those governed by other forms of collective bargaining, either in the private or the public sector. As a matter of fact the median weekly wage thus fixed is below that for those with no national agreement. This latter fact gives a clue to the nature of the criticism, in that it is not that wages councils are actually retrograde. They operate usually in difficult areas where, no doubt, wages would be lower without them. On the other hand they are not nearly as effective as voluntary systems of collective bargaining and may actually inhibit the development of a badly organized area into a well organized area. Consequently, at the present time, there is no pressure to establish new councils, but considerable pressure to facilitate the machinery for their considered abolition. We shall, therefore, mention only the functioning of and machinery for abolition of wages councils.

The Royal Commission pointed out the similarity between wages council bargaining and voluntary national bargaining. In either case, wherever local bargaining also exists, the national standard has been treated as a floor from which to work upwards. A raising of the floor will, in both cases, normally mean an automatic raising of actual rates, even if already higher than the new floor. As with national agreements, so local bargaining in a wages council area will become the effective instrument wherever conditions make this possible. In the case of wages councils this tendency is considerably enhanced by the fact that the functions of the council are limited to wage rates, holidays and holiday rates. Wage fixing can be conducted for sections of those covered by a council but is usually done across the board and is for this reason even more likely to give place to local distinctions.

The structure of a wages council provides a misleading impression of its function. It is tripartite (including a small group of 'independent' members) and, theoretically, reaches decisions by means of a vote of each of those elements. In practice it would be unrealistic for employers and independents to impose unacceptable terms on employees. Normally, therefore, the major effort of the independents will be to secure agreement between the two sides so as to avoid a vote.

Before the passing of the Industrial Relations Act a joint application for abolition of a wages council was the normal method for winding one up. Immediately before that Act the then Secretary of State for Employment was, apparently, prepared to assist a union desiring abolition to secure the support of the employers to that end. The Act permits any organization of workers which represents a substantial proportion of the workers covered by the Council to apply on its own initiative on the ground that the existence of the Council is no longer necessary for the purpose of maintaining a reasonable standard of remuneration for the workers with respect to whom the Council operates. The question of abolition is now referred to the CIR which has already recommended the abolition of one council.

THE INDUSTRIAL ARBITRATION BOARD

This body, which was never a court in any accepted sense, was originally called the Industrial Court. It was established in 1919 at the time of the first great attempt to assist voluntary collective bargaining in this country. It was intended to act as an independent tribunal for industrial arbitration at the request of both parties to a dispute. In practice it is composed, on each occasion on which it sits, of one member from each of three panels, the President, who is a lawyer, normally sitting as the independent member. When a dispute concerning women is being considered, a woman must sit. At the present time the employees' representative is normally the only full-time salaried member of that panel, who is also a woman. When only women are concerned, the sole women's representative on the independent panel also sits as an additional member. The President may vary this arrangement but normally does not do so. It is possible, however, for a reference to be decided by a single person. Assessors may be appointed to assist the board, and representation by solicitors or barristers may be permitted. Neither of these powers is commonly exercised. The chairman exercises a casting vote if the board is not unanimous. The parties bear their own costs, but the cost of running the board is borne by the Exchequer.

The award is usually announced on the same day as the hearing. This is possible largely because, though the decision sets out the arguments which have been put to the board, it does not express any view as to their relative merits (save that implicit in the decision), nor, normally, does it give reasons for the decision. This practice of not giving reasons has become standard in British industrial relations arbitration. It may be that in future, when dealing with matters referred to it by the NIRC under the terms of the Industrial Relations Act, the board will find it necessary at least to summarize its reasoning.

The jurisdiction of the board stems from a number of diverse sources:

1. *From 'trade disputes'*
Under its original jurisdiction the board may deal with matters arising out of a 'trade dispute', as defined in the Trade Disputes Act 1906. The definition, which presumably survives for this purpose despite the anomalous areas where it is not coincidental with the new definition of 'industrial dispute', is:

' "trade dispute" means any dispute between employers and workmen, or between workmen and workmen which is connected with the employment or non-employment, or the terms of the employment, or with the conditions of labour, of any person. The expression "workman" means all persons employed in trade or industry, whether or not in the employment of the employer with whom a trade dispute arises.'

Once the Secretary of State has consented to the reference the parties must attempt to draw up agreed terms of reference. The board will decide the terms from the two separate statements if no agreement can be reached. It is obvious that parties who have, as is necessary, agreed to refer the matter in the first place will tend to accept the award. If they do not there is no machinery for compelling acceptance. There is, on this issue and in those circumstances, no implication of the terms of the award into the individual contracts of employment of those affected.

Anyone can be a party to a reference under this provision, but in 449 cases between 1958 and 1966 analysed by Wedderburn and Davies in their excellent work on the old system of collective bargaining in this country (*Employment Grievances and Disputes*

Procedures in Britain, California U.P. 1969), none came from an application by a single employee or an unorganized group of employees.

2. *Allegation of disregard of the Fair Wages Resolution*

The Fair Wages Resolution represents a method of writing into all government contracts basic standards of union recognition and the observance of standards and conditions of work. In practice many local authorities include the terms of the resolution in their contracts. It has no force of its own because it is a resolution of only one House of Parliament. So the sanction for non-observance can only be, in the last resort, withdrawal of the contract or refusal to enter into other contracts. The sanction is not, therefore, very effective since in many cases the employer concerned is the only company with which the government can feasibly make such a contract. The most significant provisions of the resolution are:

'1. (*a*) The contractor shall pay rates of wages and observe hours and conditions of labour not less favourable than those established for the trade or industry in the district where the work is carried out by machinery of negotiation or arbitration to which the parties are organizations of employers and trade unions [i.e. organizations of workers] representative respectively of substantial proportions of the employers and workers engaged in the trade or industry in the district.

(*b*) In the absence of any rates of wages, hours or conditions of labour so established the contractor shall pay rates of wages and observe hours and conditions of labour which are not less favourable than the general level of wages, hours and conditions observed by other employers whose general circumstances in the trade or industry in which the contractor is engaged are similar.

4. The contractor shall recognise the freedom of his work-people to be members of trade unions.

6. The contractor shall be responsible for the observance of this Resolution by sub-contractors employed in the execution of this contract.'

The resolution is becoming less significant as its basic elements are increasingly accepted by employers. No doubt it will eventually be almost obsolete, but there is at present, and will continue to be for some years, a trickle of applications under it. It may be observed, for instance, in support of the argument for its continued validity, that paragraph four, using the general definition of 'trade union' rather than that in the 1971 Act, extends freedom of membership beyond the registered organizations to which it applies by statute. Moreover, the contractor must furnish an assurance that he has for the previous three months complied with the resolution before he is permitted to tender.

The resolution requires a question of non-observance to be put to the Department of Employment and to be referred by it to an independent tribunal. In practice this tribunal is always the Industrial Arbitration Board. It does not matter who brings the question to the attention of the Department. Sometimes this is done by individual workers.

As has been said, the finding of the board would only indicate whether or not there had been a breach of contract between the contractor and the government. The employee concerned acquires no rights by implication into his contract, either from the existence of the resolution or the finding of the board. The board is apt to construe the requirements strictly. It has been held, for instance, that recognition of the freedom to join a trade union need only extend to those unions normally recognized in the industry or area and not to all unions.

3. *Statutory requirements of fair terms*
In the case of a number of industries, requirements as to the observance of fair terms and conditions have been imposed in return for monopoly concession or as part of a qualification for the grant of a licence to operate. In these cases the right to complain of non-observance is usually reserved to representative organizations within the industry. The sanction, if it were only withdrawal of the licence or concession, would be rather unreal. In some cases, therefore, the method adopted is that of the implication of an individual contractual right.

In private road haulage, complaint against applicants for, or holders of, licences is, exceptionally, permissible from individuals. The merits are assessed by broadly defined standards of fairness, and the board, in relevant cases, has power upon such a complaint to fix a proper wage. The award of the board becomes an implied term in the contract of employment and, subject to variation by the board, its observance is compulsory for three years. In three other cases – civil aviation, the film industry and the British Sugar Corporation – the implied term method is applied. In civil aviation the standard of terms is set by a requirement of comparison with those in the nationalized airlines.

4. *Claims to extend observance of collective agreements*
In many other industrial countries provision exists for the compulsory extension of collectively agreed terms and conditions to minority employers or work groups which do not voluntarily adhere to them. In this country there is only a very rudimentary system of doing this contained in section 8 of the Terms and Conditions of Employment Act 1959 (the only section of that Act still in force and now considerably amended by the 1971 Act). The final version is contained in Schedule 7 of the 1971 Act as follows:

'Where a claim is duly reported to the Secretary of State under this section:

(*a*) that terms or conditions of employment are established in any trade or industry, or section of a trade or industry, either generally or in any district, which have been settled by an agreement or award, and

(*b*) that the parties to the agreement or to the proceedings in which the award was made, are or represent, organizations of employers and organizations of workers, or associations of such organizations, and represent (generally or in the district in question, as the case may be) a substantial proportion of the employers and of the workers in the trade, industry or section, being workers of the description (hereinafter referred to as "the relevant description") to which the agreement or award relates, and

(*c*) that as respects any worker of the relevant description an employer engaged in the trade, industry or section (or, where the operation of the agreement or award is limited to a district, an employer so engaged in that district), whether represented as aforesaid or not, is not observing the terms or conditions. . . .'

the Secretary of State may take any steps which seem to him expedient to settle, or to secure the use of appropriate machinery to settle, the claim and shall, if the claim is not otherwise settled, refer it to the Industrial Arbitration Board.'

Claims may now be made in respect of workers governed by a wages council, but not as regards wages or terms and conditions fixed in pursuance of any other enactment. The report to the Secretary of State must be in writing and can only be made by a registered trade union or a registered employers' association which is, or is represented by, one of the parties to the relevant agreement. The report is not 'duly' made until the Secretary of State is satisfied that it contains sufficient particulars.

On a reference of this type, if the board is satisfied that the claim is well founded it must make an award requiring the employer to observe the recognized terms and conditions as respects all workers of the relevant description, unless it can be shown that the employer is observing terms and conditions not less favourable. The award of the board takes effect as an implied term in each contract of employment from a date fixed by the board not earlier than the date on which, in the opinion of the board, the employer was first informed of the claim. The term is, however, abrogated by the coming into operation of an agreement varying, or abrogating, the recognized terms and conditions. It must be remembered that this last provision does not mean that the employer concerned can contract out of the award. This matter is still in doubt. All it does certainly mean is that the award ceases to have effect along with the standard forming agreement on which it was based.

'Section of trade or industry', as in the Industrial Relations Act, refers to function rather than geographical location. So, although 50 has been held to be a substantial proportion of 350 workers, a representation in that proportion at a single plant would not be representative of a substantial proportion of the section as a whole.

5. *Failure to bargain with a sole agent*
One of the two new matters added by the Industrial Relations Act to the jurisdiction of the board is a claim by a registered trade union, made initially to the NIRC, that an employer subject

to a sole bargaining agency order of the court (not a voluntary sole bargaining agreement) is failing to take a step which might reasonably be expected of an employer ready and willing to bargain with the agent. When such a complaint is made to the NIRC this is the only course, apart from dismissing the complaint, which is available; that is to say, the normal remedies of declaration, order, or compensation are not available. The award of the board becomes an implied term in the contract of employment of each employee in the bargaining unit.

6. *Disclosure of information*
The same effect follows an order made under the other aspect of jurisdiction conferred on the board by the Industrial Relations Act. Complaint can be made to the NIRC of a failure to disclose to officials or representatives of a registered trade union information relevant to collective bargaining, or information which it would be in accordance with good industrial relations practice to disclose to them. This duty was considered in the previous chapter.

THE COMMISSION ON INDUSTRIAL RELATIONS

The most important body, from the point of view of the development of industrial relations, is not the NIRC but the Commission on Industrial Relations. The CIR was originally established as a Royal Commission following the Donovan Report, with the object of examining individual bargaining arrangements and recommending improvement of them. Before the alteration of its powers in the Industrial Relations Act it was anxious to avoid any suggestion that it was more than an advisory body. Despite a very slow start it achieved a number of notable successes, even persuading employers who had not previously recognized trade unions to enter into bargaining procedure agreements.

It consists of between six and fifteen members, most of whom are part-time, and all of whom are appointed for five years at a time, subject to resignation. A large secretariat is primarily concerned in the process of ascertainment of facts and the discussion of alternatives. The commission's practice has been, in the past, to place each reference in the hands of a particular member assisted by a defined section of the secretariat. Discussion with the other members will take place from time to time and, of course, before formulation of the final proposals.

The commission has a long list of functions, most of them concerned with determination of the key issues in any collective bargaining question referred initially to the NIRC.

Firstly, however, it has an original power to consider and make recommendations upon any question relating to industrial relations, generally or in a particular industry, undertaking or part of an undertaking. In particular the following possible topics of reference are mentioned:

'(a) the manner in which employers or workers are, or ought to be organized for purposes of collective bargaining, including any question as to amalgamation of, or co-operation, or other relations between, the bodies in which employers or workers are organized for those purposes;

(b) procedure agreements, or the need for procedure agreements where they do not exist;

(c) any matter for which a procedure agreement can provide; [i.e. consultation machinery, negotiating rights, facilities for officials of organizations of workers, dismissal and disciplinary procedures, and grievance procedures]

(d) recognition and negotiating rights;

(e) disclosure of information to employees or officials of organizations of workers having negotiating rights;

(f) facilities for training in industrial relations and collective bargaining.'

It must be explained that the commission can only make recommendations through the Secretary of State on these matters.

In addition, however, the Commission has the following powers:

(a) Agency shop applications:

(i) consideration of postponement of the application pending settlement of a bargaining dispute;

(ii) scope of the ballot (i.e. the size and nature of the unit of employment to be covered);

(iii) arrangements for ballot (similar power in ballots for revocation);

(iv) report to NIRC on result of ballot (similarly for revocation ballot). Similar powers exist in respect of permitted closed shop agreements.

NB. Upon a favourable report an obligation to enter into an agreement arises immediately without the need for further action by the NIRC.

(b) Remedial powers in respect of procedure agreements:
    (i) consideration of whether the unit concerned suffers from one of the specified defects;
    (ii) consideration of whether the unit should be revised and the formulation of proposals;
    (iii) promotion and assistance of discussions between the parties to secure agreement on new or revised provisions;
    (iv) failing, or additionally, to such agreed changes, consideration of, and report upon, own proposals.

(c) Recognition of sole bargaining agency:
    (i) application for withdrawal of the reference on the ground that a satisfactory and lasting settlement has been reached;
    (ii) consideration of extension of the scope of the unit;
    (iii) consideration of the appropriateness of the unit;
    (iv) consideration of the necessary qualifications of the proposed agent;
    (v) arrangements for, conduct of, and report upon, ballot;
    (vi) promotion and assistance at discussions to settle dispute over revocation of the order;
    (vii) consideration of appropriate unit for revocation ballot;
    (viii) arrangements for, conduct of, and report upon, revocation ballot.

(d) Emergency procedures:
    (i) assistance, at the request of the NIRC, in formulating an order for a ballot;
    (ii) conduct, or supervision, of a strike ballot.

(e) Wages councils:
All the functions of a commission of inquiry in respect of wages councils. At the moment this will largely involve consideration of applications for the abolition of wages councils.

The commission has power, for the purposes of any ballot, to serve a written notice on any employer requiring him to furnish the names and addresses of employees within the descriptions specified in the notice with specified particulars of the positions held by such employees.

The commission also has a general power to take such steps as it thinks fit for the purposes of securing the remedying of any defect which, in the opinion of the commission, exists in the arrangements out of which any question contained in the foregoing list arose.

THE NATIONAL INDUSTRIAL RELATIONS COURT

The composition of this court has been dealt with in Chapter 1. In so far as material exists on its method of operation this has been considered in Chapter 9. (See also: Rideout, *NIRC Practice and Procedure*, Sweet and Maxwell 1973.) Its industrial relations functions are numerous but largely concern the receipt of complaints and the making of orders following the report of the CIR on the vital issues. They can be set out as follows:

1. *Agency shop applications through statutory machinery*
(*a*) receipt of application from trade unions or employers;
(*b*) consideration of whether the application is barred because made within the prohibited period of two years after the matter was previously under consideration;
(*c*) consideration of whether the union, or unions, constituting the proposed agent has negotiating rights in respect of the descriptions of worker to whom the application applies;
(*d*) request to Commission on Industrial Relations to consider the application further;
(*e*) receipt of subsequent reports from CIR; but no further action required on them (section 11) if they are affirmative of the advisability of an agency agreement;
(*f*) consideration of any complaint that an employer has failed to enter into or carry out an agency shop agreement following a successful ballot and affirmative CIR report on the application. The court may make an order declaratory of the rights of the men and the employer and a further order requiring

the employer to take such action in compliance with the duty as it considers within his power and such as he ought to take (102);

(g) if the ballot does not produce the necessary majority, the making of an order that no agency shop agreement shall be made in respect of the applicant unions covering any of the workers covered in the unsuccessful application (13(3));

(h) receipt of application for revocation of an agency shop and ascertainment of whether it accords with statutory requirements;

(i) request to commission to hold a ballot for revocation if so satisfied;

(j) receipt of commission report and making of appropriate order.

2. *Approved closed shop agreements*
Similar powers as exist for agency shop agreements in respect of receipt of the application and consideration of satisfaction of statutory requirements; with the addition of:

(a) making of an order allowing between one and three months for request for a ballot upon the report of the CIR in favour of such an agreement. Receipt of such a request and ascertainment that it is made by one-fifth of the workers in the unit;

(b) making an order approving the draft proposals following a positive ballot.

3. *Exemption from statutory machinery on unfair dismissals*

(a) receipt of joint application for exemption and consideration of whether the conditions contained in section 31 of the Industrial Relations Act 1971 are satisfied;

(b) making an order designating the agreement as a substitute for the statutory procedure;

(c) receipt of joint application, or application by the Secretary of State, to make the substitution order. Making of revocation order if all parties desire revocation or if the conditions for its making are no longer satisfied. Transitional provisions may be contained in the order.

4. *Interpretation and enforcement of contractually enforceable collective agreements*
Sole right.

5. *Remedial action in respect of local procedure agreements*
(a) receipt of application by one of the parties or Secretary of State on ground of defective procedure agreement;
(b) where application is made by a party, ascertainment that notice of it has been given to Secretary of State;
(c) decision as to whether there are reasonable grounds for believing that the unit suffers from absence or unsuitability of a procedure agreement and from resort to unconstitutional strike action and that, by reason thereof, the development or maintenance of orderly industrial relations in that unit has been seriously impeded or there have been substantial and repeated losses of working time;
(d) reference to the CIR;
(e) receipt and confirmation (if no objections are received) of proposal as to the scope of the industrial unit to be considered;
(f) receipt of final report of CIR;
(g) upon an application within six months by one of the parties the making of an order specifying the unit and the parties and making the terms of the new procedures contractually enforceable, unless this order is considered unnecessary to secure observance;
(h) revocation of the agreement upon a joint application by both parties or by one party if the court is satisfied that the order is no longer necessary to secure compliance with its provisions.

6. *Sole bargaining agencies*
(a) receipt of application for establishment of agency;
(b) determination whether application has been made within a precluded period, whether the parties have made adequate attempts to settle the matter voluntarily and whether reference to the CIR is necessary with a view to promoting a satisfactory settlement;
(c) exercise of discretion not to refer matter to court wherever the application does not substantially differ from one under consideration within two years;
(d) receipt of report from CIR on extension of scope of the reference (i.e. widening of the unit) and extension if no objections received. Otherwise consideration of the degree if any to which extension should occur;

(e) receipt of report from the CIR as to recognition of the agent for the unit specified;

(f) receipt within six months of application to give effect to the report after a ballot, and determination whether any conditions imposed by the commission have been satisfied. Request to CIR to conduct ballot;

(g) if the ballot is successful, the making of an order specifying the unit and the agent and recquiring recognition of the agent;

(h) receipt of application for revocation of a sole agency and determination of whether the statutory requirements have been satisfied. Request to CIR to proceed to deal with the application;

(i) receipt of report of CIR on ballot. If ballot is not in favour of continuance of agency making of order to discontinue and not re-grant the agency.

7. Emergency procedures

(a) receipt from Secretary of State of an application for an order forbidding the taking of industrial action for up to sixty days in a defined area of employment;

(b) consideration of adequacy of the grounds for the application and making of order if it is concluded that the Secretary of State has grounds on which he can be satisfied of that adequacy. Order defines area covered;

(c) extension of order not originally made to cover sixty days up to a maximum of sixty days;

(d) extension of order to cover persons other than those originally specified;

(e) receipt of application from Secretary of State for a ballot to be taken on proposed or existing industrial action.

(f) making of order for ballot if sufficient reasons to satisfy Secretary of State that necessary grounds exist. Order defines area covered. Order also forbids industrial action during the taking of ballot;

(g) extension of order to cover persons other than those originally specified;

(h) receipt of report on ballot and publication thereof.

The Registrar is under a duty to state a case for the opinion of the NIRC at the request of the complainant or the organization to which the complaint relates in respect of complaints concerning the passing of resolutions under the Trade Unions (Amalgamations etc.) Act 1964.

CONCILIATION AND ARBITRATION

CONCILIATION

The powers of conciliation of the Department of Employment originated in the Conciliation Act 1896, which provides that where a difference exists or is apprehended between employers and workmen, or between different classes of workmen, the [Secretary of State] may:

'(b) take such steps as may seem expedient [to him] for the purpose of enabling the parties to the difference to meet together, by themselves or their representatives, under the presidency of a chairman mutually agreed upon or nominated by the [Secretary of State] or by some other person or body, with a view to the amicable settlement of the difference;

(c) on the application of employers or workmen interested, and after taking into consideration the existence and adequacy of means available for conciliation in the district or trade and the circumstances of the case, appoint a person to act as conciliator or as a board of conciliation.'

Resort can be had to this process at any stage in the dispute, although it has been the practice of the Department of Employment not to intervene until the agreed procedure has been exhausted or, if there is no agreed procedure, until the parties have attempted to settle the dispute.

Immediately before the 1971 Act the Department's conciliation service acted in about 400 cases a year, one quarter of which involved a stoppage of work. The majority of interventions developed from approaches by workers' organizations.

No doubt, however, increasing involvement of government in the regulation of wages makes it more difficult for the conciliator to be regarded as unidentified with any side so as, effectively, to help the parties to find a mutually acceptable basis for settlement. This feeling has undoubtedly developed and joint CBI-TUC efforts are being made to establish an independent conciliation and arbitration system. The Industrial Relations Act, however, strengthens the conciliation powers of the Department in such matters as the formation of bargaining units whilst transferring some of the opportunities away from the Department as such.

The Secretary of State, or an affected employer, or recognized trade union may apply to the Industrial Court on the ground that existing procedures for dealing with industrial disputes are inadequate. The NIRC has power, with the assistance of the CIR, to devise a new and enforceable procedure. It is provided that before he makes an application the Secretary of State must consult the affected parties and this would, no doubt, be used to provide an opportunity to induce voluntary improvement. The CIR, during the process of consideration, will obviously also seek voluntary improvement. The Act itself assumes this by making provision for the incorporation of agreed processes as well as CIR recommendations. The same duty of prior consultation is imposed before the Secretary of State makes an application in respect of the recognition of a sole bargaining agent. So also before he applies for a ballot under the emergency procedures.

In the case of either of the first two applications being made by one of the parties, prior notice must be given to the Secretary of State and he must offer such advice and assistance to the parties as he considers appropriate with a view to promoting agreement between them on the matter. Either party is free to proceed with the application, but the NIRC must not deal with a reference for a sole bargaining agency unless it is satisfied that the parties have endeavoured voluntarily to settle the matter and, for that purpose, have made adequate use of facilities for conciliation available to them. In this preliminary process of advice the CIR can be asked to examine any resultant question referred to it.

The CIR may, at any time before it reports to the NIRC, on either reference, request that the reference be withdrawn on the ground that a satisfactory and lasting settlement has been reached. Plainly this implies that the CIR will be expected to work towards voluntary settlement.

This implication comes out even more strongly in the procedure for revoking a sole bargaining agency where, at the outset, the NIRC must allow the CIR reasonable time to promote and assist such discussion as in their opinion might lead to a settlement.

The Registrar of trade unions, upon receiving a complaint from an applicant for membership of a trade union or employers' organization, a member thereof or a person who has ceased to be a member otherwise than voluntarily, of a breach by the organization of the 'guiding principles' or of its rules, may refer the complaint to the settlement machinery of the organization, if he considers that machinery adequate and if it has not already been used. If, having done so, the complainant reapplies, the Registrar must 'endeavour to promote a settlement of the matter . . . without its becoming the subject of a complaint to an industrial tribunal'.

The NIRC is specifically required to provide parties coming before it with opportunities for conciliation. No machinery or more detailed provision is made available. Presumably the court would use the services of the Department of Employment or any other person or system which seemed most appropriate.

Finally, the Secretary of State must appoint conciliation officers to act where complaints have been made of unfair dismissal, or infringement by an employer of the individual trade union rights granted by section 5 of the 1971 Act. The conciliation officer may either act on the joint request of the parties or on his own initiative if he thinks there is a reasonable prospect of success. His object is, again, to promote a settlement of the complaint without it being presented to an industrial tribunal. Particularly, in dealing with dismissal, he is to seek to promote re-engagement on terms which appear to him to be equitable. Failing this, because it is for instance not desired or not practicable, he is to seek to promote agreement on the amount of compensation. In this case it is provided that anything communicated to a conciliation officer in the course of conciliation is not admissible in evidence before an industrial tribunal or the NIRC without the consent of the person who communicated it. There is some doubt about communication of information in other circumstances. Early practice of the NIRC would seem to raise doubts as to whether that court would exclude 'without prejudice' communications.

ARBITRATION

It is still correct to say that the consent of both parties is always necessary before a substantive dispute is referred to arbitration, although a conciliator may persuade the parties to resort to arbitration and a number of procedure agreements include a provision for automatic resort to arbitration as a final stage in the process. As we have seen, procedural disputes may be compulsorily referred to the CIR and a settlement compulsorily imposed under the remedial procedures of the Industrial Relations Act.

A single arbitrator may be appointed under the Conciliation Act 1896, so that it is possible for a conciliator to be given power to become an arbitrator. Otherwise the powers of the Department of Employment to refer a dispute to arbitration are contained in section 2 of the Industrial Courts Act 1919. They may not be used until there has been a failure of the agreed procedures.

The Industrial Arbitration Board may be appointed to arbitrate, or the dispute may be referred to one or more persons appointed by the Secretary of State, or to a board composed of equal numbers of persons (although there is usually only one from each side) nominated by employers and by workers, and chaired by an independent person appointed by the Secretary of State. Awards rarely contain reasons and are not published. The great advantage of the process is its informality and speed and the fact that hearings normally take place at the place of dispute.

Boards of arbitration follow the same principles although they are usually more formal. The employer and worker representatives, nominated either by the Secretary of State or by the parties, are never from the industry concerned, nor involved in current disputes of a similar kind in other industries. Generally boards are said to be appointed to deal with the more important disputes, but there is no rigid policy and all the disputes referred to boards could be referred to single arbitrators or the Industrial Arbitration Board, had the parties so wished.

ENQUIRY

Enquiries by a Committee of Investigation or, more formally, by a Court of Enquiry, are sometimes established into disputes of a particularly serious and, usually, prolonged character. The object of such an enquiry is to establish the facts of the dispute and, by publishing its findings, to focus opinion on the shortcomings of either or both sides. The main categories of such references appear to be:

(a) where the bulk of workers in an industry is concerned and a national strike threatened;

(b) when there is likelihood of strike action which would have a disruptive effect on a wide section of the public;

(c) occasionally where an isolated dispute looks like having severe secondary effects;

(d) where persistent disputes reveal the existence of an underlying problem producing a 'trouble spot';

(e) where no further arbitration or negotiation machinery is left.

(McCarthy and Clifford, 'The Work of Industrial Courts of Inquiry' (1966) 4 BJIR 39, and Wedderburn and Davies, *Employment Grievances and Disputes Procedures in Britain*, 1969, at p. 227.)

It follows from the object of publicity that reports of Courts of Enquiry are invariably published and laid before Parliament. The fact-finding function very often leads to a settlement. Courts are sometimes, but rarely, appointed without the consent of one side, but it is very uncommon for either party to refuse to give evidence, since they are generally considered to be helpful.

Part IV

Individual Employment

Chapter 11

Dismissal

We have already discussed the rights of the individual in respect of trade union membership and activities. The trade union official, however, will frequently be asked questions concerning dismissal from, or discipline in, employment, redundancy payments, and compensation for injury. These topics are not part of trade union law, upon which this book has concentrated, and they are also large and complicated subjects. It is always possible that a little knowledge, if unwisely used to draw further conclusions, will prove a dangerous thing. With that warning, however, some attempt will be made briefly to outline each of the three topics.

THE BASIS OF THE WORKER'S PROTECTION

An employee now has two largely separate rights. Firstly, he has a right to complain of a breach of his contract of employment and seek damages (possibly even reinstatement) from common law courts. The scope of the action will depend entirely on what is expressly or implicitly contained in his contract. So, if an employer has specified that a person one minute late may be dismissed without notice, an employee so dismissed without good reason will not be able to complain before a common law court under this heading. Secondly, from March 1972, whatever is contained in the contract, an employee may complain (initially to an industrial tribunal) of an unfair industrial practice if he is unfairly dismissed. In the example just given, he could almost certainly bring a successful action under this method.

COMMON LAW REMEDIES DEPENDING ON CONTRACT

An employer is entitled to dismiss or impose discipline as provided by the individual contract of employment, and not otherwise. The difficulty lies in determining what is contained in the contract. As will readily be appreciated, most of the contract is usually made by word of mouth and, even then, little may be said on a number of important points. Of course, what employers call a 'section four statement' will be given to each employee after thirteen weeks of service, but this statement is often rudimentary, may well simply refer to other documents such as collective agreements and, when it does so, may be 'kept up to date' by changes in these other documents without further notification. Even where a formal written contract is issued it will usually only contain the framework of the terms.

The terms of a contract of employment come from several main sources:

(a) expressly (either in writing or by word of mouth) in the contract itself;
(b) by implication from collective agreements (see Chapter 9);
(c) from the common law itself, which implies certain fundamental rights and duties.

The third of these needs more careful examination, partly because it has not previously been considered, and partly because most of the legal problems of discipline, and particularly of dismissal, have arisen in this area.

The common law, apparently drawing upon what it considers to be the distinctive characteristics of employment, has built up a group of rights and duties of employer and employee. Breach of the rights by an employee will, if sufficiently serious, entitle the employer to terminate the contract of employment, or, as lawyers more precisely regard it, to accept the repudiation of his contract implicit in the employee's conduct. Breach by the employer entitles the employee to treat his employment as at an end, and leave. In each case, because the offender has repudiated his obligation no notice by the other is necessary. In either case there is no requirement that the repudiation should be accepted unless the party guilty of the breach refuses to continue with the contract. Since this is regarded as a personal contract, there is usually no legal way in which he can then be compelled to continue. Since these are only implied terms they may be altered by express provision. The situation may be tabulated thus:

Characteristic	Duty of Employee	Duty of Employer
Service	(a) to be ready and willing (sickness and other incapacity apart) to work; (b) to offer personal service; (c) to take reasonable care in the exercise of that service (including care of employer's property); (d) not wilfully to disrupt the operation of the employer's business (This has only recently been suggested in the context of industrial action, and is doubtful)	To pay agreed wages in return for such *willingness* to work
Control	To obey reasonable orders as to time, place, nature and method of the service	To take reasonable care for the employee's safety (but, probably, not the safety of the employee's property)
Trust and confidence	(a) to work only for the employer in the employer's time; (b) to disclose information relevant to the employer's business (except information detrimental to the employer or his fellow employees); (c) to hold for the employer the benefit of any invention etc. relevant to the business on which the employee is engaged; (d) to respect the employer's trade secrets; (e) generally to do nothing to destroy the trust and confidence necessary for employment of that kind	(To treat with proper courtesy – depending, probably, on what one might reasonably expect in the particular job)

Characteristic	Duty of Employee	Duty of Employer
(Proximity – probably not now a general characteristic)		(Formerly, and still possibly in very personal employment, to provide board, lodging and medical attendance)
Agency	(a) to account for all profits received in the course of employment (including the returns from inventions etc.); (b) to indemnify the employer for loss (including that resulting from damage to third parties for which the master is also liable) caused by the employee	To indemnify the employee for loss (other than personal injury) sustained in service

Not every academic lawyer would agree with all the suggested derivations of rights and duties, but they demonstrate how and why the rights and duties are built up and, to some extent, how they become more or less significant, or even disappear for practical purposes. Much more detail would be necessary to provide an answer in most individual borderline cases. There is no room in this book for such detail, even if, at the present time of considerable change, it could be relied on as more than a guide to what might happen. The question of payment of wages during sickness and of suspension without pay seem to be of sufficient importance to warrant some special treatment.

SICKNESS
In practice many employees will find that this matter is dealt with expressly by their contracts. Indeed, one of the benefits of so called 'staff status' is usually a much extended right to payment during sickness. In many cases other workers have rather minimal rights to payment while away sick (although, of course, they will usually be entitled to receive national insurance sickness benefit). If no provision is made in the contract of employment, the common law will imply that the worker is entitled to go on receiving his wages until his contract of employment is ended. That is to say, usually (unless his illness is very severe or prolonged so as to be regarded

as 'frustrating' the purpose of the contract) until his employer clearly tells him his contract is at an end. The common law explains this by saying that he is ready and willing to work if circumstances would permit him; so he has performed his part of the contract and the employer is obliged to perform his. If the employee is wholly dependent on piece-work earnings it would appear to be correct to say that he earns no pay unless he is actually working. In such a case, therefore, a sick man might remain employed but not be entitled to any wages because none were earned. Of course many such employees have guaranteed minimum wages and these would be payable during the guarantee period. This is actually a very interesting point because it illustrates very effectively how the development of collective agreements has removed the possibility of pressure upon legal principle to provide an answer to what would have been been a very difficult legal problem.

SUSPENSION

So long as he continues to pay the wages due, an employer is under no duty to provide work, save in very rare cases (as for instance of an actor) where it could be said to be so essential to the employee that he should maintain his public standing that the provision of work was an implied obligation. The need to 'keep one's hand in' would not be considered sufficient reason. In the case of piece-workers, at least if largely remunerated by that method, however, it is unlikely today that a court would hold that the employer had no obligation to provide the means of earning wages. It must be understood, however, that this is no more than an assumption of the probable solution the courts would provide if faced with this problem. As we have said, collective agreements usually relieve them of this need.

Suspension with pay is, therefore, entirely within the employer's rights. Suspension without pay is, surprisingly to most employers and workers, a breach of contract unless the contract expressly or impliedly permits it. The better view is that it is not to be regarded as a termination of one contract and a restarting of a new contract on the same terms at a later date. The problems really arise from the situations in which the right to suspend may be implied. Almost certainly most well-known practices of disciplinary or other forms of suspension will be held to establish customary practices in the industry or factory, thus giving an implied contractual right to suspend. It may sound surprising if this is thought to produce a situation where what has usually been done can be done again and, conversely, what has not been done cannot be done, at least without a fresh agreement; but that is roughly so. In practice it seems likely that some suspensions occur which are really a breach of the contract to continue to pay wages.

The common law action for damages for wrongful dismissal will not arise if the employee is in fundamental breach of contract. In that case the employer is entitled, at common law, to dismiss the employee without notice. It is difficult to say precisely what is sufficiently serious a breach to permit summary dismissal. It seems best to apply common sense to the situation. If, in all the circumstances, the breach seems a small matter, it can reasonably be assumed that dismissal without notice will produce a right of action at common law, and vice versa. A sufficient reason which comes to light after the dismissal will suffice to justify it.

NOTICE

The *common law* right of action will also be lost if, although no reason, or no sufficient reason, exists, 'proper' notice is given. The minimum statutory periods of notice are:

For an employee of more than 13 weeks and less than 104 weeks seniority – 1 week

For an employee of more than 104 weeks and less than 5 years seniority – 2 weeks

For an employee of more than 5 years and less than 10 years seniority – 4 weeks

For an employee of more than 10 years and less than 15 years seniority – 6 weeks

For an employee with more than 15 years seniority – 8 weeks

('Seniority' here means continuous service with the dismissing employer. The contracts of Employment Act 1963 contains the rules for deciding what amounts to continuous service.) The minimum notice required to be given by an employee of more than thirteen weeks seniority is one week, however much greater is his seniority than that. In both cases the requisite periods can be extended, but not decreased, by the contract of employment. The amount of notice required from white-collar workers, for instance, is frequently four weeks or more.

Although the giving of notice by an employer, without a reason, destroys the common law right of action it would lay an employer wide open to statutory action for unfair dismissal. On the other hand if a reason existed sufficient to make a dismissal fair, the same reason would in most cases also justify summary dismissal for common law purposes, so that notice would be unnecessary to avoid liability under that head. It may, therefore, be asked whether notice rights have any purpose to serve, since it would appear that, if good reason exists, dismissal without notice is justified under both heads, whilst if no good reason exists no amount of notice will prevent liability for an action under the statutory head.

In fact this generalization is not correct in all situations. There are a few situations, some involving large numbers of dismissals, where the reason will prevent the dismissal being unfair but where the reason does not involve a breach of contract by the employee so that, at common law, he is entitled to notice. They are:

Redundancy,
Sickness (wherever the need to replace the employee will justify the dismissal for statutory purposes),
Incompetence (arguably).

A word may be added on the last of these. If a man is taken on for a particular job he usually impliedly undertakes that he is competent to do it (if he did not the only other likely situation would be a probationary employment). In that case, if he proves incompetent, he has broken his undertaking, the contract is repudiated, and he may be dismissed without notice. If, however, he changes jobs whilst with the same employer one of three situations may exist:

(a) he may, indeed, undertake that he is competent;
(b) more likely he will agree to 'have a bash', in which case he undertakes no particular competence; or
(c) because the employer either trusts him or trusts the retraining, which the employer himself may have provided, no warranty of competence is sought and none would be implied.

The NIRC has also utilized the concept of notice as a practice of good industrial relations so as to fix a standard for compensation for unfair dismissal.

STATUTORY REMEDIES DEPENDING ON THE CONCEPT OF UNFAIR DISMISSAL

Whatever the contract of employment may provide, an action for unfair dismissal is available to most employees of more than 104 weeks' standing (unless subject to a jointly agreed exempt dismissal procedure) if they are dismissed in circumstances in which an industrial tribunal takes the view, 'in accordance with equity and the substantial merits of the case,' that the employer acted unreasonably in treating the established reason for dismissal as a sufficient reason. If no reason is established, then there would be a conclusive presumption of unfair dismissal.

It is for the employer to show the reason, or the principal reason, and to show that it was a substantial reason of a kind such as to justify the dismissal. A few such reasons are listed (as examples, not as a comprehensive list of fair reasons). They are:

(a) a reason relating to the capability (assessed by reference to skill, aptitude, health or any other physical or mental quality) or qualifications (degree, diploma or other academic, technical or professional qualification relevant to the position which the employee held) of the employee for performing work of the kind which he was employed to do;

(b) a reason relating to the conduct of the employee;

(c) redundancy;

(d) the fact that for the employee to continue in that job would be a contravention, either by the employee or the employer, of some statutory restriction, e.g. that a mine manager must be certificated.

This list is not very helpful because it is far too general. A reason relating to an employee's conduct may or may not be sufficiently substantial to justify dismissal. The list is, indeed, so general that it comprehends almost all reasons that may exist. The result must be that in all cases, the employer must show the reason to be 'substantial' and the tribunal will *then* ask whether it was reasonable to treat it as 'sufficient'. What 'substantial' and 'sufficient' mean, and what, if any, is the difference between them, are questions to which at the moment no clear answers can be given. It may help to look rather at those grounds which do not permit of fair dismissal.

In one situation, stemming from entirely separate provisions in the Industrial Relations Act, the establishment of the reason will always establish what amounts to unfair dismissal. All forms of dismissal, penalization or other discrimination, or refusal to engage a worker because of his exercise of the trade union rights discussed in Chapter 3, and all prevention or deterrence from the exercise of those rights by an employer or a person acting on behalf of an employer, constitutes an unfair industrial practice. Since complaint lies also to an industrial tribunal dismissal for these reasons will, no doubt, be treated in the same way as unfair dismissal except that, once the ground is established, no question can arise that the dismissal was, in the circumstances, reasonable. It should be noted also that this ground of complaint is wider in scope than any other, extending not only to employees, but to 'workers', thus including the self-employed, and also being available to any worker, however short a period his engagement has covered.

Where a certificate signed by a Minister of the Crown is submitted stating that dismissal was for the purpose of safeguarding national security, the certificate is conclusive evidence of that fact and the tribunal or NIRC must dismiss the claim.

All other cases where dismissal is said to be unfair in the Act are situations in which the complainant can show that he has been picked for dismissal in a situation, involving redundancy or strike action, where a number of other employees were similarly involved but have not been dismissed. Dismissal of an employee because he is on strike or is taking part in other industrial action (whether or not it is 'irregular'), or is redundant, is expressly stated not to be unfair. It becomes so, in either case, if the dismissed employee can show that one or more of those similarly placed was not dismissed (or in the case of industrial action was offered reinstatement at the end of the period of industrial action) *and* that the reason for the discrimination was that the dismissed employee was exercising his trade union rights as specified in section 5 of the Act. This raises considerable difficulty since it may be asked what is the position if the selection is for some other reason which on its own would not justify dismissal. It may be argued that the Act is really asking the tribunal to say that the principal reason for dismissal is not the strike or the redundancy, since if it were the obvious question would be why all the others were not so involved. Perhaps, however, the Act is merely saying that in the specified circumstances the principal reason must be deemed to be the exercise of trade union rights whilst in other dual reason situations it is for the tribunal to decide. Whichever is the correct answer we may deduce that in all cases of dismissal of strikers or dismissal for redundancy the dismissed employee is free to allege that the principal cause of his dismissal was some other reason. In such an allegation the fact that others in the same position were not dismissed would be strong supporting evidence. That being so, industrial tribunals are likely to experience grave difficulty, since in many redundancy dismissals a selection is made based on reasons other than the mere fact of redundancy. Is it then true to say that redundancy, or the reason for the selection, is the principal reason for dismissal of the individual concerned?

The other specified situation of selection is not of a kind with these others. In a redundancy situation similar selection is unfair if it is in contravention of a customary agreement or accepted procedure and without special reasons to justify the contravention. This is the only really clear exception to the general rule of looking for the real reason. Here the real, indeed the only established, reason is redundancy but, because of the method of selection, it is to be considered not a justification.

The way the Act is constructed would seem to suggest that in any of these three cases, where the fact of discrimination for the specified reasons is established it is not open to the tribunal to say that, nevertheless, the equity and justice of the case justifies dismissal.

It has constantly been made clear that, however good the reason for dismissal, the method may be such as to render it unfair. The absence of opportunity to speak in his defence, for instance, will probably give the employee a successful right of action; though the amount of compensation may be reduced because of his conduct. From this, if for no better reason, it can be deduced that dismissal cannot be justified by a reason that comes to light after the event.

Not all employees are in the same position as to the right to complain of unfair dismissal. The following employees have no such right in any circumstances:

(a) the husband, wife or close relative of the employer;
(b) a registered dock worker;

(c) a share fisherman;

(d) a teacher to whom section 85 of the Education (Scotland) Act 1962 applies;

(e) one under a contract which normally involves employment for less than twenty-one hours weekly;

(f) one under a fixed term contract (other than a contract of apprenticeship) made before the end of February 1972, where the dismissal consists only in the expiration of the term;

(g) one under a fixed term contract (including a contract of apprenticeship) made after the above date, where at some time during the currency of the contract the employee has agreed in writing to exclude any such claim arising merely from the expiration of the term;

(h) where, under his contract, the employee normally works outside Great Britain. This does not include employment on a British ship, unless the employment is wholly outside Great Britain, or the employee is not ordinarily resident in Great Britain.

The following employees may only claim where the reason (or the principal reason) for the dismissal was that the employee had exercised, or indicated his intention to exercise, any of the trade union rights within section 5 of the Act:

(a) one employed in an undertaking in which immediately before the effective date of termination there were no more than two employees (other than the employee dismissed) who had been continuously employed for thirteen weeks or more;

(b) one continuously employed for less than 104 weeks with the employer concerned;

(c) one who, on or before the date of termination, had reached the normal retirement age or the age of 65 (60 for a woman).

This particular complaint, as already noted, is available to self-employed persons, who have no right to complain on any other ground.

As with redundancy the claimant must show that the employer has terminated the contract. In the case of unfair dismissal, there is no exception to permit a claim to be made where the employee has left because of the conduct of the employer. This leaves a dangerous gap in the protection, since it is quite feasible for an employer to force an employee to leave rather than to dismiss him, thus avoiding the possibility of a claim. An employee who has already received notice of dismissal retains his right to claim compensation for unfair dismissal, as he does to claim at least a proportion of a redundancy payment, if he gives written notice, within the obligatory period of notice, to leave before the expiration of the employer's notice.

For example, employer gives six weeks' notice to employee for a reason insufficient to justify dismissal. Employee finds another job, and, after three weeks, gives written notice to leave in one week's time. The employee retains his right to claim compensation for unfair dismissial provided that he is entitled, by his contract, to receive more than three weeks' notice.

Dismissal by way of a lock-out, whether it occurs at the beginning of or during the lock-out, will not be considered unfair if the employee *is offered* re-engagement as from the date of resumption of work. He must be offered his old position or a different but reasonably suitable position. Despite the working of the Act this is really more akin to saying that such a temporary dismissal is not to be considered as a dismissal at all for these purposes. This impression is enhanced by the provision that if the employee is not taken on again at the end of the lock-out it is the reason for that failure, and not for the original termination, which is relevant to the determination of the question of fairness.

PROCEDURE

A common law claim, on its own, may exist where, for instance, the employee alleges that though a reason like redundancy exists which would prevent a successful action for unfair dismissal, that reason does not involve a breach by him of his contract but that, nevertheless, he has not received the notice to which his contract entitles him. In such a case, at the moment, the case would have to be commenced either in a County Court or the High Court. Provision does exist in the Industrial Relations Act for transferring this jurisdiction to the industrial tribunals. Until such transfer is effected, however, the process is, rather awkwardly, entirely separated from that for determining an unfair dismissal.

Common law rights may be entirely observed and the employment terminated by proper notice. In such a case the only claim is the statutory one of unfair dismissal. Such a claim is made on the appropriate form to the nearest industrial tribunal. There is a general right of audience before these tribunals so that the claimant may either fight his own case, be represented by a trade union official, or a lawyer, or anyone else. Generally the parties pay their own costs. Unless barristers are briefed, and this should not be necessary in most cases, these costs are not likely to be high.

All industrial tribunals possess conciliation officers. They have power to operate in two situations: either,

(a) where a claim has been made to a tribunal of unfair dismissal; or

(b) where no such formal claim has been made but, *after he has ceased to be employed*, a request is made to the conciliation officer by either the employee or the employer on the ground that the employee alleges that he was unfairly dismissed.

NB. A conciliation officer cannot be brought in before the employee has ceased to be employed, e.g. during a period of notice. The NIRC has said that this need not be adhered to where the period of notice is a long one.

The conciliation officer, in either situation, may act either if he is jointly requested to do so by the complainant and the employer or if, without such a joint request, he considers that he could act with a reasonable prospect of success. Necessarily the decision on this latter point will involve on his part a certain amount of determination of the justice of the claim. The Department of Employment are anxious to point out that, in the absence of a joint request, conciliation officers will not only intervene where they consider the dismissal to be unjustified. It is plain that they will not always intervene in unjustified dismissals, if only because the employer's attitude will often make it clear that he is not open to conciliation. The object of the conciliation officer is obviously to attempt to ameliorate the position in any way he can, but the Act particularly requires him to seek to procure reinstatement of the employee on terms appearing to the conciliation officer to be equitable, or, failing that, to promote agreement as to the amount of compensation.

This latter is, of course, the normal process of 'settling out of court'. It may be objected that it allows the employer to get rid of an employee provided he is prepared to pay and that, by avoiding the bad publicity of a tribunal hearing, it saves the employer from any really meaningful sanction. This is largely true but it is impossible to insist on parties fighting a case when both are prepared to settle. The position of the conciliation officer, therefore, is only beneficial in that he provides independent advice in the settlement process; rather than leaving it to the parties with the danger that the employee will ill-advisedly accept a lump sum.

ALTERNATIVE PROCEDURE

The entire right to complain to an industrial tribunal of an unfair dismissal may be removed if there exists a designated grievance procedure applicable to the employee concerned. All the parties to a procedure agreement, acting jointly, may apply to the NIRC to designate the procedure agreement in place of the normal right of complaint to an industrial tribunal. The NIRC may make such an order, but only if it is satsified that the procedure agreement conforms to the following requirements:

'(a) all the organizations of workers party to the agreement must be independent;

(b) the agreement provides for procedures for dealing with claims that an employee has been, or [presumably meaning "and"] is in the course of being, unfairly dismissed;

(c) availability, without discrimination, to all employees falling within any description to which the procedure agreement applies;

(d) remedies provided which are "on the whole as beneficial as (but not necessarily identical with)" those provided by the Act;

(e) provision of a right of independent arbitration or adjudication where a decision cannot be reached by the other means provided;

(f) reasonable certainty as to whether a particular employee is one to whom the procedure applies.'

Most difficulty seems likely to be occasioned by requirements (c), (d) and (e). Most voluntary dismissal procedures negotiated by trade unions will provide that the procedure is not available to non-members of the unions party to the agreement. A 'description' of employee within (c) seems likely to be a job description – as elsewhere in the Act. It can hardly be right to say that 'all grade A craftsmen who are union members' is a 'description' of employee, otherwise it would be equally reasonable so to describe 'all grade A craftsmen who are Anglicans' and the whole purpose of the requirement would be lost. So a large number of agreements would have to be altered before they could qualify for exemption. It is unlikely that trade unions would wish to agree to this. The only statutory remedy, failing agreement to reinstate, is compensation. The normal remedy in voluntary procedures would be reinstatement. A right to compensation will certainly never be the principal voluntary remedy, and may well not appear at all. It may be almost impossible to compare radically different remedies to discover whether they are 'on the whole as beneficial as' each other. It is probably safe to say, however, that, if it is desired to submit a voluntary procedure for exemption, it should provide at least a residual right to compensation if, for good reason, the employee does not desire reinstatement. Finally, employers are not generally ready to entertain the idea of 'independent arbitration', even as a final procedure where all other methods fail to produce agreement. There is, in any event, a shortage of people with sufficient experience to act in this capacity and employers are not anxious to train arbitrators by trial and error. There is also considerable fear that an arbitrator appointed for a particular unit tends to feel that decisions for management must roughly balance those for employees.

A voluntary procedure has, however, the great advantage of saving a great deal of time in preparation of a case to present to an industrial tribunal not acquainted with the nature of the job or the organization of the work and factory. The further one removes the adjudication, no doubt the more dispassionate it becomes. It also becomes increasingly ill-informed and inexpert. If tribunals are heavily worked they will not have time to acquaint themselves fully with such necessary detail. A more reliable decision might well emerge at plant level.

REMEDIES

The common law remedy appropriate to wrongful dismissal has consistently been the award of damages for breach of the contract of employment. Save in very unusual circumstances the courts would never decree reinstatement. Their refusal was based on the ground that it was contrary to public policy, if not impossible, to compel A to work for B, or B to employ A. It might be argued that in the light of the impersonal nature of many large employers today there is nothing particularly undesirable in ordering British Railways or ICI to employ an individual. This may be so, but there is a rule that A cannot obtain 'specific performance' of a contract against B unless B also had the right to the same remedy against A. So, unless justification can be found for making orders in favour of both the employee and the employer, neither can be permitted.

Recently, however, the Court of Appeal considered the case of what it took to be an employee willing to be reinstated and an employer willing to reinstate, the cause of the dismissal being trade union pressure. A majority of the court took the view that in such a case a contravention of public policy would not be produced by an order to reinstate. The interesting sequel was that though the plaintiff was reinstated, the other thirty or so employees similarly placed were immediately given the appropriate notice of dismissal, suggesting that the employer's willingness is not an abstract concept but is to be viewed in the light of all outside pressures to which the employer is subject.

Upon a claim for unfair dismissal an industrial tribunal may recommend, but not order, reinstatement. If it makes such a recommendation which is not acceded to by the employer, compensation may be increased, whereas, if the employee does not accept an offer of reinstatement, compensation may be reduced. Otherwise, upon finding a case proved, the tribunal may, if it considers it just and equitable to do so, grant a declaration of the rights of the complainant and the employer and/or award compensation to be paid by the employer. An award of compensation for unfair dismissal must not exceed an amount representing 104 weeks' pay for the complainant or £4,160 (that is to say, 104 weeks' pay at a maximum of £40 per week), whichever is less. In practice this amount is unlikely to be awarded because the complainant is required to mitigate his loss, and, if he fails to do so, will be treated as if he had taken such steps in mitigation as are reasonable. In this connection the main effect is that if there is a reasonable prospect of employment for a person unfairly dismissed he may receive no more compensation, possibly even less, than he would under his common law claim, because he will either find a new job quickly or will be expected to have done so.

At common law, because the claim is founded on breach of contract, the courts have always said that if an employee is dismissed without good reason or proper notice all he has lost is his contractual right to such notice. So if an employee was entitled to four weeks' notice, the most compensation he would receive at common law for wrongful dismissal would be an amount equivalent to four weeks' pay. In dealing with a claim for unfair dismissal an industrial tribunal is not limited in this way. It may award 'such amount as [it] considers just and equitable in the circumstances having regard to the loss sustained by the aggrieved party in consequence of the matters to which the complaint relates'. The NIRC has held that four main elements must be considered. . . . Firstly the amount of wages that would have been received during a 'proper' notice period. No reduction is to be made for money actually earned in this period. Secondly, compensation for loss of fringe benefits, but not for the manner of the dismissal. Thirdly, an amount, probably small, for loss of job security. Finally, there is a relatively large element to represent the loss of accrued right to a redundancy payment resulting from the fact that the dismissed employee will have to start building up that right all over again. This the Court has said should be one half of the amount of compensation that would have been received upon a redundancy.

It may be that though the employer has dismissed the claimant unfairly he has done so largely because of industrial pressure or a threat thereof. This fact does not affect the claimant. He is entitled to proceed against the employer disregarding the possibility of such pressure. The employer is not entitled to defend the claim by alleging such pressure. The employer, however, in such a situation, can seek to recoup his loss against those who have sought to put pressure upon him in one of two ways:

(a) He may bring a separate action against those responsible for an unfair industrial practice if the pressure has been produced by strike or other irregular industrial action short of a strike which those responsible have called, organized, procured or financed or which they have threatened so to do, with the principal purpose of knowingly inducing an unfair dismissal or a breach of section 5.

NB. Only the employer can bring this action. The dismissed employee's action lies only against the employer. The employee is not entitled to proceed against those who have imposed the pressure.

(*b*) When a claim for unfair dismissal or breach of section 5 is
brought against him an employer may join those responsible
for the above-mentioned types of pressure and seek from them,
in one and the same action, a contribution to the compensation
he has to pay. The amount of the compensation is such as the
tribunal or court considers just and equitable in the circumstances, even up to a full indemnity.

The practical difference between those two courses will probably
lie in the fact that the first will be used where pressure is being
brought to which the employer has not yielded, since an order can
then be obtained forbidding continuation of the pressure. Where
dismissal has already taken place there is little point in bringing a
separate action and so the second alternative of joinder will be
used.

THE CODE OF PRACTICE AND DISMISSAL PROCEDURES

So far as the common law is concerned no procedural requirements
for dismissal are laid down. An employee, in particular, is not at
law entitled to a hearing before dismissal. The Industrial Relations
Act, introducing the new concept of unfair dismissal, rather un-
certainly, founds that concept both on the substantive reasons for
dismissal or alternatively on procedural defects. So it appears that
in considering whether there has been an unfair dismissal the
question of the procedure adopted is entirely irrelevant. On the
other hand it would seem that once it is determined that there has
been an unfair dismissal a bad procedure will not justify increasing
the amount of compensation awarded.

In practice, however, it is probable that both tribunals and
courts will also lean against an employer who has ignored the
procedural provisions of the Code of Practice. These are that the
procedure:

(*a*) should specify who has authority to take various forms of
disciplinary action and ensure that supervisors do not have
power to dismiss without reference to more senior management;

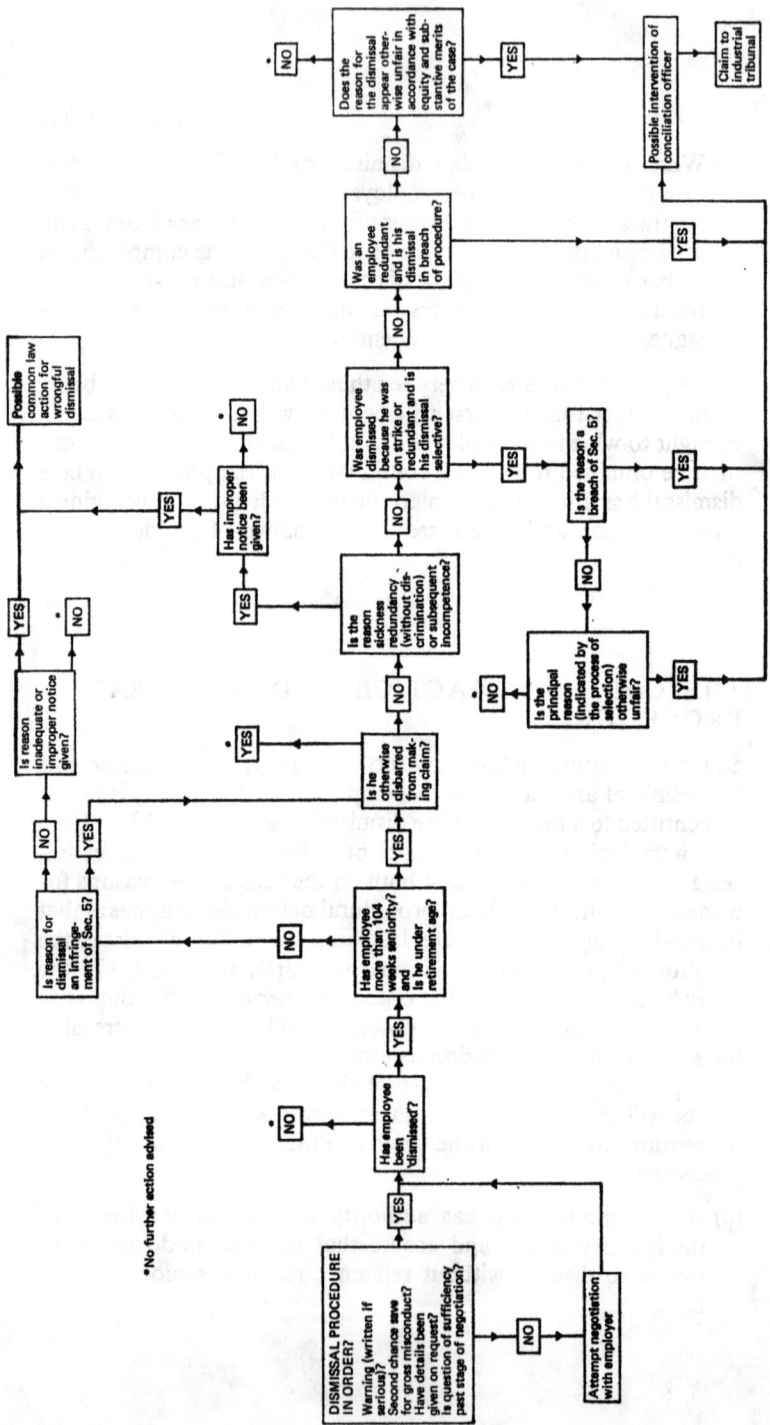

*No further action advised

DISMISSAL PROCEDURE IN ORDER?
Warning (written if serious)?
Second chance save for gross misconduct?
Have details been given on request?
Is question of sufficiency past stage of negotiation?

Attempt negotiation with employer

Has employee been 'dismissed'? — NO → *
— YES ↓

Has employee more than 104 weeks seniority? and Is he under retirement age? — NO → Is reason for dismissal an infringement of Sec. 57?
— YES ↓

Is he otherwise disbarred from making claim? — YES → *
— NO ↓

Is reason for dismissal an infringement of Sec. 57? — NO → Is reason inadequate or improper notice given? — NO → *
— YES → YES →

Is reason inadequate or improper notice given? — YES → Possible common law action for wrongful dismissal

Has improper notice been given? — NO → *
— YES → Possible common law action for wrongful dismissal

Is the reason sickness redundancy (without discrimination) or subsequent incompetence? — YES → Has improper notice been given?
— NO ↓

Was employee dismissed because he was on strike or redundant and is his dismissal selective? — YES → Is the reason a breach of Sec. 57? — YES →
— NO ↓

Is the reason a breach of Sec. 57? — NO → Is the principal reason (indicated by the process of selection) otherwise unfair? — NO → *
— YES →

Was an employee redundant and is his dismissal in breach of procedure? — YES → Possible intervention of conciliation officer
— NO ↓

Does the reason for the dismissal appear otherwise unfair in accordance with equity and substantive merits of the case? — NO → *
— YES → Possible intervention of conciliation officer → Claim to industrial tribunal

(*b*) should give the employee the opportunity to state his case with the right to be accompanied by an employee representative;

(*c*) should provide for a right of appeal, wherever practicable, to a level of management not previously involved;

(*d*) should provide for independent arbitration if the parties *to the procedure* wish it. (One might assume that if both parties to a procedure agreement wished for arbitration it would inevitably be provided for!);

(*e*) should provide, as a first step, for an oral warning of misconduct, or, in more serious cases, for a written warning;

(*f*) should provide for dismissal only in the case of gross misconduct;

(*g*) should provide for a written record of action, such as final warning, suspension without pay, or dismissal, taken upon any further misconduct;

(*h*) should provide for written details of the disciplinary action to be given to the employee and, at his request, to his employee representative;

(*i*) should provide that no disciplinary action should be taken against a shop steward until the circumstances have been discussed with a full-time official of the union concerned.

Chapter 12

Redundancy

Dismissal on grounds of redundancy is, as we have seen, not 'unfair'. Provided that proper notice of dismissal was given, it has never been possible successfully to claim compensation for such a dismissal at common law. It must also be admitted that trade unions as a whole had failed to secure, by voluntary agreement, any widespread system of compensation for redundancy. The law may concentrate on individual loss but it tends only to take major steps forward when sufficient numbers of individuals are affected to produce a social problem. This situation developed in the 1960s, if not before, as major 'rationalizations' of industry began to produce mass dismissals. Frequently these occurred in areas where unemployment was already a problem. The reaction of trade unions was naturally to attempt to prevent such dismissals and it is not surprising, given the union philosophy of the strong protecting the weak, that the protection sought was often by way of work-sharing so that everyone worked less and earned less; but, at least, no one was dismissed. From the point of view of the spread of Christian principles this was a very healthy development. Economically it was apt to be disastrous, especially if it meant that large contingents of skilled or potentially skilled labour were under-employed in one industry or area, whilst in another expansion was held back for lack of manpower. The philosophy behind the Redundancy Payments Act 1965 is, therefore, undoubtedly of encouragement of willingness to dismiss, and accept dismissal of, surplus or redundant labour. There can be no doubt that this purpose has been achieved. Save in areas of severe unemployment, the fear of redundancy has sharply declined to the point where it is often not difficult to secure enough volunteers for dismissal for redundancy. Strikes over threatened redundancy have sharply decreased. The principal point of failure of the design lies in the fact that there has not been as a result of the Act a particularly noticeable increase in the desire to move to a different area, or even to retrain for a different industry. It is probable, however, that few people would have expected such changes to result from the payment merely of a few hundred pounds compensation. There seems to be a widely held view among redundant employees that the receipt of compensation has enabled them to take more time and care in seeking other work so that the ultimate choice is likely to prove more satisfactory and permanent.

The legal provisions of the statutory system of compensation for redundancy are considerably more technical and complex than those examined in the previous chapter in connection with unfair dismissal. In the case of unfair dismissal considerable discretion is permitted to a tribunal considering both the substantive question of unfairness and the amount of compensation. Redundancy, as we shall see, is much more rigidly defined and the scale of compensation is virtually fixed. There is little doubt that this legalism was increased during the first five years' operation of the Act by the fact that appeal from decisions of industrial tribunals was to the Divisional Court of the Queen's Bench Division and then to the Court of Appeal. Appeal now lies firstly to the NIRC and there are already signs of a more flexible approach to the law.

SCOPE OF THE SCHEME

Any employee with more than 104 consecutive weeks' continuous service with the employer concerned, immediately before the dismissal for redundancy, may qualify, provided he is not over 65 (60 in the case of a woman) and that the qualifying service occurred after the employee reached the age of 18. Weeks only count if they are covered by a contract which normally involves employment for twenty-one hours or more. So a full-time employee will continue to be able to count those weeks when he is on short time and actually works less than twenty-one hours; but an employee who, for instance, regularly works alternate weeks of eighteen and twenty-five hours would never have more than one week of continuous employment. Even within the general class of employment to which redundancy payments are usually available there are a number of specific exceptions:

(*a*) a contract (including a contract of apprenticeship) where, during the currency of the contract the employee has agreed in writing not to claim a redundancy payment merely because of the expiration of the term;

(*b*) an employee covered by an exemption order made by the Secretary of State where there is a satisfactory collective agreement in force providing for compensation for redundancy;

(*c*) employees of the Crown (note that civil servants and other Crown employees, except members of the armed forces, have a right to claim for unfair dismissal;

(*d*) employees of the National Health Service;

(*e*) holders of certain public offices;

(*f*) registered dock workers (who have their own scheme);

(*g*) share-fishermen;

(*h*) employees employed solely by their own spouses;

(*i*) domestic servants closely related to the employer;

(*j*) employment which, under the contract, normally involves work outside Great Britain (or Northern Ireland where employees come under an almost identical Act) unless the employee is in Great Britain upon his employer's instructions when the contract is terminated;

(*k*) employees of the government of an overseas territory. (This will include overseas government agencies like TASS, the Soviet News Agency);

(*l*) any other employee excluded by statutory instrument made by the Secretary of State for Employment.

NB. All self-employed persons are excluded.

DISMISSAL

No redundancy payment is due unless the claimant has been dismissed with or without notice, or where his contract, being a fixed term contract, expires; or where the contract is terminated *without notice* by the employee in circumstances such that he is entitled by reason of the employer's conduct to do so. The death of a personal employer, the dissolution of a partnership or the winding-up of a company are also to be treated as involving a dismissal.

This requirement of dismissal is strictly construed and great care must be taken by an employee particularly:

(*a*) where he has received warning of impending redundancy; since for instance, if he finds another job and initiates the leaving himself he will not have been dismissed;

(b) where he has cause to leave; since if, to be on the safe side, he gives proper notice, instead of leaving without such notice, he will have failed to satisfy the strict terms of the requirement.

Once notice has been given by the employer it cannot be retracted save with the consent of the employee. Once dismissed for redundancy, therefore, an employee may proceed with his claim even if the employer purports to withdraw the notice.

The NIRC acting in one of its first cases on a redundancy appeal, however, has held that where an employer informs his employees who are on strike that he will dismiss them if they do not return by a certain day and, when they return a day later, insists on engaging them on new contracts, the period will count as one on strike rather than as one of dismissal. Failure to reinstate a man for a short period immediately after the strike will count as a temporary cessation. In both cases continuity will be maintained. In either case it is still true to say apparently that if such a man is not subsequently re-engaged he must be considered to have been dismissed immediately.

It had been held that termination dates from the time at which proper notice expires if the employee works out his notice. If he is paid wages in lieu of notice or dismissed without notice, whether or not that course is a proper one, termination of employment, as the better view had it, occurred when the employee finally left work. It must be assumed that the view of the NIRC as to the date of dismissal for the purpose of the Industrial Relations Act will now replace that of the Industrial Tribunals for the purposes of the Redundancy Payments Act. In that event the assumption is that the date of dismissal is when the proper period of notice has, or would have, run out. This assumption will be displaced if there is an agreed termination or the employer indicates his view that dismissal is to take effect immediately. This will affect primarily the qualification period of 104 weeks' continuous employment. Obviously it would be sensible to have the same rule for a similar calculation in both situations.

At common law, if a contract of employment is varied by agreement it would probably be said that one contract had ended and a new contract begun. If this view were allowed to stand for purposes of redundancy payment there might be said to be a dismissal upon each change and this would produce problems in some cases about suitability of the new job. The Act, therefore, expressly provides that it shall not be so and the doctrine of consensual variation has developed. If both parties freely accept a change in the contract there will be no termination of employment. The fact of continuing to work under the new arrangement, but with a clearly expressed protest, will probably reveal an absence of agreement sufficient to dispose of the suggestion of a consensual variation. Where there is a change of employer by agreement this cannot be said to be a consensual variation.

Finally it may happen that an employee, having received notice of dismissal for redundancy, will find another job while working out his notice and wish to leave before the expiration of the period of notice he has been given. This is another situation where a natural reaction to an employer's readiness to be helpful could be unfortunate. If the employee leaves early, with or without the agreement of the employer, even though he is already under notice of dismissal, his leaving will be his own act and will not count as termination for the purpose of claiming a redundancy payment. The Act provides a way round this but it must be carefully adhered to in every detail. In order to maintain his claim, the employee must give notice of his desire to his employer in writing and such notice can only be effective if it is given within the compulsory period of notice that the employee is entitled to give.

Example: Employee with six years' service entitled under the provisions of the Contracts of Employment Act to four weeks' notice, and whose contract does not provide for any longer period, is given eight weeks' notice of dismissal for redundancy by his employer. Within two weeks of the receipt of this he finds a new job and wishes to take it up the following Monday. He cannot give an effective counter-notice, however, for a further two weeks; that is until he moves into the last four weeks of his notice period representing the compulsory period of notice.

There is no magic in this. It merely stems from the clear wording of the Act. The employer may well be sympathetic to some defect in the procedure but should take care before making a payment which is not due because of such an error. There have been recent signs of an increased tendency not to make payments of rebate where the redundant worker is not entitled to the payment he has received.

An employer is not obliged to accept the counter-notice. He may, in writing, before the expiration of the counter-notice, require the employee to withdraw the counter-notice and work out the original period. If the employee wishes to ignore this requirement and take up his new job he must accept that his claim for a redundancy payment will have to be made to an industrial tribunal and that the tribunal (in one of the few areas of discretion it has) may, on the merits of the case, decide what, if any, proportion of the redundancy payment which the employee would normally have received it is just and equitable for him to receive in the circumstances.

REDUNDANCY

There is a presumption that all dismissal is for redundancy and it is for the employer who wishes to resist a claim to show that that was not the reason for dismissal. Obviously, the easiest way to do this is to show some other reason, but it is sometimes possible for an employer who fails to prove any other reason for the dismissal nevertheless to prove that the reason was not redundancy. Strong evidence that there was no redundancy would, for instance, exist in the fact that the dismissed person's place had immediately been filled.

Many situations arise in which redundancy is not the only reason for dismissal. In all cases of selective redundancy, for instance, there must be a secondary reason for the selection. The relevant reason is the primary one and some difficulty may be caused, for instance, where there is obviously a potential redundancy situation but the employer has not dismissed for this reason previously. If he dismisses an employee alleging incompetence, the employee, whilst not disputing this possibility, may reply that the real reason is redundancy. The courts have indicated that on the whole, provided the reason given by the employer is that which genuinely motivated him and that he acted in good faith believing in that reason, it does not even matter that in reality the reason did not exist. The enquiry, therefore, is always 'why did the employer think he was dismissing the employee?' Even this may sometimes be difficult to settle, but at least it indicates that the primary reason is that which motivated the employer and not that which actually existed.

In deciding the real reason for dismissal it will be necessary to determine what the claimant was employed to do. An employee may well be engaged to be ready to undertake a much wider range of tasks than he has previously been asked to do. So a general labourer may only previously have been employed to clean machines. If he is told that because new and more easily cleaned machines have been installed, so that one of the two men previously engaged on such cleaning is not required, he will in future clean the floors and washrooms, no breach of his contract occurs. If he refuses and is dismissed, the employer is entitled to say that he was dismissed for refusing to carry out his contractual obligations and not because of the diminution in work. The same is true where work runs out at one place and the employee is asked to undertake the same work, but in another location. If the employee's contract requires him to be available to move that distance, and this may be a question of what obligation can reasonably be implied, then dismissal following a refusal to move will not be dismissal for redundancy. In both these examples, however, there is obviously a redundancy situation and the question is simply whether that is the primary reason for dismissal. If dismissal would not have occurred had the employee, as he was obliged to do, accepted the move, then the primary reason for dismissal will be his refusal to move. The very fact of the offer indicates that there is still work within his contractual area. If, however, the employee is not obliged to move or undertake the other work, the termination occurs by the very fact of the new requirement. If the employee had accepted the change there might have been a consensual variation, but as he does not accept it the change must involve the end of his original contract. No offer to continue within the terms of his contract is made. The reason is clearly that there is insufficient work of the contractual kind in the contractual place and that is plainly a redundancy. At this stage in the enquiry the offer of the new job is irrelevant. Yet another situation may arise. If an employee is obliged by his contract to move or to undertake other work but the employer does not rely on that obligation preferring to say: 'I have no more work of this kind here: I must dismiss you, but I can offer you employment of that kind there,' he has expressly terminated the original contract and offered a new one, although he need not have done. Once again the other work is irrelevant and the answer to the question why the contract was terminated is redundancy.

The statutory definition of redundancy is an exhaustive specification of the situations in which compensation will be paid. These are where:

(a) the employer has ceased, or intends to cease, to carry on the business for the purposes for which the employee was employed by him, or has ceased, or intends to cease, to carry on that business in the place where the employee was so employed, or

(b) the requirements of that business for employees to carry out work of a particular kind, or for employees to carry out work of a particular kind in the place where they were so employed, have ceased or diminished or are expected to cease or diminish.

It is probable that this covers virtually all cases of over-staffing. It has been said that it does not extend to one of the classic redundancy situations, where an employer has, for some time, been employing ten men to do the work of eight, because the employer's business has not diminished nor have his requirements for employees of that kind since they have always been as low as they now are. It is at this point that the weakness of this argument lies. It is unlikely that an employer would have taken on more employees than he needed, bearing in mind that there is no absolute standard of necessity, so that even if he did take on more people than some might think necessary that number was his requirement at the time. At some stage his requirement must have diminished either by a decline in work or by his realization that, though the amount of work remained the same, he did not require so many people to do it as he did in fact employ. So it is not the definition but the facts which are likely to cause trouble. Suppose, as occurred in one well-known case, six employees were originally fully employed. The nature of the work radically changed but they were all fitted into the new structure. Later (it may have been because too many were fitted in or because, as the employer alleged, the quality of the claimant's work was such that people would no longer pay an economic rate for it but would rather have inferior work for which they paid less), the employer found it desirable to dispense with the services of the employee. On one view there was a redundancy situation within the meaning of the Act even though it had existed for some time before action was taken. On the other, the answer will depend entirely on how one defines the original work and how one defines the work for which people will now pay. If one could call the first that of a cabinet maker and the second that of a carpenter and joiner, there would again be a redundancy situation. If, however, both were the work of a carpenter, simply differing in quality, then it is possible to say that there had been no diminution in work of the particular description. That being so, one is bound to say that there could not have been a dismissal for redundancy and that the real reason was that, to the employer, the claimant was not worth what he was paid.

Two main problems arise from interpretation of the statutory definitition of redundancy, namely: the meaning of 'work of a particularly kind' and of 'the place where the employee was so employed'. In the case just mentioned, the importance of defining the kind of work the employee was employed to do has been shown. If a man is a captain of cargo ships, then decline of coastal trade balanced by an increase in ocean-going trade does not produce a decline in his kind of work. If, however, he is a coastal waters captain such a change does result in a decline in his kind of work. A garage mechanic who worked nights partly produced his own redundancy because he declined to work them if he was not able to occupy the flat over the garage. The employer then discontinued the night service. It was held that the employee was a garage mechanic, not a night-mechanic, and as work was available in the day there was no redundancy. One interesting case which went to the High Court on appeal concerned a middle-aged barmaid who was dismissed to be replaced by young and more attractive barmaids, more in the 'bunny-girl' style. The industrial tribunal eventually concluded that there had been a decline in the requirement for work of the dismissed barmaid but that she had been replaced. The Divisional Court found this contradictory. Had it been possible to conclude that the two jobs were of a different type the decision would have been easy. In a way that seems to be what the tribunal was trying to say: With a middle-aged barmaid work had so declined that she was no longer required. The employer then replaced her with a different type of barmaid so as to attract custom again.

This case raises not only the problem of the description of the job but also two other questions; that of inevitable future redundancy if changes are not made, and that of the evidential value of a replacement. Before we consider these, however, there should be a final warning on job description. Not every clear change in requirement will be said to involve a new type of work. The manager of a relatively low-class gentlemen's outfitters is the manager of a gentlemen's outfitters. If the standard rises and his language or attitudes do not suit the new customers he can be dismissed for unsuitability, but he is not redundant because such a manager is still required. But is a manager of a machine shop engaged in the repair of goods redundant if that shop is turned over to the manufacture of those goods? Obviously there are different types of machine shop with different types of managers and the type may differ because of the sophistication of the work rather than the goods dealt with. The difficult question will always be when this change is a change in the 'kind' of work.

The next problem has been answered by the courts. It is not infrequent that an employer should anticipate that the uneconomic nature of his operations will lead to eventual redundancy. In face of this he may offer his employees new contracts and, in the event of them not accepting, dismiss them. It cannot be said that they have been dismissed for refusing to do a job they were contractually bound to do, since this is not the case. It seems reasonable to argue that the dismissal was for redundancy. The NIRC has rejected this view, which had been taken in earlier decisions. The present approach is that, however uneconomic the job, the requirement for it still exists. The fact that there is now only a requirement for it to be carried out on different terms of employment is irrelevant within the definition of redundancy. It would now seem that termination of contract in such a case would be unfair.

It has been said that if there is a replacement it is very difficult to show that the dismissal was for redundancy. As the case of the barmaid shows it should not be considered impossible. Suppose the facts of the above argument and ask whether redundancy was inevitable if, for instance, a male employee does not take a cut in salary. He declines and is dismissed and replaced by a lower-paid female employee, doing exactly the same job. Up to now it has usually be said that when replacement is achieved by the fact that jobs are doubled up so that two are being done by one person, there is no redundancy of the dismissed employee who used to do the other job. The fact that it was not alleged that the barmaid would inevitably have been redundant had she continued in the job she was doing demonstrates the strength of the idea that replacement is virtually fatal to a claim even though it is replacement on terms designed to avoid loss of the work because of the uneconomic nature of the previous employee. It may still be possible success-fully to argue, however, that the change of circumstance is suffi-cient to amount to a change of job; depending, for instance, on whether it can be said that the new arrangement is one of a lower status.

There is already one situation where replacement is not fatal to a claim and that occurs where the employee engaged to replace the person dismissed is himself moved from a redundant position with the same employer. Here tribunals, stretching a point a little, are sensibly enough prepared to say that the dismissal is because of redundancy.

Conversely, where there is no replacement, this fact is very strong evidence of redundancy. The position is, however, not so clear as the converse. As we have seen, one of a group of employees may be dismissed because he is too much of a craftsman to work fast enough to be economic. The work is there and his dismissal may well be held not to be for redundancy even though there is no replacement. In part this is often because the remaining members of the group absorb the work so that, in a sense, replacement may be said to have occurred.

LAY-OFF AND SHORT TIME

It is obvious that redundancy can be concealed by under-employ-ment. Indeed it was pointed out at the beginning of this chapter that one of the main purposes of the Act was to avoid such a situa-tion. It is accordingly expressly provided that an employee placed on short time (less than half his normal week's employment) or laid off for more than four consecutive weeks, or six weeks in any thirteen, may leave his employment but claim redundancy pay-ment as if he had been dismissed. The employee must give notice in writing to his employer of his intention within four weeks of the end of a period giving rise to such a claim. Provided the employee does then leave his employment after proper notice of termination, he may claim a redundancy payment unless the employer, within seven days of receipt of notice of the employee's intention, gives written notice of dispute of the claim. Unless this counter-notice is withdrawn in writing, the issue of whether a redundancy payment should be made must be determined by an industrial tribunal. Presumably the employer may dispute the facts. The Act also expressly provides that the employee's claim will fail if the employer can show that within four weeks of the original notice he would be able to offer at least thirteen consecutive weeks of full employment. Since most cases take about ten weeks to be dealt with by a tribunal this defence will be fairly easy to substantiate. the employee, of course, when making his original decision whether, in face of the employer's notice of dispute, to leave work and chance his claim, will have to speculate on this matter without the benefit of the information available to the employer. This is obviously a case where negotiation with the employer, against the background of the legal rights, is preferable to the blind reliance upon legal rights.

ALTERNATIVE OFFERS

In order to facilitate a rearrangement of work in face of redundancy the Act makes provision for the establishment of a defence to a claim for redundancy payment on the ground that a suitable alternative offer has been made. Two main situations are dealt with, both of which apply only where the offer has been made before the termination of the first contract:

(a) where the new terms do not differ from the old ones and the new contract will run straight on from the old one;

(b) where the new offer (which must be in writing) does differ from the old contract but is, none the less, an offer of suitable employment in relation to the employee, made before the termination of the former employment, and the new job will start, at the latest, within four weeks of the termination of the former job.

If the employee can be shown unreasonably to have rejected the offer in either case he will forfeit his right to receive a redundancy payment.

For those purposes such an offer can only be made by: the employer; an associated company; a person who has taken over the employer's business; the personal representatives of a deceased employer (in which case an eight-week period is permitted for the start of a new job).

The offer must be sufficiently fully detailed to enable the person to whom it is made to ascertain the nature of the job and its suitability, although the necessary details may be contained in several documents. It is not necessary that the offer (in writing where so required) should be made personally to each affected employee, but the claimant will succeed if he can show that it never reached him because steps which were short of those adequate to ensure this were taken. It follows that a notice on a company board will suffice if the employees could reasonably be expected to read and understand it. It is no defence to the employer to show that he took all reasonable steps. He must show that the offer was adequately communicated.

Some confusion may be felt as to the meaning of reasonable refusal in face of an offer held to be suitable. In practice no sharp division is made and tribunals not infrequently describe a factor as making an offer unsuitable when it would seem more rational to say that it renders a refusal reasonable, or vice versa. (So the bad health of the employee's wife has been held to make the job unsuitable.) Broadly speaking it may be said that the suitability of the offer is to be determined by looking at the circumstance of the job from the point of view of the person to whom it is offered, whilst the reasonableness of a refusal is tested by considering the circumstances of the person in relation to the job. Obviously on this formula the two will overlap. A job may become unsuitable solely because it is offered to a man with one arm. A refusal may be reasonable because, given the offeree's heart condition, the job is too heavy. The distinction is really only a means of reminding one-self that the facts are to be looked at from each of two directions, namely that of the employer having the job primarily in mind and that of the worker condsidering his own personal circumstances.

Obviously, tribunals may exercise a good deal of discretion, and there is some evidence that there has recently been a tendency to extend the view of the adaptability to be expected of the redundant employee. It will probably prove best to give some examples of single factors on either side in order to demonstrate the working of this provision, bearing in mind that the question is one of fact to be determined by the tribunal and that these are only guides and not invariable rules. It should also be borne in mind that the single factors are usually combined so as to produce a conflict or to support each other.

Suitable Offer	*Unsuitable Offer*
Some pay loss compensated by staff benefit	Loss of pay
	Loss of bonus, car, trade, contacts and status)
New job at a greater distance from home	New job involving change of residence (but this, usually considered under reasonableness, depends on circumstances)
	Adverse effect on health
	Downgrading in status (even if there is hope of improvement)
Job requiring retraining which employee might be expected to undertake	But not if new job involves strains which a man who had attained former job would not expect

Compensating factors

Prospect of rapid upgrading. Overtime possibilities to make up decrease in pay. Increase in wages, particularly in face of rise in travelling time.

Reasonable Refusal	*Unreasonable Refusal*
Desire to retain skill by continuing old job with another firm	
Loss of craft status in return for staff status	Job requiring overtime which would overlap with wife's job so that children would be alone
	Uncertainty about long-term security of job
Where job requires change of residence:	
Ill health of parents who live near; Children at critical stage in schooling	
Substantial wage drop if combined with other factors	Drop in wages on its own
Increases in travelling time	

Where an offer within the procedural provisions dealt with in this section, i.e. satisfying all the conditions for alternative offers excluding those of suitability and reasonableness (which acceptance, as it were, renders irrelevant), is accepted, employment will be considered continuous for the purpose of any future redundancy.

If an offer were accepted and then the employee found it unsuitable and voluntarily left, or the employer found the employee unable to cope with it and dismissed him for incompetence, no redundancy payment could be claimed. If, therefore, the redundant employee feels doubtful as to whether he will like, or be able to cope with, the new job offered, he would be well advised to accept it on a trial basis. If within the trial period either party terminates the contract because of such unsuitability the effect of the original acceptance is wiped out and a redundancy payment can be claimed based on the redundancy which caused the termination of the first job. The existence of and amount of a redundancy claim depends on the period of 'continuous' employment. We shall now examine the various provisions for overlooking what appear to be interruptions in this continuity.

CONTINUITY

1. CHANGE OF EMPLOYER

As a starting point it would, without some special provision, be generally correct to say that if an employer disposes of his business to another the employees could claim to have been dismissed for redundancy. Obviously the requirements of the employer for their services would have ceased and the new owner would be offering new contracts. The Redundancy Payments Act solves this problem, however, by providing that if there has been a 'transfer of business' the transferee is in the same position as the former employer to make an alternative offer. If he does so and it is accepted, the period of employment from one employer to another will be treated as continuous. The problem is to decide the difference between transfer of a business and transfer merely of some of its assets. Unfortunately the employee may have to settle this question as best he can for himself, for, if he accepts the new employment and, say, twelve months later is dismissed for redundancy by the second employer, the decision of a tribunal that there was no sufficient transfer will rob him of a claim against either. His claim against the first employer is barred after six months, whilst his claim against the second, since the two periods are not continuous, does not commence until he has been employed by the new employer for two years. Even then it excludes any compensation for what may have been a long period in the first employment.

It is necessary to decide what is the essential substance of the business. Thus merely to sell a factory is not a transfer of business but only of one of its assets. On the other hand if the factory is sold with its machinery as a going concern and is operated as such without a break on the same terms of production it may be held that it does not matter that the vendor continues to carry on his business elsewhere for he has sold a separate and identifiable business. This idea of business as 'a going concern' is the best available test. Very often, but not always, one of the key points to look for is the transfer of goodwill, that is to say, the surrender by the vendor of his right to continue to trade with his former customers or in the same locality. In the example just given, however, it was demonstrated that this is not necessary if there are other sufficient indications of the transfer of a complete going unit. Neither is it necessary in those industries such as agriculture where goodwill is not significant.

From what has been said, it is also clear that sale of part of a business will not suffice unless the part is clearly and completely separate.

Obviously, complete sale of the assets to a purchaser who intends to strip out the old machinery and start some other form of manufacture will not amount to a transfer of business. It is fatal to such a claim that a different type of product is being manufactured. Conversely, failure to transfer the machinery because the purchaser wishes to instal new machinery will not prevent a transfer of business if the same production is to be carried on with the same potential customers.

2. TEMPORARY BREAKS IN THE EMPLOYMENT CONTRACT
Whilst serving the same employer there may be times when the employee's contract is terminated but he later returns to the same employment. The Act makes provision for several such situations. If the contract continues, however, and is a contract which normally provides for twenty-one hours or more work a week, then the period of employment for redundancy payment will be taken to be continuous even if no work is actually done in any given week.

(a) Strikes
A strike is usually regarded at common law as a breach of contract, but there is no need for the employer to terminate the contracts of employment. If he does not do so and the strike took place after 6 July 1964, the period during which the employee was on strike

does not count as part of his period of employment, but it does not break continuity of the periods before and after the strike. If the employer does terminate the contracts during the strike, the question arises of whether it is part of the dispute procedure or whether it really was intended as a dismissal. The National Industrial Relations Court has decided that where a token dismissal of this sort occurs there will be no termination for purposes of redundancy payments until the employer finally decides not to reinstate the employees. Even if there were considered to have been a termination it might be held to have been 'temporary' within exception (c).

(b) Sickness

If an employee is off work sick, or his contractual employment is reduced below twenty-one hours a week, even if he has no further entitlement to sick pay, his contract will continue until he is actually dismissed. Until then no problem of continuity arises. From that time the Act allows twenty-six weeks of absence for sickness without contract to count as part of the period of continuous employment, provided that the employee returns to the former employment as soon as he is fit for it. It follows that he might take a light job in the interval while he is still unfit for the heavier employment but he must return as soon as it can be shown that he is fit. The most complicated situation likely to arise would be something like this:

Weeks 1–2	– Employee off work sick and on full pay;
Weeks 3–13	– Employee off work sick without pay;
End of week 13	– Notice of dismissal;
Weeks 14–28	– Employee off work;
Weeks 29–39	– Employee engaged on light work;
Week 40	– Employee certified fit and returns to former employment.

The period without contract with the original firm is just twenty-six weeks and so the whole of the time off work will count as continuous employment with the original employer. It has been held that absence because of pregnancy is not within the meaning of absence for sickness.

(c) *Temporary Cessation*

Presumably in order to avoid hardship to the employee whose contractual employment is interrupted only temporarily but who would, without some special provision, be forced to start again for purposes of redundancy payments, the Act provides that a period of 'temporary cessation of work' for the whole or part of a week shall count as a period of continuous employment. In view of the somewhat unexplained nature of this provision it is odd that the meaning of temporary cessation is nowhere defined in the Act. The House of Lords has, however, established that 'cessation' does not cover a case where the employee takes the initiative in leaving, but applies only where the employer terminates the employment of the particular employee. It is not necessary that all work of that kind shall have been terminated, but merely the work made available to the complainant. It was not made clear by the House of Lords whether only situations where the employer had no work to offer were covered or whether the provision extended to those situations where the employer chose not to offer work which he had available. There is no reason, based on the wording of the Act, for distinguishing these situations, and it seems from subsequent decisions that tribunals are not inclined to make such a distinction.

Whether, given a 'cessation', it is to be considered 'temporary' is a question of fact for the tribunal to decide. The method of making the decision has, however, been subject to comment by the High Court which, after considerable change of mind, has decided that the matter is to be determined by asking whether, in all the circumstances, the cessation has turned out to be temporary. This may not appear particularly helpful but it does make clear that the decision does not, as was first suggested, depend on the intention of the parties when the interruption began. Accordingly an interruption may initially be intended to be temporary, but broaden into a permanent one although, by chance, the parties eventually come together again. Conversely, the parties may initially intend to sever relations permanently, but unexpected circumstances may arise which produce a renewal of relations within, say, a few weeks. The fact that the employee takes another job in the interval is, of course, some indication of his own intention, although an equivocal one, but is otherwise irrelevant.

It may occur to the reader that it would be theoretically possible for someone who, for instance, regularly worked in a London hotel during the winter, and a seaside hotel (owned by another employer) in the summer, to claim that either job temporarily ceased while the other was being done. If this were so, two continuous periods of employment for the purposes of the Act would develop concurrently. It is, indeed, quite likely that this provision of the Act had the seasonal worker specially in mind, since otherwise that worker would never be entitled to a redundancy payment. If the situation were as clear cut as that set out, it might be difficult not to arrive at the suggested answer. Normally, however, the second period would be covered by a number of jobs so that no second presumption of continuity would arise. Otherwise a tribunal might decide that it was the employment, and not the cessation of it, which was temporary; that is to say that the claimant had been a temporary employee, even though he might have returned to the same firm over a number of years.

(d) Custom or arrangement
'If in any week the employee is, for the whole or part of the week absent from work in circumstances such that, by arrangement or custom he is regarded as continuing in the employment of his employer for all or any purposes . . .' the week in question is to count as a period of continuous employment for the purposes of the Act. At one time when the idea of temporary cessation was being construed much more widely than is now the case, it looked as if this provision could easily be absorbed within it. Now it is clear that it is a residual provision designed to pick up those cases where either the cessation could not reasonably be described as temporary or the initiative was not that of the employer. (Some authorities suggest that the matter should be looked at the other way so that temporary cessation is regarded as the residuary category. It does not seem to matter much.) The requirement is, however, that the cessation must be, as it were, within the employee's rights by being permitted. It is probable that the agreement or custom must precede the cessation, so that subsequent ratification is not within the provision.

The sort of situation the provision has in mind is one, for instance, where an employee is on call in the sense that the employer who has a job to be done may require the worker to enter into a contract of employment while such a job is done. It is probable that in this situation it does not matter whether it is the job that is interrupted or the interruption which is broken by the job because the provision merely talks of absence from work. It is also clear that in this provision the contemplation of a continued relationship is normal, whereas the others so far discussed normally contemplate a clear break in that relationship.

(e) *Absence abroad*
Periods when the employee was, for the whole or a part of a week, employed outside Great Britain do not count as part of the period of continuous employment, but such periods do not break continuity between the preceding and succeeding employment in Great Britain.

CALCULATION OF PAYMENT

The amount of redundancy payment to which an employee dismissed for redundancy is entitled is determined by reference to a normal week's pay, assessed at the end of the period of employment.

(a) A *time worker*, that is one who is paid according to the amount of time he works, who works a standard fixed week without overtime presents a simple position. The last week of employment is taken, assumed to be a week of full employment, and the wage for the full standard week (i.e. the standard hourly rate multiplied by the standard hours) is multiplied by the appropriate number of years of service to produce the total amount of compensation.

(b) A *piece-worker* who, under his contract, has a fixed working week is treated in the same way on the assumption that there is enough work to fill up the fixed hours. His hourly pay is assessed by dividing the amount earned in the four weeks immediately preceding termination by the number of hours actually worked. This means, of course, that the piece-worker will suffer from any decline in work in that period. Even weeks on short time are counted so long as some work is done.

OVERTIME
In both the above cases the working of overtime introduces a complicating factor.
(a) where a standard week is fixed with overtime payment if it is

exceeded that overtime is ignored in the calculation which is based solely on the standard week;

(b) if the contract fixes a number of hours overtime on top of the standard week the whole period is counted but disregarding any overtime premium, i.e. the extra amount above the normal hourly rate paid for overtime hours.

It should be observed that even if overtime is compulsory it will be ignored if the standard week is specified. There is, however, a very extensive case law on the question of when overtime is compulsory and when it is voluntary, and also upon the determination of whether a fixed week includes or excludes overtime. It is impossible to deal with it here and the reader should refer to Grunfeld on *Redundancy*.

A *'week's pay'* is an uncertain concept and the tribunals and courts have had to consider claims for the inclusion of a number of factors in it. Firstly it is clear that it is gross earnings that will be taken into account so that no income tax and national insurance deductions will be made. (The redundancy payment when made is not subject to tax.) Commission or allowance which is contractually due and which does not vary with the amount of work done, will be included even if it is not due to be paid until a date which, as it turns out, is after the dismissal. A gratuitous bonus which, though habitual, is not bound to be paid by the employer will not be counted.

Specific travelling allowances are not counted, but it may be that a round sum is expressed as 'expenses' when it is really payment for the job. An employee, for instance, may be paid for using his own car in his work. In such a situation the Divisional Court has been prepared to hold that the expenses are part of his remuneration. No very precise line can be drawn between the two forms. If in doubt, the item is worth putting before the tribunal for its consideration. The payment must, however, be quantified in monetary terms. So use of a flat will not be valued and added to the amount of money payment unless, indeed, the contract does this. If, for instance, the contract states that wages will be £20 plus a flat valued at £4 when there is an established rate for such workers of £24, it is likely that a tribunal would take both amounts together.

The rather anomalous lines of distinction continue in decisions on tips. Remuneration or pay, it has been held, is that which comes from the employer in return for the work. So tips paid direct to the employee by customers will not be quantified and added to the week's pay for the purpose of assessing compensation. If, however, the tip is expressed as a gratuity in the bill and is then paid out by the employer, it will be counted.

If after he has left employment a retrospective pay rise is granted which would have been payable to the claimant, it should be taken into account. He can therefore make a supplementary application (within the permitted time) even if the redundancy compensation has already been paid.

SHIFT AND ROTA WORKERS

An employee whose times of working during the day or night differed from week to week during the last twelve weeks or longer so that the amount payable varied from one week to another is classed as a shift or rota worker. In this case the week's pay is calculated by multiplying the average weekly hours over the last twelve weeks before termination by the average hourly rate of remuneration. Weeks in which no remuneration is paid are replaced by earlier weeks to make up the number to twelve. Only remuneration actually paid for work done is taken into account and items such as payment for a guaranteed week or premium rates are discounted.

NO FIXED HOURS

An employee with no fixed hours is treated in the same way, save that weeks where less than twenty-one hours are worked are replaced but only so as to bring the number up to eight.

Once the appropriate week's pay has been determined, this is multiplied by the weighted number of year's seniority of the claimant according to the following table.

For years of employment between the ages of 18 and 21 – $\frac{1}{2}$ week's pay

For years of employment between the ages of 21 and 40 – 1 week's pay

For years of employment between the ages of 40 and 64 – $1\frac{1}{2}$ weeks' pay

The total number of years' service that can be counted is twenty, but these can be the most beneficial so that the maximum number of weeks' pay that can be received is thirty. No pay over £40 per week can be counted, so that the absolute maximum payment would be £1,200. During the final year before normal retirement however (59–60 in the case of a woman, 64–65 in the case of a man), the amount due is reduced by one-twelfth for each month of that year. So an employee on the normal retirement age receives no redundancy payment.

An employee will not suffer from the bankruptcy of his employer because it is provided that in such a case the compensation due can be recovered from the Department of Employment which will then have the right to proceed for it in the bankruptcy proceedings.

ALTERNATIVE SCHEMES

'If at any time there is in force an agreement between one or more employers or organizations of employers and one or more trade unions [in the sense of organizations of workers] representing employees, whereby employees to whom the agreement applies have a right in certain circumstances to payments on the termination of their contracts of employment, and, on the application of all the parties to the agreement, the [Secretary of State] having regard to the provisions of the agreement, is satisfied that [the obligation to make payments under the Act] should not apply to those employees, he may make an order under this section in respect of that agreement.'

Under this provision, therefore, joint applications for the exemption of schemes such as early payment of pensions may be made. Applications can be made in the same way, or on the initiative of the Secretary of State, for revocation of the exemption.

While the exemption order is in force the voluntary scheme takes the place of the statutory scheme, but disputes as to entitlement to payment must be taken to an industrial tribunal. Payments made under approved alternative schemes qualify for the rebate payable under the statutory scheme to the employer, which is currently 50 per cent of the total compensation.

Chapter 13

Compensation for Industrial Injury

The purpose of this chapter is to provide an understanding of how the law operates in considering claims for compensation for industrial injury rather than, as in previous chapters, to answer the more important legal questions arising from the relevant claim. In cases of industrial injury the trade union official or member must rely on his union and its legal services even more than in other fields. Many cases are simple enough, but the minority in which difficult problems arise could not be dealt with in a chapter of this size. This is, of course, true of the more detailed points which might arise under any of the other headings dealt with, but in these cases a general framework of explanation can safely be attempted, while here any attempt to solve a particular problem from a general framework might very well be misleading.

THE NATURE OF LIABILITY

There is in English common law no general rule governing compensation in cases of industrial injury. It is not, for instance, possible to conclude that compensation must be available once there has been an injury at work. At common law compensation is only obtained when someone can be shown to have been at fault in creating the situation which led to the injury. Many injured persons would, therefore, be without any form of compensation were it not for the system of National Insurance (Industrial Injuries) benefits (and its predecessor, the Workmen's Compensation Acts) which provides standard compensation for industrial injuries from a central fund irrespective of any question of fault. The injured workman may claim both at common law and under the national insurance scheme. His common law compensation will be reduced by one-half of his estimated national insurance compensation in the first five years.

His common law action may itself be divided into three separate elements which we will call Direct Negligence, Vicarious Liability and Breach of Statutory Duty. We will examine these in more detail, but it is worth observing how one may supplement another. There is now recognized an almost universal duty on everyone to take reasonable care to protect from physical injury anyone they can reasonably foresee as likely to be injured by the effects of an absence of such care. An employer, therefore, will owe a duty of care under this broad general principle to his employees, to self-employed people working for him, and (for the condition of his premises and the operations thereon) to visitors. He will even owe a similar duty to the passer-by in the street who, for instance, may be struck by something thrown from his window. Though this action is called 'negligence', the same liability attaches to deliberate acts as to accidents. The duty is one to take reasonable care to prevent injury.

In the past the generality of this duty has not been so widely recognized, and the books and cases still talk as if subdivisions like 'employer's liability' and 'occupier's liability' raised important points of distinction. Employer's liability is even sometimes still subdivided into liability to provide safe premises, safe plant, competent employees and a safe system of work. These are, no doubt, useful headings under which to group the cases, but they no longer represent the limits of liability if, indeed, they were ever intended so to do. It is, however, correct to say that the care reasonably to be expected of an employer in relation to his employees is greater than that expected, for example, of a member of the public to other members of the public in the street, or of the householder to visitors on his premises. So an employee will virtually never use the Occupier's Liability Act against his employer because the common law of negligence offers him more protection.

The employer is usually a limited company. Although the average employee regards management, or at least senior management, as the employer, they are, more often than not, fellow employees. The actions of the disembodied employer in carrying out his duty of care are, therefore, delegated to individuals who work for him. The law is quite plain, however, that it is no defence to an employer to say that he left the duty in someone else's hands. The question is always: has the employer shown reasonable care? It is, of course, reasonable for him to employ people to exercise this duty but, having done so, he (that is the company) must take reasonable care to see that they are qualified to do the job and do it properly. An improperly trained supervisor may be negligent himself. His employer will also be negligent in putting him on a job he was not qualified to perform. If he is qualified but is merely careless, the employer may still be directly liable if he knew or should have known of this tendency and taken steps to guard against it. But one reaches the point where the employer has done everything he could reasonably be expected to do to prevent the fault, which none the less occurs. A well-known example of this situation in the past occurred where the employer obtained a machine or tool from a thoroughly competent manufacturer. When used, however, it was found that the machine or tool had a defect which the employer could not reasonably be expected to have discovered by examination or tests and, as a result, the operator was injured. The employer is, as we have said, under a duty to take reasonable care to supply safe tools or machinery. He cannot say that he has entrusted the supply to others but he can say that, by going to a competent contractor and making such examination and tests (if any) as were reasonable, he had carried out his duty. In the case of faulty machines, tools and equipment used in the course of employment this position has recently been reversed by statute and the employer made liable in all cases, whether he was negligent or not. This was done because it was thought better that the employer should be left to recover his loss from the supplier with whom he had a contract than that the worker should have the difficult task of proving that the manufacturer had been negligent. The common law position holds good in other cases so that, for instance, the employer who has taken all reasonable steps will not be directly liable for his own negligence if an employee causes injury by his unforeseeable negligence.

In this case the vicarious liability of the employer for the faults of others enters the picture. Since many cases of alleged direct liability of an employer involve, as we have shown, the actual negligence of another employee, the two matters are often alleged together. It will not, of course, be possible to obtain double damages, but it will mean that if the case fails on one ground it may succeed on the other. Vicarious liability may not always be available simply because of the technical rules which govern it and in particular the rule that an employer is only liable for the negligence of an employee when the employee is 'acting in the course of his employment'. Finally, vicarious liability may be the only ground of liability worth pleading because it is apparent that the employer has done everything he reasonably could and the fault is entirely that of an individual employee. A person injured by this fault may, none the less, bring his action against the employer because the law will hold the employer liable for the negligence of employees acting in the course of their employment. Socially this is a very useful doctrine because it means in practice that few people bring their action, as they are entitled to do, against the negligent employee. He is not insured and will almost certainly be unable to pay the damages awarded against him. A plaintiff will, therefore, always be advised to bring his action against the employer if possible. Employers' insurance companies have virtually all undertaken not to use their right to seek an indemnity from the negligent employee whose employer is found vicariously liable. So in practice one arrives at a position where, to a large extent, the enterprise bears the liability for the individuals it employs.

To pause at this stage to give an example of how these various heads of liability will operate:

A is a factory owner who desires some repair work to be done. He draws up the specifications and generally organizes the operation but engages two specialist contractors to do the work. X, the employee of contractor B, is injured by the negligence of Y, an employee of contractor C. Contractor B has taken no steps to guard against the possibility of this situation arising and A has merely left the organization of the site and the work on it to B and C.

It is quite likely that A will be held liable for negligence in that he owed to those he knew would be on his site a duty to take reasonable steps to see that the work was properly organized. B will be liable as an employer, but on exactly the same principle. It may be, however, that a higher degree of care might be expected of B than of A, and if blame is being apportioned A might bear less liability than B. C could be liable on the same basis as A but it is more likely that C will be held vicariously liable for the negligence of his employee.

In addition to these forms of liability any person may be liable in a civil action for damages if injury is caused to another by that person's default in performance of a statutory duty designed to protect the other. In employment the most obvious example of this arises from breaches of duty under the Factories Act and similar legislation covering mines, quarries, shops, offices, railway premises, agriculture and merchant shipping. Here statute obliges an employer, for instance, to securely guard dangerous machinery. It is obvious that this is designed to protect those working in the appropriate premises. The Act may provide a criminal penalty for breach of the duty, but if an individual worker is injured because of this breach he will succeed in an action for compensatory damages for his injury.

It may well be that an action for breach of statutory duty will succeed where actions based on negligence fail. This is usually because the Acts impose higher basic standards. So the duty to fence dangerous machinery contained in the Factories Act is described as 'absolute'. Apart from modification by regulations issued under the Act there is no defence that no fence could reasonably be provided, or that the fence was as safe as it was reasonable to make it. Apart from such modifications by regulations it is, for instance, true to say that if a fence is put over a grindstone leaving a one inch gap between the bottom of the fence and the table on which the workpiece is placed there is a breach of statutory requirement because the stone is not securely fenced. If proof of this is needed, the fact that the operative inserted his thumb under the fence and touched the grindstone is enough. It is useless for the employer to protest that this must mean that he cannot comply with the Act and continue to use the grindstone. On the other hand there are situations where the Act will afford no basis of action, whilst negligence might. These depend largely on the interpretation of the scope of the statutory requirements. The fencing requirement in the Factories Act, for instance, is that every dangerous part of a machine must be securely fenced. It has been established by the courts that a failure to fence dangerous material being worked in the machine is not a breach of the Act, unless the danger arises from interaction between the machine and the material in the normal course of operation, e.g. a dangerous nip created when steel bars are fed through banks of rollers. A failure to fence against dangers from material may, however, give rise to an action for negligence if the standard of reasonable care is not satisfied.

As with negligence, an employer may not delegate his duty under a statute. If the standard of statutory duty is that something should be done 'so far as is reasonably practicable', it may be that casual mistakes or negligence by an employee who is carrying out the task of performing the duty will not be considered a breach by the employer. He may be considered to have taken all reasonably practicable steps to see that the job was done properly; although it is worth remarking that 'reasonable practicability' imposes a high standard than 'reasonable care'. If, however, the requirement is absolute, the duty must be carried out and the mere fact that it has not been performed renders the employer liable.

It is proposed now merely to draw attention to some of the more important points under each of three heads of vicarious liability, negligence and breach of statutory duty.

VICARIOUS LIABILITY

An employer will be liable for the civil wrongs (and, primarily, the negligence) of his employee if the wrong is committed by the employee in the course of his employment. Thus vicarious liability for most practical purposes can be regarded as limited to liability for employees. It does not extend to self-employed workers. We have not considered the definition of an employee so far, and it will be necessary very briefly to do so now.

Originally the courts defined an employee as one who was subject to the orders of an employer as to the manner (as distinct from the end result) of his work. Over the years this was given a less nineteenth-century air by substituting 'control' for 'orders' and replacing the idea of that control actually being exercised by the right to exercise it. Even so it became obvious, first with professional and then with skilled employees, that a search for a right of control was akin to looking for a mirage. One pretended it could be there and then purported to find it. Because of this the courts tried to find some real substance, suggesting that an employee is one who comes within the employer's organizational structure. This is too vague to be very satisfactory and the courts soon discarded it in favour of an attempt to compile a list of the normal indications of employment, such as payment of regular wages, stamping of cards, the right to dismiss, and so on. Some of these may seem to beg the question. Whether a person's card is stamped or whether he does it himself depends in the last resort on whether he is employed or self-employed. None the less the fact that some-one does it for him at least indicates that he is regarded by himself and that person as employed. So we might add to our list of indications that of the intention of the parties. It is, of course, only evidence, like all the other factors, because both parties may have got it wrong, but it is some help. Finally the courts adopted a two-stage approach saying, in effect, that one first decided on general impressions such as this what type of contract appeared to have been created, asking primarily for a distinction between the dependent worker and the small businessman. Then the court would seek to weigh those factors for or against that prima facie conclusion. Obviously this is a very imprecise method, but it is probably the best possible. The outcome may well depend on the purpose for which the definition is required. Dependence on another may be more significant when deciding upon entitlement to unemployment benefit; control may be more important when deciding on vicarious liability.

This element of difference of emphasis of particular factors for different purposes is made very clear by the courts when a question arises as to whether the loan of an employee to another employer has transferred the burden of vicarious liability. It is very difficult in such circumstances to imagine a situation in which the actual parties to the relationship of employer and employee have changed. Such a change would require the consent of the employee and transfer of many more of the indications of employment than is normal. The courts have made it clear that they will be satisfied that the burden has shifted if a sufficient degree of control has passed to the borrower. It follows from this, and the courts have pointed out the proposition, that in the case of a skilled man, especially one lent with expensive equipment, it will be difficult to prove a sufficient transfer of control.

The employer is only held vicariously liable where the employee was acting 'in the course of his employment' when he committed the wrong. It is pointless to look for any semblance of authority for his actual act, since an employer is not often likely to authorize a negligent act. What the courts do is first to draw the lines of a broad framework of authorization. That is to say, they ask what the employee is employed to do. When that is determined, vicarious liability will attach to his employer whatever the employee does within that framework, however much the detail of his job may forbid him to act in that way. Suppose, for instance, the employee is employed to drive a lorry but forbidden to give lifts. The framework of authorization in which he works is driving a lorry. So long as he is doing that, the fact that he does it contrary to orders by having an unauthorized person with him in the cab will not remove the employer's vicarious liability if, for instance, the driver is negligent and injures the passenger.

Some acts may, however, be so excessive as to be outside even this broad framework. This may happen in two main ways. It may be that what the employee does does not even approach the boundaries of his job. One of the more pleasant phrases used by lawyers puts the position well. The employee is said to be 'on a frolic of his own'. The lorry driver who, coming to a crossing at which the traffic lights have failed, kindly parks his lorry and undertakes direction of traffic, will probably not render his employer liable if two vehicles collide in the middle through his negligence. Again, a garage attendant, having supplied a customer with petrol and watched him drive away, only to return to complain of the attendant's behaviour, would not be within the scope of his job in relation to that customer if he assaulted him. It could not be said that he was behaving as a garage attendant, however badly. Secondly it may be possible to argue that the detailed action was within the broad job heading but that it was so obviously an excessive exercise of authority as to remove it beyond the boundaries. An attendant at a dance hall, for instance, may be employed to deal with unruly elements. If he supposes a person to be within this definition and pursues him out of the hall he will cease to be within the course of his employment if he assaults that person outside the hall after it has become clear that the person is not unruly.

The crucial point is to discover the way in which the courts will seek to decide the basic broad framework of the job. The lawyer, as was pointed out in the first chapter, looks for the law in previous cases. If one goes back far enough and with sufficient care it is possible to find cases which suggest that this should be defined narrowly. In one, some carters were held only to be employed to transport material from point A to point C. When they dumped the material at the intermediate point B, in order to speed their journey, they were held not to be in the course of their employ ment. These days, however, this narrow approach will not be adopted. Indeed, very much the reverse is true. Recently it was held that a lorry driver is also employed to look after the employer's property. So he was acting in the course of his employment when he permitted an unqualified person to drive the lorry. The courts have, however, moved even further than this.

A was a forklift truck driver in a factory. He was driving his truck back to the warehouse where it was kept when not in use when he found, parked on the ramp leading up to the warehouse doors, a five-ton diesel lorry. He left his truck and, without warning to the men unloading the lorry, entered its cab with a view to moving the lorry. He started the engine and the lorry moved sharply backwards crushing one of the men unloading it. The lorry driver had thoughtfully left the gears in reverse so that the lorry should not run down the ramp if the brakes failed to hold it.

The Court held that A was in the course of his employment. On the facts this may not cause undue surprise. He was, after all, employed to return his truck to the warehouse and he was taking steps to do so. The Court of Appeal said, however, that where a man is on his employer's premises in normal working hours there is a presumption that he is in the course of his employment. That is to say that in such a situation it is for the employer resisting the imposition of vicarious liability to prove the contrary and not, as is usually the case, for the injured person alleging vicarious liability to prove a course of employment.

It should be observed that, in the above example, A was undoubtedly acting in his employer's interests. It is, however, not necessary in order to establish vicarious liability to show that this is so. On the other hand it is a factor that will weigh with a court. One is bound to ask whether the court would have been so keen to raise the presumption if the act had been against the employer's interest.

Though it is primarily a matter for the lawyer arguing the case, the trade union official or the injured worker involved should make sure that the circumstances of his industry are clearly understood. Judges grasp situations very well considering that few of them have ever driven a lorry or worked in a factory, but they should be assisted as much as possible. In one case, for instance, an employer appeared to give evidence and asserted that his employees had his permission to use for virtually any purpose the van in which one of them had been killed. He was attempting to show that they were in the course of their employment as demolition workers when, having spent most of the day at, or travelling to or from, a public house, they crashed the van on the final journey back to the site to pick up a colleague who had been left to hold the fort. The employer, who was insured, was no doubt engaged in some advanced industrial relations and the Court of Appeal refused to accept his contention. Had it been more clearly explained that in certain sections of the demolition industry it is common to fix a time for the job and leave the workers to do it when they see fit, he might have been believed.

NEGLIGENCE

The key to the enquiry as to whether the employer has been directly negligent is whether he can be said to have taken, deliberately or accidentally, sufficient care, either by action or inaction, to avoid injury to the complainant.

The duty is owed to the individual and so must take into account characteristics which were known or could reasonably be foreseen. It is, for instance, reasonably foreseeable that any employee will himself be careless. Reasonable steps must, therefore, be taken to protect him from his own folly, carelessness or tiredness. An employee with only one good eye risks much more severe injury than the employee with two good eyes. The employer knows this and so, because negligence is essentially a reasonable balancing of risk and feasible measures of prevention, must take greater care of him. A warning notice may, in some cases, be sufficient to satisfy the duty of care. It would not be so if the employee were known to be unable to read. The employer would have to show that the danger had been brought to the employee's notice in some other way. The employer's duty in this branch of the law does not extend beyond what is reasonable. He is not to assume that his employees are unfit to be out on their own. He is, perhaps surprisingly, not expected to exhort them to use the safety devices that they know are readily available for their protection.

If safety precautions are reasonably necessary, however, the employer must take reasonable steps to see that they are taken, and that reasonably necessary safety devices are provided. Some devices cannot be considered to be provided if they are not as readily available as might reasonably be expected. Obviously some are expensive or liable to be stolen and must be kept locked up while not in use. If, however, access is not reasonably easy, the courts will hold that they have not been provided. The same may be true if they are at the other end of the factory so that it would be unreasonable to expect an operative to leave his machine for so long as is necessary to find them. The type of safety device is also a matter for discussion. An employer is expected to provide the best one reasonably available. As has been said, negligence is essentially a matter of balancing risk and prevention methods, and a very expensive device will be held unnecessary if the risk is small. The method by which the courts assess the factors is very well illustrated by some fairly straightforward facts which arose in one case.

A operated an engineering factory, part of which was flooded one morning by an unusually heavy storm. The water lifted grease, which normally flowed into ducts in the floor, and, as it subsided, deposited the grease on the floor and the duckboards which covered it in places. A spread a large quantity of sawdust, but his supplies ran out before the whole of the affected areas had been treated. During the afternoon an operative, while obtaining tea from an urn, slipped on the grease and was injured.

It was held that A had made reasonable provision of sawdust bearing in mind the unlikelihood of the event. A was not unreasonable in deciding to continue to operate the factory rather than cease production while the floors were cleaned, bearing in mind the very low risk (as it appeared to the court) of such an accident occurring.

In considering negligence cases, the determination of what is reasonable depends a great deal on what is normal practice. This is not to say that evidence that a safety precaution is in accordance with normal practice will always lead to the conclusion that no more is reasonably to be expected. On the other hand, a decision the other way means that the normal practice adopted, probably by large numbers of employers for some time, has been, and is, negligent. It will, therefore, be difficult to persuade a court to reject the sufficiency of normal practice.

A somewhat similar problem arises when a practice is approved, for instance by a joint safety committee. Unfortunately this has led many trade union officials to consider whether they should continue to serve on such safety committees so as to give approval to safety precautions which may turn out to be inadequate to prevent injury. There is no doubt that the existence of such approval makes proof of reasonableness more easy, but it probably goes no further than that. If a safety device was one that would have been approved had the machinery for approval been operated it is one that the courts would be very likely to consider to satisfy the duty of reasonable care.

The employer's duty of care exists irrespective of whether the employee is in the course of employment or not; although it is, of course, true to say that an employer may have little difficulty in showing that he could not reasonably foresee and guard against a departure from the course of employment. The duty also extends to premises, other than his own, upon which his employees are working; although again, what can reasonably be expected from him on the premises of another may be much less than on his own property. It should not be forgotten that an employer, even operating on another's premises, owes a duty of care to others whom he could reasonably foresee as likely to become involved in his operations.

The plaintiff, in order to establish his claim, must show that his injury was caused by the defendant's negligence. In its simplest forms this is an obvious proposition. It is also true that no great difficulty is produced where the injury results from the negligence of two people, even if one of them is the injured person himself. Where the negligence of two separate persons other than the plaintiff contributes to his injury, he may bring his action against either of them for the whole injury. Normally he would sue both in the same action. If one turned out to have some form of defence he would succeed against the other. If he chooses only to sue one, he cannot be faced with the argument that the other is also involved. That is a matter purely between the two negligent persons (lawyers call them joint tortfeasors), who can claim contribution from each other.

Where the plaintiff is to blame in part for his own injury, a different principle applies. The courts will apportion the blame on a principle known as contributory negligence. It must be shown that the injured person has himself been negligent and not merely made a slip which he could not reasonably avoid. For this reason the courts have shown some reluctance to hold a workman partly to blame for the effects merely of monotony or tiredness. It is fair to say that the courts on this issue show a very realistic appreciation of the pressures and strains upon an employee, and certainly do not expect him to behave impeccably. If he is considered partly to blame for his injury this is expressed as a proportionate reduction in the amount of compensation he would otherwise receive. Obviously such an assessment can only be a rough estimate.

Finally, however, the question may be raised of whether the alleged negligent act has contributed at all to the injury. Suppose, for instance, that A is negligent towards B, and B, in order to avoid the consequences, takes action which is negligent in respect of C, who is injured by B's act. Can C claim against A? It is impossible in a chapter of this nature to attempt any useful answer to the complications which arise out of this question of causation. The advice of a lawyer would always be essential because almost every fact situation is different from any other. Only two major points can be made here. A plaintiff who has reacted negligently to the negligence of the employer may find the courts prepared to say that the plaintiff's negligence is the sole cause of his injury and that the employer's previous fault merely produced the situation providing the explanation of why the plaintiff took action at all. Suppose, for instance, that the employer fails to provide proper equipment. He is obviously negligent. But if, following this, a skilled and experienced man with full knowledge of the risk finds his own inadequate equipment and uses it, he may be held to be the sole cause of his own injury. It would be otherwise if the job were a 'one-off' situation, or the employee had insufficient skill or experience. In that event he would, at most, be considered contributorily negligent.

More startling is the proposition that if safety equipment is not provided because the employer knows that his employees will not use it, it cannot be said that the failure to provide it has caused the accident. The courts have accepted the argument that as the accident would have happened even if the safety equipment had been provided, it cannot be said that it resulted from such failure. In some cases the courts showed themselves strangely ready to infer, in cases where death had resulted, that the deceased would not have used the safety device. Such inference has been drawn from the normal attitude in the trade of not using it and the absence of any suggestion that the injured workman's attitude would have been different. There have, however, been other cases, which it is suggested should be followed, where there has been no such readiness to make such an inference without clear evidence.

BREACH OF STATUTORY DUTY

It is impossible in one section of a single chapter to make even a token attempt to summarize the range of statutory safety, health and welfare provisions that exist. Some attempt to provide a form of index of the general structure of the major statutes dealing with safety is given at the end of this chapter. Here all that will be attempted is to give some idea of the type of pitfall that the lawyer will be searching to avoid; in order that the union official or individual supplying him with the facts of a case may appreciate the complexity of the information that may be required. For this purpose we will use only the safety provisions of the Factories Act 1961.

There is no general law applicable to all workplaces and so the first problem is to ascertain that one is dealing with a workplace within the particular definition covered by the statute. The definition of a factory is very lengthy, but basically a factory must consist of a place (though not necessarily a building) where people are employed to manufacture, clean, finish or otherwise prepare goods for the purpose of profit. A factory will include any building incidental to these purposes within the general factory boundary. If, however, there is an ancillary building outside that boundary, like a pumping station, it will have to be a factory in its own right. A pumping station of this type would not be a factory because nothing is done to the goods which pass through it. Building and construction sites are specifically brought within the statutory definition of a factory, although not all the statutory provisions are applied to them.

The duty to observe the Factories Act rests primarily, but not exclusively, on the 'occupier' who will usually be the owner and so, normally, the employing company. Many of the detailed regulations made under the Act applying to particular industries or processes, however, impose the duty on others such as site contractors and 'persons performing' the work. Other statutes use other terms like 'employer'. Each of these words raises its own problems of definition and the lawyer must ensure, so far as he is able, that his action is brought against the person upon whom the duty is laid, otherwise he will have to start afresh. Whereas the main duty on the occupier may oblige him to supply the safety device and even to ensure that it is used, the Act also requires the individual worker not wilfully to interfere with or misuse such safety devices. It will be seen that these duties overlap. The occupier who has provided the device will have failed to ensure its use if an employee wilfully interferes with the device as, for instance, by taking a guard off a machine. So far as an action for damages is concerned this overlap will produce a situation, similar to that arising where there has been contributory negligence, in which the damage must be apportioned.

The duty under the Act is to protect all those on the premises for the purposes of the work done there. This applies whether they are employees or self-employed persons and also for whoever they are primarily working. It has been held, however, that the duty does not extend to such workers as brigade firemen or policemen on the premises for their normal business, since they are not there for the purposes of the factory.

The Factories Act establishes a system of inspection and provides criminal penalties for breach of the Act. As we said at the beginning of this chapter, the possibility of civil action for damages for injury is not mentioned in the Act but is superimposed by implication. There are about 600 inspectors with almost 300,000 factory premises, within the statutory definition, to visit. The policy is to pay frequent visits to trouble spots rather than to attempt to visit every factory at regular intervals. The policy of the inspectorate is, however, to use the criminal sanction very sparingly. Only about 2,500 prosecutions each year are brought and although they almost always result in prosecutions this is a minute fraction of the number of infringements recorded by inspectors, let alone the number that occur. In one survey of 200 firms over a period of four and a half years inspectors noted 3,800 violations. No consideration of any sort was made in 3,140 of them. Of the remaining 660, notification of a matter requiring attention was given in 74·5 per cent of the cases and prosecution was undertaken, even by the end of the period, in only 10 cases, or 1·5 per cent of those which were even considered for action. This is a considered policy. The view is taken that if fines are exacted as a matter of course they will merely be regarded as a charge upon production, whereas if they are reserved for serious breaches they will carry a moral stigma which will act as a better deterrent. So although a number of the statutory duties are, as we have noted, absolute, criminal liability is only imposed where there is considerable moral fault. No doubt this policy is sound in principle but it seems not unreasonable to suggest that it has been carried too far. Examples can be found of blatant disregard of warnings of serious breach over a period of years where no prosecution by the inspectorate is in sight. It is worth pointing out that a private individual, such as a full-time district official, could bring a prosecution. The power is not reserved to the inspectors. The difficulty, which results in such a course being very rare indeed, is probably that of obtaining the necessary information. Inspectors have powers other than the bringing of a prosecution and in particular they may apply to a magistrate's court for an order to stop the use of a dangerous machine or of dangerous premises. There seems little reason why this power, at least in relation to a particular machine, should not be used more extensively than is at present the case.

Whether a criminal prosecution is brought or not, an individual injured because of breach of the statutory safety requirements can bring an action for compensation. Such a claim should, of course, be made if it seems to have a reasonable chance of success. It is as well, however, that the technical difficulties to be faced if the employer's insurance company decides to require that he contest the action should be understood. First of all it may be worth stating the obvious point that everything will depend on the evidence and that it is most important to acquire details of the state of the machine and the nature and cause of the injury. Section 14 of the Factories Act, the most famous provision in all the safety legislation, requires that every dangerous part of a machine shall be securely fenced. A later section requires the fence to be maintained and kept in position while the machine is in motion or in use. This may appear on the face of it to be relatively straightforward, but the following are some of the problems that arise:

MACHINE	Only covers 'factory machinery' in the sense of machines in use in the factory. So a machine being made or tested in the factory is not covered.
	Does not cover the non-mechanical aspects of the machine, e.g. those arising from a vehicular characteristic of movement as distinct from the mechanical operation of, say, the engine.

PART	Does not include material in the machine unless the danger is caused by interaction between the machine and the material in the normal course of operation.
DANGEROUS	No part is, as it were, inherently dangerous. A part is dangerous only if danger can reasonably be foreseen. Once some danger can be foreseen, however, the part is dangerous and it is irrelevant that what actually happens could not be foreseen.
SECURELY FENCED	Without much basis in the Act the courts have held that the requirement is only of a fence to keep the worker and his clothing out, and not a fence capable of keeping the machine in. This is despite the fact that many machines have a considerable tendency to throw pieces off.
MOTION OR USE	A machine may, obviously, be in motion without being in use, but the courts seem apt to hold that 'motion' in this context means something like the normal working speed; so that a machine being turned over by hand or by an 'inching' device is not within the requirement that the fence should be maintained.

It will readily be appreciated that one or other of these pitfalls may explain why it is wise to allege negligence as well as breach of statutory duty. Finally, breach of statutory duty suffers as much, if not (because of the technical requirements) more, than negligence from the problem of 'causation'. Suppose, for instance, that the Building Regulations require that stairways in unfurnished buildings should be provided with a handrail and that the stairway in question has none. A worker is climbing the stairs carrying a large sheet of glass. The wind blowing through the unfinished building catches the glass causing the worker to lose his balance and fall over the unguarded edge of the stair. A court held that the accident could not be said to arise out of the breach of statutory duty because the rail was not required to be on the open side. Had it been on the other side the workman would not, in the circumstances, have been able to use it to steady himself, so that he would have been just as likely to fall even if the statutory duty had been carried out.

FAULT LIABILITY

It will be appreciated that an injured workman may lose his chance to recover compensation under any of these heads simply because no one is at fault. Vicarious liability fills some of the gap in that provided he can show that some employee was to blame, the injured man does not have to show which one it was. Even so, it may reasonably be objected that the damage is the same and arises from employment whether there is fault or not. Several suggestions are current for a system of compensation for industrial injury irrespective of fault. Compensation would probably have to be paid from a central fund maintained from contributions into which also went the proceeds of any liability the administration of the fund could establish in cases where there was, in fact, fault. At the moment, in this country, the nearest approach to this system is under the National Insurance (Industrial Injuries) Act. No attempt will be made to examine the operation of that system here, but it may be pointed out that its existence adds yet another means of obtaining compensation to the list already examined, without achieving a comprehensive and reliable insurance against injury. The object of this chapter has been largely to explain the nature of the complexities of this area rather than to provide an answer in any specific situation. The final warning that should be conveyed again is that these complexities are such that an injured workman should never accept lay advice as to the likelihood of any claim succeeding, and should certainly never accept an offer of compensation to settle his claim, without taking reliable legal advice.

Comparative Index of Major
Statutory Provisions

Reference is to
section numbers

COMPARATIVE INDEX OF MAJOR

FACTORIES   MINES

	FACTORIES	MINES
Duty imposed on:	*Occupier*	*Owner*
	Owner of machinery used in factory and in certain respects, of tenement factories	Mine manager or under-manager 152
	Director, manager, secretary or other officer of company neglectfully facilitating, consenting to, or conniving at breach by company 155	Person in charge of part of mine affected by excessive concentrations of gas 79
	Parent of young person consenting to or conniving at employment in breach of statute 158	Surveyor where relevant 11
	Person employed if wilfully interfering with or misusing safety appliances or endangering himself 143	Certain permitted delegates of owners' duties 152
		Parent of young person consenting, conniving at or in wilful default in respect of employment in breach of statute 160
		Individual workmen Regs. and 51, 80, 89, 90, etc.
		Deputies 53
		Shotfirers
Duty to protect:	All persons working in the factory (Regulations may be limited to persons employed)	Persons employed
Defences	Owner of machinery may be substituted for occupier 163	That it was impracticable to avoid or prevent the contravention 157
	Breach of duty imposed on employed person and occupier not shown to have failed to take reasonable steps to prevent breach 155	To criminal proceedings for under-manager to show that breach took place in part of mine outside his jurisdiction 158
	Person charged may bring	To criminal proceedings for person prosecuted to

STATUTORY PROVISIONS

SHOPS AND OFFICES	AGRICULTURE
	NB. In agriculture, because the statute depends almost entirely on the making of regulations, account has been taken of regulations
Occupier	*Employer*
Owner of leased building in respect of common parts 42 and 43	
Director, manager, secretary or officer of company as for factories 65	Director, manager, officer, etc., of company as for factories 14
Any person wilfully and without reasonable cause doing anything likely to cause danger or removing equipment 27	Employees wilfully interfering with or misusing any safety equipment 13
Persons employed (under a contract of service)	Persons employed (under a contract of service)
To prove that the person charged used all due diligence to secure compliance 67	To prove that the person charged used all due diligence to secure compliance 16

COMPARATIVE INDEX OF MAJOR

FACTORIES	MINES
actual offender before court and prove that person charged had used all due diligence to enforce and that offence committed without his consent, connivance or wilful default 166	show that duty expressly imposed on someone else and that person prosecuted used all due diligence to secure compliance 156

SAFETY
Absolute duties

Secure fencing: Prime movers 12 Transmission machinery 13 Every dangerous part of other machinery 14 Substantial construction and constant maintenance of fence 16 Sound construction, adequate strength and proper maintenance of hoists and lifts 22; and chains and lifting tackle 26 Testing and thorough examination of chains and lifting tackle 26; and of cranes, etc. 27 Sound construction and maintenance of floors and steps, etc. 28; and of ladders Sound handrails 28 Provision of breathing apparatus in places where fumes likely 30 Sound and adequate steam boilers 32; maintenance and examination Sound and adequate steam receivers and containers 35 and air receivers 36	NB. All duties are limited by the general defence of practicability. Duties are very detailed and the following is a selection Provision and maintenance of safe access to every place of work 87 Safety in places where liability to fall ten feet 87 All parts and working gear of all machinery used as equipment of good construction, suitable material, adequate strength and free from patent defect 81 Every flywheel and dangerous exposed part of machinery securely fenced 82; fence properly maintained and kept in position Provision of two outlet shafts 21 and 24 with communication between them 23 Proper maintenance and availability of shaft machinery 29 Making and keeping safe of mine shafts and staple pits in use 30 Provision and proper maintenance of barriers

STATUTORY PROVISIONS (*cont.*)

SHOPS AND OFFICES   AGRICULTURE

Secure fencing: every dangerous part of any machinery   17

NB. This Act is operative by regulations made under the provisions of section 1

Sound construction and proper maintenance of floors, steps, passages, etc.   16

Provision and maintenance of hand rails on stairs   16

Fencing of stationary machinery, power take-offs and shafts
Substantial construction, proper maintenance and guarding of circular saws
Safety in relation to threshers and balers
Guarding of field machines
Field machines must be maintained so as to be safe in use
Handrails on stairs
Ladders, steps and trestles of good construction, sound material and properly maintained
Openings in floors must be guarded

COMPARATIVE INDEX OF MAJOR

	FACTORIES	MINES
	Fire escapes properly maintained and free from obstruction 41	at shaft entrances. Efficient barriers to impassable roads 31
Duties limited by practicability	Fencing of low vessels containing scalding, corrosive or poisonous liquids 18 Gates to hoist and lifts constructed before ·1937 22 Openings in floors 28 Prevention of dust explosions 31 Explosive gases in pipes or vessels 31 Prevention of inhalation of dust 63	Roads in good repair 34 Prevention of vehicles, animals, ropes and harness rubbing road walls 36 Prevention of walking in roads in use by mechanized vehicles Refuge holes in road walls 40 Special provisions for winding apparatus, explosives, support and adequate ventilation
Duties limited by reasonableness	Provision of fire escape 40	
Duties limited by reasonable practicability	Floors, steps, etc., free from obstruction or slipperiness 28 Safe means of access to place of work 28 Workplaces from which liable to fall more than 6 ft 6 in. 28 Requirements of special regulations under section 76	'Minimizing' of inflammable or injurious dust 74 Obligation on manager to make regulations as regards roads save where, in the circumstances, it would serve no object 37
Provision of suitable devices	Steam boilers 32 Steam receivers and containers 35; and air receivers 36 Protection of eyes 65	To prevent vehicles running away 41 Apparatus for carrying persons through unworkable roads 28 Suitable and sufficient lighting 61
HEALTH Absolute	Clean state of premises, free from effluvia 1 Lifting of weights likely to be injurious 72	

STATUTORY PROVISIONS (*cont.*)

SHOPS AND OFFICES	AGRICULTURE
Effective means of fire alarm 34	Employees must not sit on drawbars of field machines
	Children must not drive or ride on tractors, self-propelled machines or agricultural implements or drawbars
	Poisonous spraying
Openings in floors	
Appropriate means of fire fighting 38	
Provision of fire escapes 28	
Floors, steps, etc., free from obstruction or slipperiness 16	Each stairway and floor as safe as reasonably practicable
Clean premises, furniture and fittings	Young persons not to lift weights likely to injure 2
No accumulation of dirt 4	
Lifting of weights likely to injure 2	No employee to lift weight greater than 180 lb.

COMPARATIVE INDEX OF MAJOR

	FACTORIES	MINES
Provision of effective means	Drainage of floors likely to be wet 6	
Provision of sufficient or suitable standard or method	Removal of dirt and refuse 1 Ventilation 4 Lighting 5 Provision, cleaning and maintenance of sanitary conveniences 7 Certain provisions for underground rooms 69	Provision, cleaning and maintenance of sanitary conveniences 94
Specific or periodic	Washing of smooth walls 1 Repainting of walls 1 Weekly cleaning 1 Overcrowding 2	
Standard of reasonableness	Temperature 3	
Standard of practicability	Rendering harmless fumes and dust 4 Keeping windows clean 5	
WELFARE	Drinking water 57 Adequate and suitable washing facilities 58 Adequate and suitable accommodation and drying for clothes 59 Suitable seating facilities 60 First aid 61 Power to make regulations as to meals (prohibited in certain places), protective clothing, first aid rooms, seats, and supervision of employees	Adequate facilities for first aid 91 Power to make regulations for washing facilities, changing and drying rooms and canteens 96
Duties upon employees or persons working	Persons employed not wilfully to interfere with safety devices or misuse them or endanger themselves 143	Offence to lose safety lamp or to take matches, cigarettes, etc., into safety lamp area 65 and 66 Offence to remove, alter or

STATUTORY PROVISIONS (*cont.*)

SHOPS AND OFFICES   AGRICULTURE

Ventilation   7
Lighting   8
Provision, cleaning and proper main-   Provision, cleaning and proper
  tenance of sanitary conveniences   9   maintenance of sanitary con-
                                            veniences   3 and 5

Weekly cleaning   4
Overcrowding   5

Temperature. Opportunity for persons to warm themselves   6

Control of noise or vibrations
  (regulations)
Keeping windows clean   8

Drinking water   11

Adequate and suitable accommoda-
  tion and drying for clothes   12

Suitable seating facilities   13 and 14

First aid   24 and 26   First aid   6
Suitable eating facilities for persons
  taking meals in shops   15

No person wilfully and without   No employee wilfully to interfere with
  reasonable cause to do anything   or misuse any safety equipment 13
  likely to cause danger nor remove
  safety equipment   27

COMPARATIVE INDEX OF MAJOR

FACTORIES	MINES
	tamper with any safety device without permission 90
	Offence wilfully or negligently to act or omit to act in a matter affecting safety 90
Cleaning	Not to be done by women or young persons if risk of injury from moving part of that or another machine 20	
Training	Young persons working at designated machines 21	No person to be employed unless either properly instructed and competent or under instruction and supervision of someone who is 88

ADMINISTRATION

Inspection: Powers

FACTORIES	MINES
Enter and examine any factory or warehouse (with constable) 146 and 7	Enter and inspect any mine or rescue station (with constable) 145
Demand production of records	Demand production of records
Examine and enquire as to public health matters and to enter with medical officer of health and sanitary inspector 9	To demand facilities from persons within those area of activity the matter lies
To exercise such other powers as may be necessary	Question employees and to take samples
To question employees and require them to sign declaration of truth of statements	To order improvement of roads 34 and 35
Apply to magistrates for orders to stop use of machines or premises 54 and 55	To serve restrictive notice where mine is dangerous 146
	To take possession of dangerous machinery 145
	Sole power to conduct prosecutions 164
Conduct prosecutions 149	

STATUTORY PROVISIONS (*cont.*)

SHOPS AND OFFICES   AGRICULTURE

Not to be done by young person if
risk of injury from moving part   18

No person to work at specified
machines unless trained or under
supervision   19
Effective steps to instruct on escape
in case of fire   36

As for factories   Enter any agricultural land at all
                              reasonable hours (but not a dwell-
                              ing house without 24 hours' notice)
                              10
As for factories   Demand production of records, etc.
                              Undertake necessary examinations
As for factories   and enquiries

As for factories   53

As for factories

Apply to magistrates to prohibit   Serve notice requiring provision of
absolutely or until repair use of   safety requirements   3
machinery, premises or operations
causing risk of bodily injury or injury to health   22 and 32
Conduct prosecutions   70 and 71

COMPARATIVE INDEX OF MAJOR

	FACTORIES	MINES
Other inspection	Local authorities 8 Fire authorities 40 Medical 11 Factory inspector in conjunction with other authorities 9, 10, 41, 45	By panel of experienced persons representative of majority of persons at mine, either generally or after an accident 123
Certification	Fire 40 Underground rooms 69	Management 4
Miscellaneous	Notification 80-2, 137 Information and research 177 Formal investigation Keeping of records 140-2	Notification: plans 18, accidents 116 Formal investigation 121 and 122 Records 133-40

STATUTORY PROVISIONS *(cont.)*

SHOPS AND OFFICES
Fire authority   30

AGRICULTURE
Sanitary inspectors with above-mentioned powers   11

Fire   29

Notification of accidents   48
Information   49 and 50

Notification of accidents   8

Keeping of records

Keeping of records   8

Labour Law Books

The following list of books is, of course, by no means complete. It is offered as representing a comprehensive cover of the subjects dealt with in this book without too much repetition and with an endeavour to select some of the best books on each topic. This is an invidious task and readers may have their own differing views, in which case they should obviously be followed. The list is designed to be generally useful in the branch office.

General
C. D. DRAKE *Labour Law* Sweet and Maxwell, 1969 or R. W. RIDEOUT *Principles of Labour Law* Sweet and Maxwell, 1972 or SIR W. M. COOPER AND J. C. WOOD (ed.) *Outlines of Industrial Law* Butterworth, 1972
K. W. WEDDERBURN *Cases and Materials on Labour Law* Cambridge University Press
K. W. WEDDERBURN *The Worker and the Law* Penguin, 1971
An Encyclopaedia of Labour Law Sweet and Maxwell, 1972. Looseleaf. Very useful for reference, but expensive.

The Industrial Relations Act
C. CRABTREE *The Industrial Relations Act* Charles Knight, 1971 or N. SELWYN *Guide to the Industrial Relations Act* Butterworth, 1971
The free guide from the Department of Employment is also very good.

Collective Bargaining – The Voluntary System
K.W. WEDDERBURN AND P. DAVIES *Employment Grievances and Disputes Procedures in Britain* California University Press, 1970
Report of the Royal Commission on Trade Unions etc. 1965–1968 HMSO Cmnd 3623
and in particular among the invaluable research papers produced for this Commission:
 Nos. 1 and 10 on Shop Stewards
 No. 2 Part 2 on Disputes Procedures
 No. 5 Part 1 and No. 6 on Trade Union Structure and Growth

The Contract of Employment and Unfair Dismissal
B.A. HEPPLE AND PAUL O'HIGGINS *Individual Employment Law* Sweet and Maxwell, 1971

G. DE N. CLARK *Remedies for Unjust Dismissal* P.E.P., 1970 Proposals made before the introduction of unfair dismissal in 1972.

AIKIN AND REID *Employment, Welfare and Safety at Work* Penguin, 1971

Redundancy
C. GRUNFELD *The Law of Redundancy* Sweet and Maxwell, 1971
S. R. PARKER AND OTHERS *Effects of the Redundancy Payments Act* HMSO, 1971

Safety and Compensation
J. H. MUNKMAN *Employers' Liability at Common Law* Butterworth, 7th edn, 1971
A. REDGRAVE *Factory Acts* Butterworth, 1966

Trade Unions
It is to be regretted that no book has been written or revised since the Industrial Relations Act covering trade union law in general. The most useful one on pre-1971 law is:
C. GRUNFELD *Modern Trade Union Law* Sweet and Maxwell, 1970

Law Reports
All sets of law reports are expensive. If one of the general sets can be afforded, one or other of the following is advised:
All England Law Reports Butterworth
Weekly Law Reports Council of Law Reporting
Both are published in weekly parts and can then be bound in three annual volumes. Both, however, contain a vast amount of material of no interest to industrial relations. The best specialized set is:
Industrial Court Reports Incorporated Council of Law Reporting, Lincoln's Inn, WC2A 3XN. Monthly parts and bound volume. £20 per year.
Industrial Tribunal reports are published in monthly parts by HMSO. Industrial Tribunal cases and appeals therefrom are published monthly by HMSO. They are sometimes summarized (or, in the case of appeals, reported) in *Knight's Reports*. Appeals are sometimes reported in the *All England*, or *Weekly Law*, Reports.

Attention is also drawn to the most useful fortnightly summaries of collective agreements and developments, legal and otherwise, in industrial relations published by Incomes Data Services Ltd, 140 Great Portland Street, London W1N 5TA.

Index

ACCOUNTS
Audit of 30, 35, 68, 70
Duty to keep 30, 68–9, 70
Inspection of 69
Submission of 30, 69–70
ADMISSION
Eligibility for 34
Method of 51
Procedure for 34
Rejection, complaint of 61–6
Right to 49–50
Trade unions, to 48–51
AGENCY SHOP
Nature of 43, 95
Procedure for establishing 45, 181–2, 183–4
Recognition as pre-requisite 45, 142, 181, 183
Revocation of 46, 181–2, 184
Unfair industrial practice connected with 92, 183–4
AMALGAMATION 78–81, 186–7
ANNUAL RETURNS 69–70
APPEAL
Admission, as to 34–50
Disciplinary action, from 35–55
Exhaustion of 55, 59–61
APPRENTICESHIP
Contract of 202
Redundancy compensation in 213–14
ARBITRATION
Ad hoc 189–90
Arbitration Board, the Industrial, by 175–80
ARBITRATION BOARD, THE INDUSTRIAL
Claim to 106, 150
Extension of collective agreements by 178–9
Fair Wages Resolution, the 177
Information, duty to supply 170, 180

AUDITORS 69
AUTHORITY
Rules as to 33

BALLOT
Agency shop, for 45, 149, 181–2
Closed shop, for 47, 182, 184
Emergency procedures, in respect of 135, 137–8, 182
Forms of application for 156–7
Sole bargaining agency, for 148, 149–150, 182, 186
Sole bargaining agency, revocation of 151, 182
BANKRUPTCY
Redundancy payments, effect on 234
BARGAINING. See COLLECTIVE BARGAINING
BENEFIT
Exclusion from 74
See also FUNDS
BIAS 58–9

CLOSED SHOP
'Approved' 44, 46, 95, 184
Conspiracy to injure, as 122
Legality of 41, 42
Pre-entry 42
Reasonableness of 49
Revocation of 47
Unfair industrial practice connected with 93
See also AGENCY SHOP
CODE OF PRACTICE, THE
Dismissal procedures 209, 211
COLLECTIVE AGREEMENT
Breach of, unfair practice as 83, 94, 162–4
Content of 159

Contractual enforcement of 159–66, 168, 185
Dismissal procedure, for 205
Extension of 178–9
Form of application for 158
Implication, contract of employment, into 164–6
Interpretation of 162, 184
Order to enforce 137
Procedural:
  definition of 161
  improvement of 166–9, 181, 182, 185, 188
Redundancy procedure, for 201, 234
Restriction on right to strike in 98
COLLECTIVE BARGAINING
Arbitration Board, the Industrial functions of 175–80
Duty of 150
Information to facilitate 169–70, 180, 181
Local 140–1
Procedural:
  improvement of 166–9, 181, 182, 185, 188
  remedial procedure for 166–9
Recognition, voluntary 142, 182
Training in 181
Voluntary nature of 140
Wages councils, by 172–4, 179, 182
COMMISSION ON INDUSTRIAL RELATIONS, THE 180–3
Agency shop application 45, 181–2
Ballot, conduct of, by 138, 181–3, 184, 186
Closed shop application 47, 182, 184
General questions, consideration of 181
Procedure agreement, improvement of 167–8, 182
Sole bargaining agency 146, 147–8, 149, 182, 188
  revocation of 151
Sole bargaining unit, determination of 143–4
Wages councils, abolition of 174, 182
COMPENSATION
Award of 20–1

Contribution to 209
Measure of 20–1, 108–10
Trade unions, against 21
Unfair dismissal, for 206–7
CONCILIATION
Department of Employment, by 187–8
Industrial tribunals, in 23, 204
NIRC, in 17
Registrar, by 64, 189
Remedial procedure, before 188
Sole bargaining agency, concerning 145–6, 149, 188
Unfair dismissal, as regards 23, 189
CONCILIATION OFFICER
Duties of 103
CONSCIENTIOUS OBJECTION. See MEMBERSHIP
CONSPIRACY
Tort of 121–3
  defence to 123, 125, 127
CONTEMPT OF COURT. See INDUSTRIAL RELATIONS COURT, THE NATIONAL
CONTRACT
Breach of
  damages for 98, 197
  inducement to 96–9, 115, 116–19
  inducement to, by pickets 128
  inducement to, defence to 126
Consensual variation of 215–16
Employment, of. See EMPLOYMENT
Implied terms in 164–6, 175, 176, 177, 178, 179, 192, 193–6
CORPORATION
Dissolution of 77–8
Status of 38, 40, 67, 163
Trade union, as 39–40
COSTS
NIRC, in 19
COURTS
Appeal, of 16
Decisions of 13, 15
Law making function of 15
Precedent in 15, 17
Lower 16
National Industrial Relations. See INDUSTRIAL RELATIONS COURT, THE NATIONAL
Supreme 16–17

CUSTOM
Source of law, as 13, 15–16

DEFINITION
Dismissal, redundancy, for 214–15
Employment 26, 27–8, 240–1
Industrial dispute 87–90, 125
Industrial organization 25
Irregular industrial action 84–6
Lock-out 86–7
Procedure agreement 161
Redundancy 219
Strikes 82–4
Trade dispute 175
Worker 26, 88
DISCIPLINE
Hearing 57–9
Improper, complaint of 61–6
Methods of 34
Notice of 55, 56
Procedure for 35, 54–9
Reasons for 34
DISCRIMINATION
Elections, in 75, 76
Political Fund, as regards 74
DISMISSAL, UNFAIR
Closed shop, to maintain 47–8, 95
Compensation for 204–5
Complaint of 102
Conciliation in respect of 189
Contractual provisions as to 192–8
Discrimination as 200–1
Exemption from statutory machinery 184
Inducement to 208–9
Jurisdiction in respect of 22, 23
National security, bar to complaint, as 200
Non-unionist, of 42, 44, 47–8
Procedure, Code of Practice, under 209, 211
Procedure, voluntary, for 205–6
Procedure for claim of 203–6
Proof of 199
Reason for 217, 218
Redundancy, for 200–1, 212, 214–17
Remedies for 206–9
Standard of 199

Trade union rights, for 200, 202
Unfair industrial practice, as 95
See also NATURAL JUSTICE; RULES
DISSOLUTION
Trade union, of 77–8
DUES
Membership, for 34
Non-payment of 34

ELECTIONS 75–7
Method of 33
Officers, of 32
EMERGENCY 133–9
'Cooling-off period', order for 134, 136, 137, 186
Order, extent of 138–9, 186
Picketing 130
State of 133, 134
EMPLOYMENT
Application for 44, 95
Breach of contract of 23, 97, 193
Characteristics of 194–5
Continuity of 226–31
Contract, sources of 193
Contract of, implied terms in 164–6, 192, 193–6
Definition of 26, 27–8, 240–1
Dismissal from 192–211
Fixed term contract of 202
Notice to terminate 97–8, 192, 197–8
Notification of terms of 193
Redundancy compensation limited to 213–14
Reinstatement in 103, 192, 194, 206–7
Right to, unfair industrial practice 92,
Sickness during 195–6
continuity of 228
pregnancy as 228
Suspension from 196–7
Temporary cessation of 229–30
ENQUIRY 190–1

FAIR WAGES RESOLUTION, THE 176–7
FORMS
Sole bargaining agency, in respect of 152–8
Unfair industrial practice 104–5

FUNDS
Benefit 35, 68
Investment of 35
Liability against 71–2, 124
Ownership of 67
Political, the. *See* POLITICAL FUND
Protection of 71–2

GUIDING PRINCIPLES
Admission, as to 49–50
Amalgamation, affecting 80
Breach of 61–6, 94
Discipline, as to 55
Elections, as to 75
Exclusion of 56
Political fund, affecting 74

HEARING. *See* DISCIPLINE

INCORPORATION. *See* CORPORATION
INDIVIDUAL RIGHTS
Unfair industrial practice connected
    with 92, 94–5, 177
INDUCEMENT, BREACH OF CONTRACT
    TO. *See* CONTRACT
INDUSTRIAL ACTION
Secondary 100–2, 118–19
Sympathetic 99–100
See also PICKETS; STRIKES; WORK TO
    RULE
INDUSTRIAL DISPUTE 82, 84, 86, 87–90
Definition of 87–90, 125
Prerequisite of court action, as 24,
    124
INDUSTRIAL INJURY, LIABILITY FOR
    235–52
Breach of statutory duty, for 239–40
Compensation, general right of 251–2
Fault as basis for 235
Negligence 244–8
    contributory 246–7, 249
    duty of care in 244
    normal practice as 245–6
Statutory duty, breach of:
    civil liability for 250–1
    fencing 250–1
    imposition of duty 248–9

index of duties 254–65
inspection to ensure 249–50
Vicariously for another 237–8, 240–4
    course of employment 242–3
INDUSTRIAL RELATIONS COURT, THE
    NATIONAL 183–7
Agency shop applications to 45, 183–
    184
Answer to complaint before 105
Appeals to 20, 22
Application for membership, rejection
    of 50
Applications to, form of 104
Arbitration Board, reference to 179–
    180
Breach of guiding principles, com-
    plaint of 62, 65
Breach of rules, complaint of 62, 65
Closed shop
    application to 46, 184
    order against 42
Collective agreement, interpretation of
    184
Compensation. *See* COMPENSATION
Composition of 17
Conciliation in 17, 103, 188, 189
Contempt of 107
'Cooling off' order by 136, 186
Costs in 19
Dismissal procedure, approval of
    205–6
Establishment of 17
Hearing, oral 19
Information, order to supply 170, 180
Interpretation, collective agreements
    of 162
Jurisdiction of 20
Order, sole bargaining agency, for
    150, 184
    revocation of 151, 184
Order of 18–19, 20, 65, 66, 150, 151,
    183–4, 205
Procedure agreement, improvement of
    167–8, 185, 188
Procedure in 18, 103–6, 145, 146–7,
    171, 183, 189
Reinstatement, order of 61, 65
Remedies in 106–10, 183–6

Rules, approval of, by 36
Sole bargaining agency 45, 142, 144–145, 146–51, 152–8, 159, 182, 185–6
Time limit in 20
Unfair dismissal procedure, exemption from 184
Unfair industrial practices, complaint of 103
INDUSTRIAL TRIBUNALS. *See* TRIBUNALS, INDUSTRIAL
INFORMATION
Alternative job, offer of 224
See also COLLECTIVE BARGAINING
INTERNATIONAL LABOUR ORGANIZATION
Conventions of 36
INTIMIDATION
Picketing, in 128
Tort of 119–21
statutory defence to 126

LEGISLATION
Delegated 13, 14
Interpretation of 14
Source of law, as 13
LIABILITY
Authority as producing 96
Funds, of 71–2, 124
To action,
incorporated association, of 40
unincorporated association, of 40
LOCK-OUT
Definition of 86–7
Threat of 92

MEETINGS
Exclusion from 81
Rules as to 81
MEMBERSHIP
Complaints by 61–6
Condition of employment, as. *See* CLOSED SHOP
Conscientious objection to 43, 44
Contract of 48
Discrimination as to 43
Meetings, right to attend 81
Political aspects of. *See* POLITICAL FUND
Property, as, 55

Register of 70
Registered union, of
refusal 41–2
right to 41–2, 177
Reinstatement in 53–4, 61, 65
Resignation from 52
Right to, employer, as against 41–3, 177, 200
Termination of 34–5, 51–9
rules providing for 52
See also ADMISSION; DISCIPLINE; NATURAL JUSTICE; RULES
MERGER. *See* AMALGAMATION

NATIONAL INSURANCE
Industrial Injuries benefit 235
NATURAL JUSTICE
Exclusion of 56
NEGLIGENCE. *See* INDUSTRIAL INJURIES
NUISANCE
Picketing as 128

OFFENCES
Accounts, keeping of 70–1
OFFICERS
Election of 32
Removal of 32

PENSIONS
Trade union schemes for 31
PERSONALITY, LEGAL. *See* CORPORATION
PICKETING
Civil Liability for 128–30
Criminality of 128, 131–2
Emergency procedures applied to 130
Liability for 128–32
Police power in respect of 127
Statutory protection of 128–30
Unfair industrial practice, as 101–2
POLITICAL FUND 72–5
Discrimination, for non-contribution 74
Establishment 73
Levy, liability to 73–4
Purposes of 73
PROPERTY
Corporation, of 38–9, 67

Investment of 35, 67
Job right as 49
Liability against 35
Membership as 55

RECOGNITION 42, 45, 142, 181
Agency shop, prerequisite to 45
Encouragement to membership, as 42
Fair Wages Resolution, under 176
REDUNDANCY
Alternative offer 223–6
Compensation, amount of 231–4
Consensual variation 215–16
Continuity of employment 226–31
Dismissal,
    prerequisite of 214–17
    reason for 200–1, 212
Lay off, for 222–3
Meaning of 217–22
Policy in respect of 212–13
Presumption of 217
Scope of statute 213–14
Short time, for 222–3
Temporary cessation of employment
    229–30
Voluntary schemes for 234
REGISTRAR
Amalgamation, unions of 186–7
Cancellation of registration by 38
Complaints to:
    breach of guiding principles, of 63–
    66
    breach of rules, of 63–6
    misgovernment, of 81
Conciliation by 64, 189
Discretion of 35, 147
    complaint, breach of rules, of 64
Investigation of 66
Membership, rejection of 50, 189
Political Fund, jurisdiction over 75
Powers of 35, 147–8, 189
    amalgamation, in respect of 80
Rules, examination of, by 36, 189
Winding up, petition by 72
REGISTRATION
Annual report 31
Ballot, power to conduct, after 138
Cancellation of 36, 37

Documents, submission of 29, 30
Forms of 28
Independence, prerequisite of 28,
    147–8
Method of 29
Pension funds 31
Rules of. See RULES
Special 28, 29–30
REMEDIAL PROCEDURE. See COLLECTIVE
    BARGAINING
RULES
Admission, as to 34
Alteration of 33
Blanket offence, the 52, 54
Breach of 23
    complaint procedure 55–6, 61–6
Content of 32–6
Contravention of 35
Discipline 34, 52–4
    procedure for, 54–9
    prohibition of 53
    specification of 54
    unfair industrial practices in 55
Elections. See ELECTIONS
Interpretation of 52
Natural justice, of 54–5
Publication of 31
Reasonableness of 53
Registration of 32–6
Validity of 35

SECONDARY ACTION. See INDUSTRIAL
    ACTION
SHOP STEWARD
Bargaining by 141
Election of 32, 77
SICKNESS. See EMPLOYMENT
SOLE BARGAINING AGENCY
Agency shop deferred for 45, 142
Application for 144–5, 185–6, 188
    rejection of, discretion 159, 185
Ballot relating to 148, 149–50, 182,
    186
Conciliation in respect of 145–6, 149,
    182, 188
Conditions regarding 148, 185
Forms of application in respect of
    152–8

Order for 150, 186
Procedure for obtaining 146–50, 182,
    185–6
Revocation of 150–1, 182, 186
Unfair industrial practice 93–4, 95,
    145, 148, 150, 151, 179–80, 186
    reference to Arbitration Board
    106, 150, 180
Unit for 142–4, 167, 182, 185
Unregistered organizations as 144–5,
    149
Voluntary 93, 142, 143, 149, 182
    revocation of 150–1, 182
STRIKES
Authority to call 33
Continuity of employment during
    227–8
Criminal liability for 131
Discipline in respect of 34
Emergency powers in respect of 133–
    139, 182, 186
Financing of 92
Organization of 92
Restriction on, contract by 97, 98,
    165
Threat of 92
Tort, action in 23, 24
SYMPATHETIC ACTION. See INDUSTRIAL
    ACTION

TIME
Claim, presentation of 20
Limitation, complaint of breach of
    rules 63, 64
TORT
Availability of action in 23–4
Conspiracy, of 121–3
Defences, statutory, to 123–7
Intimidation 119–21
Statutory protection from liability in
    87, 115, 123–7
Stay of proceedings in 115, 124
TRESPASS
Picketing as 128, 131
TRIBUNALS, INDUSTRIAL
Appeal from 213
Application for membership,
    rejection of 50

Breach of guiding principles, com-
    plaint of 62, 63, 64, 65
Breach of rules, complaint of 62, 63,
    64, 65
Conciliation in 17–18, 23, 102–3
Establishment of 21
Jurisdiction of 22
Membership rights, determination by
    43
Redundancy payments, jurisdiction as
    to 217, 223, 234
Remedies in 103
Unfair dismissal, jurisdiction as to
    203, 206
Unfair industrial practices:
    complaints of, to 102–3
TRIBUNALS, NATIONAL INSURANCE 16
TRUST
Property, of 39–40, 67

UNFAIR INDUSTRIAL PRACTICE 91–114
Agency shop agreements, as to 45–6,
    92, 183–4
Arbitration board, consideration by
    150
Breach of agreement as 83, 94
Classification of 91–2
Closed shop agreements, as to 47, 93
Collective agreement, breach of 94,
    162–4
Complaint of:
    industrial tribunal to 102–3
    NIRC to 103–6
Disciplinary action, arising from 55
Dismissal, inducement to 208–9
Elections, as to 75
Guiding principles, breach of 61–6,
    94, 95
Individual rights, interference with
    94–5
Inducement to breach of contract as
    96–9
Inducement of unfair dismissal as 44
Industrial action as element in 91–2
Order to cease, extent of 137
Picketing, in 128, 130
Rejection of application for employ-
    ment as 44

For Product Safety Concerns and Information please contact our EU
representative GPSR@taylorandfrancis.com
Taylor & Francis Verlag GmbH, Kaufingerstraße 24, 80331 München, Germany